Early Modern History: Society and Culture

General Editors: **Rab Houston**, Professor of Early Modern History, University of St Andrews, Scotland; and **Edward Muir**, Professor of History, Northwestern University, Illinois, USA

This series encompasses all aspects of early modern international history from 1400 to *c*.1800. The editors seek fresh and adventurous monographs, especially those with a comparative and theoretical approach, from both new and established scholars.

Titles include:

Johannes. C. Wolfart
RELIGION, GOVERNMENT AND POLITICAL CULTURE IN EARLY MODERN
GERMANY
Lindau, 1520–1628

Early Modern History: Society and Culture
Series Standing Order ISBN 0–333–71194–7
(*outside North America only*)

You can receive future titles in this series as they are published by placing a standing order. Please contact your bookseller or, in case of difficulty, write to us at the address below with your name and address, the title of the series and the ISBN quoted above.

Customer Services Department, Macmillan Distribution Ltd, Houndmills, Basingstoke, Hampshire RG21 6XS, England

Gender and Politics in Early Modern Europe

English Convents in France and the Low Countries

Claire Walker

First published 2003 by
PALGRAVE MACMILLAN
Houndmills, Basingstoke, Hampshire RG21 6XS and
175 Fifth Avenue, New York, N. Y. 10010
Companies and representatives throughout the world

PALGRAVE MACMILLAN is the global academic imprint of the
Palgrave Macmillan division of St. Martin's Press, LLC and of Palgrave
Macmillan Ltd. Macmillan® is a registered trademark in the United
States, United Kingdom and other countries. Palgrave is a registered
trademark in the European Union and other countries.

ISBN 0–333–75370–4

This book is printed on paper suitable for recycling and
made from fully managed and sustained forest sources.

A catalogue record for this book is available
from the British Library.

Library of Congress Cataloging-in-Publication Data

Walker, Claire, 1965-
    Gender and politics in early modern Europe : English convents in France
    and the Low Countries / Claire Walker.
        p. cm.—(Early modern history)
    Includes bibliographical references and index.
    ISBN 0–333–75370–4
    1. Convents—France—History—17th century. 2. Nuns—France—Social
conditions—17th century. 3. Catholics, English—France—History—17th
century. 4. Convents—Benelux countries—History—17th century. 5. Nuns—
Benelux countries—Social conditions—17th century. 6. Catholics, English—
Benelux countries—History—17th century. I. Title. II. Early modern history
(Palgrave (Firm))

BX4220.F8 W35 2002

271′.90044′09032—dc21

                                                            2002072322

10 9   8   7   6   5   4   3   2   1
12 11 10 09 08 07 06 05 04 03

Printed and bound in Great Britain by
Antony Rowe Ltd, Chippenham and Eastbourne

Contents

List of Tables

Acknowledgements

The research and writing of this book has spanned more than a decade. When it began as my PhD thesis, I feared there was insufficient archival material relating to the convents to sustain such a study. Several years (and even more research) later, I have only scratched the surface of what is a veritable wealth of documents and literature about and by the early modern English nuns. I hope that in this book's wake, other scholars will continue to uncover the writings and history of the post-Reformation women religious, especially those cloisters I was unable to cover in depth.

Given the difficulties of locating and accessing the private (often 'lost') convent archives in England, France and Belgium, particularly from my own position of 'geographic dislocation' in Australia, I am deeply grateful to the librarians, archivists, scholars and friends who have assisted my research. It is impossible to name them all, but I must extend special thanks to the superiors and archivists of the monastic communities and diocesan archives I have visited, namely the Poor Clare Convent, Cross Bush; Oulton Abbey, Stone; the Priory of Our Lady of Good Counsel, Sayers Common; St Clare's Abbey, Darlington; St Mary's Convent, Buckfastleigh; Downside Abbey, near Bath; Stanbrook Abbey, Worcester; the Archdiocese of Mechelen-Brussels; and Westminster Archdiocesan Archives. They generously permitted me access to their documents, offered much appreciated hospitality in their guesthouses, and via correspondence have continued to answer my questions. In particular, I must single out Dom Philip Jebb OSB, who has always found time amidst his hectic schedule to welcome me to Downside Abbey's marvellous library, and locate not only those manuscripts I requested, but also others 'of interest', which invariably proved invaluable. Rev. Fr Ian Dickie of Westminster Archdiocesan Archives has similarly proffered considerable assistance and friendship, even opening the archive for me during his summer vacation last year so that I could finish my research. I must also pay tribute to the late Sr Mary Salome Wylie of the Priory at Sayers Common who offered constant advice, encouragement and friendship during my PhD research, and even persuaded the Mother Prioress and community to give me their spare copy of the *Chronicle of St Monica's* – an incomparable gift which has greatly assisted my research. It will always be a point of great sadness to me that she passed away before I submitted the thesis. Without her interest, intelligence, good humour, and confidence in my work, this book would have been so much harder to write.

Other colleagues and friends have also provided much needed support in the form of ideas, references and material. John Bossy, Craig Harline, Dom Placid Spearritt OSB, and Heather Wolfe all generously gave me their own research notes and directed me to repositories I would not otherwise have found. Caroline Bowden, Jennifer Cameron, Alan Davidson, Pascal Majérus, Sr Mildred Murray-Sinclair OSB, Anselm Nye, and the Rev. Fr Chris Smith have variously provided references, advice about other collections, and copies of their own work. Discussions (in person and via email) with Andrew Buck, Sherrill Cohen, Trish Crawford, Claire Cross, Peter Cunich, Sabina Flanagan, Christopher Haigh, Felicity Heal, Caroline Hibbard, Joanna Innes, Sybil Jack, Katharine Massam, John Morrill, Susan O'Brien, Wilf Prest, Judith Richards, Lyndal Roper, Julie Sanders, Kevin Sharpe, Jutta Sperling, Susan Wiseman, Nancy Wright, Heather Wolfe, and Charles Zika have enriched the book by helping me to clarify my ideas and to think about the nuns in new and challenging ways. I am particularly indebted to my PhD examiners, Felicity Heal, John Morrill and Judith Richards, for their advice regarding publication, and their continuing interest and support. Likewise, I would like to thank Rab Houston and Ed Muir for their helpful comments on the necessary (and unnecessary) revisions, and especially for their patience and encouragement during what became a protracted process of rewriting. Luciana O'Flaherty at Palgrave has been similarly understanding, and her assistance during the final months has been instrumental in completing the book. I am also grateful to the *Sixteenth Century Journal* for permission to reproduce Chapter 3. An earlier version appeared in vol. 30 (1999).

Many others have provided succour, both practical and emotional, over the years. The History Department at the University of Western Australia and the University of Newcastle's Research Management Committee funded several research trips to the overseas archives. The amazing librarians in the Auchmuty Library's inter-library loan service have managed to track down and obtain dozens of obscure books and articles for me, occasionally finding additional sources I had not known about in the process. In addition to the monastic hospitality I have enjoyed in England, friends and relatives have also offered bed and board on innumerable occasions. Special thanks to the Rev. Fr Chris Smith in Devon; Mike Cook, and Roseann, Colin and Oliver Lemmings in London; David, Jane, Ruth, John and Laura Beck in Oxford; Laura and

Mike Walker in Somerset; and, in particular, Jane, Mark, Holly and Rupert Hampson in London, who have let me live with them for months on end since my first visit in 1989. I am also extremely grateful to the many friends whose encouragement has made the process of researching, writing and rewriting, amidst teaching and endless university restructuring, a positive and bearable experience. I would like to thank my fellow postgraduate students in Western Australia for their camaraderie; my students (past and present) at the University of Newcastle, especially my honours and postgraduate students, for their interest; and the late Eric Andrews, Helen Brash, Nancy Cushing, Nick Doumanis, Jane Hampson, Helen Kilpatrick, Katharine Massam, Jenny Newman, Anselm Nye, Laura Walker and Susan West for being there during periods of self-doubt and crisis.

Finally, I am grateful to my parents, who have always encouraged my scholarly endeavours, despite wondering why it takes so long to produce theses and books. Likewise, I owe a great deal to Trish Crawford, who supervised my thesis, and who has continued to offer immeasurable advice and friendship over many years. However, my greatest debt is to David Lemmings. Without his incisive comments, computer skills, passion for historical research, unshakeable belief in my capacity to complete the project, and unfailing love and support, this book would never have been written.

CLAIRE WALKER

List of Abbreviations

AAM	Archives of the Archdiocese of Mechelen-Brussels
AAW	Archives of the Archdiocese of Westminster
Arundel	Poor Clares, Cross Bush, near Arundel, Archives
BL	British Library
Bodl.	Bodleian Library
Buckfast	St Mary's Convent, Buckfastleigh, Archives
CHR	*Catholic Historical Review*
CRS	Catholic Record Society
Darlington	St Clare's Abbey, Darlington, Archives
DL	Downside Abbey Library and Archives
HJ	*The Historical Journal*
HMC	Historical Manuscripts Commission
Lancs. RO	Lancashire Record Office
Lille	Archives Départementales du Nord, Lille
Oulton	St Mary's Abbey, Oulton, Archives
P&P	*Past and Present*
Priory	Priory of Our Lady of Good Counsel Archives
PRO	Public Record Office
RH	*Recusant History*
RQ	*Renaissance Quarterly*
Stanbrook	Stanbrook Abbey Archives
SCJ	*The Sixteenth Century Journal*
SJ	Society of Jesus
Versailles	Archives Départementales du Seine-et-Oise, Versailles

Note Concerning Dates, Spellings and Terminology

In the text the dates are given New Style (which the convents, located in Continental Europe, used) and the year is taken to begin on 1 January. Original spelling and punctuation has been retained in all quotations from contemporary manuscripts and printed works, but contractions have been silently expanded and i has been transposed to j, and u to v.

The terms 'nun', 'sister', 'convent', and 'monastery' technically refer to specific types of women religious and their communities. However, to avoid repetition of the same word, I use them interchangeably throughout the text. I have tried to sidestep the contested label 'Counter-Reformation' when talking about post-Reformation reform in the Catholic Church. Instead I refer to the 'post-Tridentine Church' and 'Catholic Reformation' wherever possible. Finally, place names in France and the Low Countries are given in the language commonly used by the nuns (and subsequent literature on them). The English and French spellings were more frequently used, largely because few nuns spoke 'Dutch' or its regional dialects. Hence, I refer to 'Louvain', 'Ghent', 'Bruges' and 'Ypres', rather than 'Leuven', 'Gent', 'Brugge' and 'Ieper'. They always spoke of 'Brussels'. The exception is my use of 'Mechelen', rather than 'Malines', which was cited variously in different sources, making it difficult to establish the nuns' customary usage.

Introduction

You may tell unto men, how dishonourable a thing it were unto them, for a woman produced out of the weakest part of nature, to outgoe them not onlie in morall, and supernaturall vertues; but in suffring death also for the constant profession of the Catholike faith: and before woemen you may advance this royall standard of your victorious Mother, inviting them like stoute Amazons, to bidde batayle unto the worlde, and their spirituall enemies. For I doe not reade of a more heroicall act performed by any either in our time or many ages before, then this of your Mother. Wherefore we have just cause to say, that yow are nobly discended, since yow are the daughter of her, whom God hath inriched with the crowne of Martyrdome, you tracing her steppes in a most contemplative course of lyfe: In which I do wish you, the increase of spiritt, and perseverance.

(John Mush, *An Abstracte of the Life and Martirdome of Mistres Margaret Clitherow*)[1]

Before Margaret Clitherow, a York butcher's wife who harboured priests and was well-known for her unfaltering adherence to Catholicism, was executed on 25 March 1586 she sent her hose and shoes to her eldest daughter as a reminder to serve God and to follow in her virtuous steps. This final advice was not lost on the 12-year-old Anne who subsequently ran away from home, and after imprisonment for her religious beliefs, travelled overseas to become an Augustinian nun in 1598. Both John Mush, her mother's confessor and biographer, and her religious sisters in Louvain recognised the symmetry in the lives of Margaret and Anne Clitherow. The martyr had given up her family and her life for her faith, and Anne likewise relinquished her kin to 'die to the world' through a life

1

of monastic prayer and mortification.[2] The connection between renowned Catholic women of the Elizabethan era and the English convents on the Continent was not coincidental, nor was it limited to the Clitherows. The relatives and protégées of other prominent Catholics similarly abandoned England for the cloister. The daughters of Jane Wiseman, who was also sentenced to death but reprieved, entered the Augustinian convent in Louvain and the Bridgettine house in Lisbon. Dorothy Lawson, who was named for her famous priest-harbouring and neighbourhood proselytising mother, likewise went to Louvain, her dowry provided by her grandmother, Lady Constable, who had been imprisoned in York for recusancy. As did Frances Burrows who had been raised by her Vaux aunts, the great supporters of the Jesuit mission.[3] Indeed convent registers were replete with the names of families fined, imprisoned, or executed for their persistent Catholicism. The cloister therefore presented the next generation of Catholic women with an opportunity to pursue their mothers' piety, while extending their nonconformity to the Protestant Church and State in an even more overt rejection of English religion, law, and society.

Between the Dissolution of the monasteries in 1539 and 1598 when the first post-Reformation English monastery was established, a steady stream of English women had flowed into Continental convents, but membership of 'foreign' houses had posed many logistical and cultural problems. Therefore, in collaboration with exiled lay Catholics and clergy, various women determined to begin expatriate English cloisters, which would serve their particular needs. From the late sixteenth century, in France, the southern Netherlands and Portugal, 22 such institutions were founded, which adhered to the rules of St Benedict, St Augustine, St Clare, St Brigid, St Dominic, and the reformed Carmelite constitutions. These houses predominantly recruited the daughters of the English gentry and aristocracy, who prayed for their kin and the restitution of their country to Rome. But the nuns also ran small schools and guesthouses, wrote devotional works, and sometimes engaged in overt political activities in the quest for their long held desire to return eventually to English soil. In the process, the convents became centres of English Catholic piety and activity in the towns and cities where they were located, and provided vital links between the nuns' families in England and Continental Catholicism.

Yet despite their prominence in the life and identity of the early modern English Catholic community, the contemplative houses have not figured conspicuously in the histories of either English Catholicism, or the post-Tridentine religious life for women. In almost every account of English nuns, the work of the contemplatives is completely over-shadowed by the actions of the woman who began a female apostolic order modelled upon the Society of Jesus. Mary Ward is deservedly well known. The daughter of a stalwart Catholic Yorkshire gentry family, she initially tried out the contemplative life, founding the English Poor Clare convent at Gravelines. However, a series of divine revelations persuaded her that she was being called to establish a completely new religious order which, fashioned upon the Society of Jesus, would undertake important educative and missionary work. In 1609 or 1610, Ward and her companions opened a school for young girls in St Omer and performed pastoral work in the town. The concept proved popular and, by 1628, 10 further houses of the Institute of Mary (or 'English Ladies') had emerged in the southern Netherlands, Italy and Germany. Mary Ward also sent sisters to London from 1614 to contribute to the English mission. Although she received initial approbation in 1616, opposition to the non-cloistered nuns (denounced as 'galloping girls' and 'Jesuitesses') mounted, leading to the closure of the Italian houses in 1625, and those in lower Germany and the Spanish Netherlands in 1630. In 1631 the Institute was suppressed by Pope Urban VIII, and Ward was temporarily imprisoned. Although disappointed that her visionary plans had not succeeded, Mary Ward was undaunted, and her order was re-established as a secular teaching community. She returned to England to set up schools, and died there in 1645. But her Institute and its ideals survived her to expand across Europe and the globe, with a succession of foundations in England, most notably the Bar Convent in York, operating schools secretly until Catholic emancipation in the nineteenth century.[4]

The tumultuous history of Mary Ward's courageous attempt to carve out an active apostolate for women in the face of conservative Church reform, accounts for her prominence in the historical scholarship. Yet Ward's spiritual and political achievements were matched by the efforts of numerous women who chose the Church's prescribed life of enclosed contemplation. A few – Margaret Clement, Mary Percy, Lucy Knatchbull, Gertrude More, the four Cary sisters and Mary Knatchbull – have achieved varying degrees of acknowledgement. Yet they are still discussed more or less in isolation from the 'mainstream' historiography of the English Reformation, and the scholarship on women and religion, both in England and Europe. Religious exile and strict enclosure not only removed them from their country and society at large, but apparently also marginalised their place in history. Catholic scholars, particularly members of the post-Reformation religious orders, have done much to redress this imbalance, but their work is not widely known beyond monastic periodicals and religious presses.[5]

The history of sixteenth and seventeenth century English Catholicism has been dominated by the role of the clerical mission and its internal politics, as well as Catholic conflict with the Protestant state.[6] Debates about the nature of the 'recusant' community, that is those who refused to attend Church of England services and accordingly incurred financial penalties and exclusion from public office, invariably highlighted the importance of the laity, particularly the gentry, in preserving belief and practice.[7] Yet, while many scholars commented upon the prominence of women in nonconformity, the debate tended to be as insular as the Catholic community was purported to be – limited to recusants and predominantly concerned with affairs inside England's borders.[8] The nuns have only ever been mentioned as incidental to both the English mission and the seigneurial Catholicism of gentry households. Recently there has been a little more acknowledgement of the convents' existence and their importance for expatriate Catholics, particularly in the aftermath of 1688.[9] However, emerging interest in the post-Reformation cloisters has yet to match the attention received by the medieval English nunneries, and the fate of their inmates after the Dissolution.[10]

There are exceptions. In addition to the Catholic historiography, scholars of English women's history and literature have discussed the nuns' writings, spirituality and the experiences of a few well-known cloisters.[11] Literary specialists have been at the forefront of recovering monastic manuscripts authored by women, and making them available in print. Adding to the Catholic Record Society's publication of convent registers and documents, they provide an increasing corpus of literature created by or relating to the English cloisters.[12] But to date there has been no detailed analysis of the convents to match the burgeoning literature on the early modern Continental religious houses.

In a 1988 survey of women and the Catholic Reformation, Kathryn Norberg lamented that 'studies are most rare' of female convents.[13] Accounts in English of early modern monastic life remain sparse in comparison with the wealth of literature in Spanish, French and Italian, (and particularly with respect to writings on Protestant and other nonconformist women). Yet, in the past decade, interest in the cloister, both as a feature of family strategy and as a female space, has begun to filter into English-language publications. Scholars of Renaissance Italy have been at the forefront of this research, inspired principally by the groundbreaking work of Gabriella Zarri.[14] Their studies on individual houses and the convents of particular cities and regions point to the economic, social, political, cultural and spiritual importance of the institution in early modern society, and their research is reflected in similar analyses of Spanish, French, Netherlands and German houses. Much of the debate has focused on aristocratic families' use of the cloister during an era of financial pressure, especially with respect to marriage dowries, and the forced monachisation of daughters.[15] However, recent research has analysed the convent's and the nun's significance as markers of patrician power and patronage, and there is mounting evidence that certain women engaged directly in the political sphere as patrons, reformers and advisers.[16] Indeed, nuns have been increasingly studied as agents and not simply pawns of dynastic and state ambitions. Religious women's responses (including resistance) to Church reform, their prominence as patrons of the arts, and their own creative endeavours have revealed a female dynamism in the contemplative houses to match the energy of the apostolic orders.[17] Despite clausura (strict monastic enclosure), many nuns vicariously breached the physical bounds of their cloisters to mediate between heaven and earth, most obviously via intercessory prayers, but also by facilitating lay devotion through their writings, music and church decoration.[18] In the reforming and missionary post-Tridentine Church such activities assumed a political mantle. Thus, far from separating from society and dying to the world and its concerns, the convent is considered an integral part of the early modern state, economy, social fabric and culture.

This book argues that the English cloisters were no less significant than their European counterparts. Although the convents' geographic and confessional dislocation from their homeland altered the terms of their relationship with the English Church, State and people, the religious houses nonetheless actively engaged in their compatriots' spiritual and political affairs, and became well-known symbols of Catholic nonconformity. However, the nuns were also members of the post-Tridentine Church, and thereby subject to the reforms which limited the female monastic apostolate to prayer behind walls and grilles. Like the women in Continental cloisters, they had to negotiate with clerical supervisors and lay patrons the role they envisaged for themselves. The nuns' aims, their strategies for implementing them, the obstacles impeding their execution, and the relationships they forged to realise their goals, accordingly constitute the book's scope and its subject matter. In a survey of several convents over a century, it has not been possible to cover every aspect of the monastic experience, or to offer a detailed history of individual women and houses. The study is skewed towards the communities whose archives were readily accessible, and focuses on issues germane to recent scholarly debates. Data was not collected for all 22 convents, but rather for a cross-section of monastic orders and houses situated in France and the southern Netherlands. For this reason the Bridgettine cloister in Lisbon was excluded. It also proved impossible to include any of the Carmelite houses in the database. Nor is there any extended coverage of Mary Ward's Institute, which was not a contemplative order and, as already noted, has been written about extensively in its own right.

The first chapter provides a statistical analysis of the convents' foundation and membership, and discusses the reasons for their establishment, and the factors affecting recruitment; in particular, the reasons why English women became nuns in the seventeenth century. Chapter 2 locates the organisation and governance of the monastic houses within both the post-Tridentine reform of the religious life and secular ideologies about female rule. However, it moves beyond the prescriptive literature to examine the nuns' interpretation and exercise of clausura and household order, which were often at odds with contemporary expectations. The third chapter explores the cloisters' tenuous economic situation, caused by the volatile combination of their exiled circumstances and ecclesiastical imperatives regarding monastic labour. The nuns had to realign their spiritual and domestic duties into income generating activities, which often flouted Church regulations, but enabled them to survive. The following chapter pursues this theme, discussing the convents' close links with society beyond the enclosure. It was essential to cultivate patrons to withstand the economic and political pressures of exile, but in the process of acquiring and maintaining allies, many nuns developed personal patronage networks, which they employed jointly for their community's temporal survival and to further their political aim of Catholic toleration in England. Yet, for all this worldly ambition and activity, the religious houses existed principally to pray. Chapter 5 explores the nuns' spirituality, which was by no means devoid of political intent or conflict, with several cloisters clashing with their clerical overseers and one another when interpretations of prayer and mission differed. Yet amidst the manifold constraints and sometimes damaging competitiveness, many English nuns forged meaningful devotional lives, finding solace in a range of pious activities from mystical ecstasy to seeking the divine in everyday tasks.

The English convents therefore must be considered as a vital link between the English Catholic nonconformist tradition and the Continental Church. The nuns' close economic and social ties, and fiercely maintained solidarity with their co-religionists in England, invariably coloured their perception of both their religious vocation and their membership of the universal Catholic Church. This led them into direct engagement with the often tumultuous politics of the recusant minority, the Crown and Parliament, and the post-Tridentine authorities regarding the future of English Catholicism. Yet national identity alone did not compel the nuns to challenge political, social and religious norms regarding what was appropriate action for contemplative women. They were deeply conscious of the manifold ways gender might both limit and legitimate their ambitions. Like Mary Ward, they believed that women 'might do great matters', but they chose to participate in Catholic activism from within the essentially conservative domain of the cloister.[19] Just as their mothers, grandmothers, and other recusant heroines, like Margaret Clitherow, had defied Church and State to maintain Catholic belief and practice from within the institution of marriage, the nuns understood that convent walls, like gender prescriptions about appropriate wifely behaviour, were fluid. The cloisters accordingly fulfilled their spiritual and political objectives through a combination of direct challenges to the *status quo*, and less confrontational negotiation of the barriers set against active female participation in early modern religious and political affairs. The nuns did not always succeed. But they nonetheless managed to guide their convents through the often harsh political, economic and confessional climate of the seventeenth century to become such entrenched institutions of English expatriate life that, to escape the horrors of the French Revolution, they were allowed finally to return to their homeland in the 1790s.

1

Female Monasticism Revived: Foundations and Vocations

Anno Domini
1597

The persecution beeing then great against the Roman Catholicks in england The lady Mary percy Daughter to the great earle of Northumberland, with many other persons of quality, leaving theyr owne country retyred into flaunders living ther at Brussells in much retreat and Devotion; they began to think of leading a Religious life, and errecting a Monastery... they soone resolved uppon this great worke; and to undertake St Benedict his Rule and Holy order; which of all others, had heertofore, most flourished; in that now hereticall kingdome. confiding it might happily in future times, be agayn a fit reception for them.

(Anne Neville, 'Annals... of English Benedictine Nuns')[1]

Lady Mary Percy, with the assistance of the Jesuit, William Holt, obtained the necessary ecclesiastical and civil approbation for her venture in 1598. She purchased a suitable house and, with a few other English women, took up residence. The new cloister attracted the financial support of the Archduke Albert and the Infanta Isabella, who governed the Spanish Netherlands, and English recusants resident in Brussels. It even received alms from the soldiers of a Spanish regiment quartered in the city, and commanded by Sir William Stanley. On 14 November 1599, Joanna Berkeley, who had been professed in the French abbey of St Pierre at Rheims in 1581, was solemnly installed as abbess. A week later in a ceremony attended by the royal governors, prominent English exiles, and the papal nuncio, the founder and her companions, Dorothy and Gertrude Arundel, Elizabeth (Anne) Cansfield, Frances Gawen, Elizabeth Southcott, Margaret (Winefrid) Thompson and Margaret Winefrid (Renata) Smith were clothed in the Benedictine habit.[2] Three additional nuns from St Pierre temporarily transferred to Brussels to establish regular Benedictine observance in the convent and to train the novices, who were accordingly professed on 21 November 1600.[3] The foundation of the Abbey of the Glorious Assumption of Our Blessed Lady marked the re-establishment of monasticism for English women, and it initiated a process which was to be repeated several times during the course of the seventeenth century. One by one the old religious orders revived across the Channel to await what the nuns believed was the inevitable return to their homeland.

The restoration of conventual life for English women occurred during a renaissance of female religiosity. In towns and cities across Catholic Europe houses of religious women proliferated. Over half Seville's convents were founded in the sixteenth century.[4] In Valladolid, 12 of the city's 20 female cloisters were erected between 1545 and 1650.[5] Teresa of Avila was partially responsible for the surge in Spain – 17 reformed Carmelite houses were established during her lifetime, and after her death in 1582 the order spread throughout Europe and into the New World.[6] But the Iberian peninsula was not remarkable in this respect. Convent populations in Italy exploded between the fifteenth and seventeenth centuries.[7] In Naples, the number of female religious communities increased from 25 in 1591 to 37 by 1650, their buildings 'devouring... whole city blocks'.[8] Elizabeth Rapley wrote of a similar phenomenon in France. Rheims, which had 60 cloistered nuns in 1619, boasted 300 to 400 by 1658. Similarly, between 1625 and 1629, three convents were erected at St Denis, on the outskirts of Paris, of which the Ursuline house alone contained 74 women in the 1670s – a figure which very nearly outstripped the entire number of nuns in Paris in 1600.[9] Although the new actively orientated religious orders accounted for much of the post-Tridentine enthusiasm for convent life, contemplative monasticism was not forsaken. Patricia Ranft has noted that 'experiments in women's active religious communities often were overshadowed in their contemporary world by the more familiar forms of religious life... [which] were also stirring with activity'.[10] Her view is supported by Craig Harline's analysis of the Low Countries before and after the Council of Trent which uncovered evidence of both active and contemplative sisters founding new houses and reforming older establishments. Most of the pre-1600 communities continued, and they were joined by 19 Dominican convents, 17 Sepulchrine cloisters, and several Benedictine, Augustinian and Franciscan monasteries, among others.[11] Female religious institutions were therefore increasingly prominent in the seventeenth-century urban landscape.

The reasons for the early modern convent's popularity have been widely debated by scholars. There is no doubt that many new foundations and the women who flocked to join them were the result of Catholic renewal in the aftermath of the Council of Trent. However, historians most commonly link female fervour with charitable apostolates. Although the Carmelites, the convent of Port-Royal in Paris, and innumerable other reformed monasteries attest to the dynamism inside enclosures, walls and grilles tend to be read as a disincentive rather than an attraction for women. Most scholars concede that some sisters found the cloister attractive, but it is supposed that willingly claustrated nuns were a distinct minority. The success of traditional monasticism therefore has been attributed to factors other than spiritual enthusiasm, including social pressures, demographic change, youthful rebellion and a desire to flee the world.[12] Mary Elizabeth Perry credited Seville's monastic expansion to a rising population, and parents continuing to view the convent as a desirable option for their daughters when marriage was not possible.[13] However, the cloister's lustre is most commonly ascribed to changing marriage patterns among Europe's elites, caused by exponential dowry inflation. The most extensive research has been conducted on Italian cloisters. Richard Trexler's and Judith Brown's analyses of Florentine convent populations suggest that they erupted from 933 women in the early fifteenth century to 3400 nuns (or 13 per cent of the female population) in 1552, and then to 4200 in 1662.[14] A significant proportion of these women were from aristocratic families. Indeed Jutta Sperling's analysis of Venetian cloisters has estimated that in 1581 nearly 54 per cent of patrician women inhabited them, and by 1642 this figure had possibly risen to a staggering 82 per cent.[15]

Although economic explanations for the Italian phenomenon are persuasive, recent research indicates that there were other political, moral, social and spiritual considerations which drove the numbers of nuns and their premises upwards in Italy and beyond. Sperling has pointed to the importance of patriarchal 'honour' in the decision to sequester daughters rather than allow them to 'marry out' of their social rank, and proposed that coerced monachisations can be seen as part of the Venetian 'nobility's game of conspicuous gift-giving and consumption'. Stanley Chojnacki likewise noted the political and moral stature which convents' religious charisma bestowed upon both their kin and the state. Craig Harline cited the 'symbolic and psychological' importance of cloistered monasticism in the early modern mind.[16] Elizabeth Lehfeldt identified a desire for salvation, familial proximity to the divine via the consecrated daughter, and the promotion of female chastity as reasons why Spanish families supported convents.[17] Reporting various French cases in which children defied parental wishes to enter the religious life, Barbara Diefendorf has suggested that among the myriad reasons for this insubordination, concerns about personal salvation were at the forefront.[18] It is impossible therefore to establish a single explanatory model for the early modern 'conventual invasion'.[19] Broader geographic, financial and cultural factors intersected with individual motivation to proliferate Europe's cloisters and, in many instances, the groundswell pre-dated the Council of Trent. Yet, the spiritual and political fallout of the Reformation undoubtedly provided the inspiration for several women.

This was most certainly the case for the English convents, whose foundation must be considered within the European context, but also within the circumstances of post-Reformation English Catholicism. In spite of their Continental location and a degree of local sponsorship, the cloisters were begun, populated, and supported financially by England's Catholic minority. Scholars might disagree on the origins of the English Catholic community – did it comprise a survival of pre-Reformation religiosity preserved by the Marian clergy, or was it the creation of Tridentine innovation and vitality imported by the missionary priests?[20] However, it is widely accepted that the laity, in particular the gentry, were the pillars of Catholic nonconformity. They nurtured Roman rites within their households, patronised and protected the missionary priests who came from within their ranks, and accommodated the often tumultuous politics both at home and abroad, which saw their numbers and fortunes ebb and flow, to remain a vital religious minority throughout the seventeenth century.[21] Women were particularly prominent in recusancy. Although John Bossy's assertion of a 'matriarchy' during the Elizabethan era has been qualified by other scholars, the religious leadership exhibited by wives, mothers, widows and spinsters was indisputable.[22] Principally noted for their orchestration of household religion, which often succoured the spiritual needs of their plebeian neighbours, gentlewomen also proselytised, administered the affairs of the Catholic clergy, and in public and private defiantly flouted both the established Protestant Church and the state which demanded conformity to it. As a result, they were fined, imprisoned and occasionally executed. The Elizabethan recusant women's determination to sustain and promote Catholicism for future generations ultimately took on an institutional mantle when they, and their daughters and granddaughters, decided to revive conventual life.

It was no coincidence that serious efforts towards a resumption of the female religious life came to fruition in the late 1590s. By the end of

the sixteenth century, the ambitions of most recusants had been modified from the wholesale reversal of the Reformation, whether by domestic uprising, foreign invasion or missionary reconversion of England, to
a realisation that numerically they were destined to remain a religious
minority. Accordingly, many Catholics sought to define new parameters
for organising and practising their faith.[23] The missionary priests whose
uncompromising politics and glorious martyrdoms had characterised
the Elizabethan era, had also been responsible for importing Tridentine
spirituality into their homeland. Its activist orientation struck a chord
with the recusant women's pious ambitions to preserve the faith and to
participate actively in the devotional renaissance sweeping the international Catholic Church. Convents would provide an alternative to
marriage and domestic religion, a place to educate the next generation
of Catholic wives and mothers, and an opportunity to foster and dis-
seminate a feminine Tridentine-inspired English piety. Thus, although
many Catholics were becoming resigned to the likely longevity of the
Protestant regime, they were by no means introspective or quiescent.
The religious houses represented their determination to develop nonconformity outside the dimensions of the gentry household, and to
engage with the Catholic Church beyond England's shores, in what
amounted to an overtly political act. Again the timing was significant.
Although not confident that Elizabeth's successor would restore England's allegiance to Rome, there were considerable hopes for a degree of
Catholic toleration.[24] In such an eventuality, it was assumed that monasticism, as well as the mass, would again be acceptable in England.
Setting up convents abroad was therefore considered by many (including the nuns) as a preliminary step in their eventual return to their
homeland.

This chapter will examine the emergence of the cloisters and the
women who entered them during the seventeenth century. Using data
relating to 1,109 women professed in ten cloisters between 1591 and
1710, it will discuss the factors influencing recruitment overall, and in
individual houses.[25] Although the analysis is inevitably biased towards
those communities included in the sample, trends emerging from the
data imply that although there were subtle differences among orders,
and even within houses following the same monastic rule, there was a
common sense of vocation and religious exile which was arguably shared
by all 22 cloisters. Subsequent chapters covering specific areas of the
nuns' domestic and spiritual lives confirm this assumption. Although
situated in France and the Low Countries as members of the universal
Catholic Church, and driven in many respects by Tridentine imperatives,

the convents retained a quintessentially English outlook. This can be seen graphically in the process of their foundation.

English convents refounded

The Brussels Benedictine abbey was the first post-Reformation cloister, but it was not the sole refuge for English gentlewomen who desired to take the veil. Since the dissolution of the last religious houses in 1539, a trickle of Catholic women and men had entered institutions on the Continent. Some former members of pre-Reformation monasteries journeyed abroad. In 1548, Elizabeth Woodford of Burnham Abbey, which had been suppressed in 1539, joined the Augustinian convent of St Ursula's in Louvain.[26] Other dispossessed nuns had banded together across the Channel in the hope that they might continue the contemplative life. The best known example is that of the Bridgettine nuns of Syon Abbey. A small group fled to the Low Countries where they led a nomadic existence for 55 years, forced to and from various resting points by the Dutch revolt against Spanish rule in the Netherlands. They were invited back to England during the reign of Mary I, but Elizabeth's accession saw them return to the Continent. Finally, in 1594, they established themselves in Lisbon.[27] Similarly, some of the Dominican nuns from the Dartford convent, suppressed in 1538, regrouped in England during the 1550s. In 1559, they travelled to the Spanish Netherlands with the Bridgettines, and ultimately sought refuge in a Flemish cloister of their order.[28] There is also mention in an Ursuline chronicle of a small group of English Poor Clares fleeing England to Veere in Zeeland in about 1572, arriving in Gravelines in 1574 or 1575, then finally joining the Poor Clare convent in St Omer.[29]

It was not only former nuns who continued the monastic tradition abroad. The daughters of English exiles in French and Flemish towns entered local cloisters. Margaret Clement, whose parents had moved to Louvain during the reign of Edward VI, joined the Augustinian monastery of St Ursula's there. Her sister, Dorothy, became a Poor Clare in the town.[30] Hence, when the decision was made to revive monasticism, founders were able to begin convents with experienced English nuns from Continental cloisters. As we have seen, the first abbess of the Brussels Benedictines came from a French abbey. Likewise, when Mary Ward established the Poor Clare convent in Gravelines, it poached five English choir nuns and two lay sisters from the Walloon cloister in St Omer, much to the fury of its abbess.[31] In 1618, the Carmelite foundation in Antwerp attracted five English nuns from local Teresian houses in Antwerp, Brussels and Louvain.[32] The newly established Third Order Regular Franciscan convent in Brussels tried unsuccessfully in 1622 to wrest Clara Williams from her Annonciade house to become their abbess.[33] In 1609, the Augustinians in Louvain had merely transferred most of their number from the Flemish community into the new English establishment.[34] As late as 1629, Lady Mary Lovel enlisted an elderly English Bernadine sister, Margaret Lin, to help found a Carmelite convent in Bruges.[35] The availability of recusant nuns indicates that in the 60 years between the Dissolution and the monastic revival, the contemplative life for women had not died in English minds. Those with the means to do so joined the tide of European women seeking the life of institutionalised prayer and godliness offered by the convent.

Certain nuns chose Continental religious communities for pious reasons. Catherine Gascoigne, one of the founders of the English Benedictine convent at Cambrai, had originally desired to join the strict abbey of Paix in Douai where, without the distraction of her countrywomen, she hoped she 'might the more seriously attend to God alone'.[36] Yet the devotional advantage of isolation was commonly mitigated by grave cultural and spiritual difficulties. Many English nuns lacked sufficient language skills to communicate with their religious sisters and their confessor. The St Omer Poor Clare house where Mary Ward entered as an external lay sister in 1606 was tri-lingual. But even the presence of several other English women, including her novice mistress, could not alleviate her spiritual desolation, when she began to doubt her vocation and had only a Walloon confessor whose language she did not understand.[37] The English nuns at St Ursula's in Louvain were unaccustomed to the Flemish diet of coarse rye bread and herb porridge, and they found the work they were expected to undertake too strenuous.[38] There were also insufficient places for the English in houses which had been founded ostensibly for local women. In their petition to begin an English cloister, the nuns of St Ursula's argued that many vocations were lost because their devout countrywomen could find no convent to admit them.[39] Moreover, several women felt that in foreign communities they were on the margins of the struggle to restore the faith in their homeland. It was partially this conviction that led Mary Ward to leave the St Omer Poor Clares and found an English house of the same order. The English at St Ursula's were compelled by the same desire to maintain the custom of female monasticism, and to keep alive the memory of their families' sufferings for the faith.

The existence of a semi-permanent group of English exiles on the Continent advanced the cause for separate English establishments. As

an expatriate community, they nurtured the tradition of religious perse- ✓
cution, and looked to their children to maintain the faith. Colleges, like
Douai and St Omer, schooled boys for the task ahead; the female cloisters would prepare their daughters. The religious houses would also
provide liturgies which the laity could attend. Thus, the convents
would become focal points for worship and community identity
among the exiled recusants. The extent to which they fulfilled this
objective was abundantly evident in accounts of expatriate generosity
to the new foundations, and lay attendance at the clothing and profession ceremonies of nuns.[40] Nonetheless, it still took the efforts of determined women like Lady Mary Percy and Mary Ward to initiate the
process. Mary Percy and her friends had been living a quasi-monastic
life in the Low Countries; the Brussels cloister emerged from their desire
to formalise the lifestyle they had assumed. Mary Ward's unfortun-
ate experiences in the Walloon cloister inspired her to found a Poor
Clare house sensitive to English needs. The Louvain Augustinians determined to split from their Flemish sisters when they deemed that St
Ursula's was becoming less tolerant of their exiled circumstances. The
success of these early houses inspired women in England to voyage
abroad and found further communities. Thus, while the initial impetus
emanated from the expatriate recusants, their vision and actions reson-
ated with the ambitions of gentlewomen in England who rushed to
support the re-establishment of monasticism.

By 1610, there were three English communities for women – the ✓
Benedictine abbey in Brussels, the Poor Clare convent at Gravelines,
and the Augustinian nuns in Louvain. All were abundantly successful
in attracting recruits during the first three decades of the seventeenth
century. Brussels professed 22 women from its beginning in 1598 up to
1610. The Poor Clares enlisted nine nuns between 1608 and 1610.
Alternately, the Augustinians, who did not separate from their mother-
house until 1609, only attracted three new nuns in the 1600s, in stark
contrast to the 23 English women who took their vows at St Ursula's in
the 1590s. The slump in recruitment to the Flemish cloister (attributed
to the foundation of the Brussels Benedictines) was another factor
behind the English Augustinian filiation. In the next decade, the Brussels professions peaked with 26 women making their final vows. Likewise, between 1611 and 1620, Louvain acquired 27 new nuns, and
Gravelines conducted an astounding 41 professions.[41] This phenomenal
wave of enthusiasm for the monastic life resulted in a plethora of new ✓
cloisters in the 1620s, of which the Augustinian filiation to Bruges in
1629 provides just one example. The Louvain house professed 45

women in the 1620s, and conditions in the enclosure had become cramped and uncomfortable. The chronicler reported

we here finding our monastery so burthened with persons that we had not convenient room to receive many more, agreed in our Counsel and yearly consultation to seek for to amplify our Order by setting up of another monastery, whereby sending there ten nuns we should make room here to receive more persons.[42]

There were also filiations from Gravelines and Brussels which can be attributed in part to their successful recruitment. The Poor Clares added another 33 nuns to their ranks in the 1620s, although the Benedictines attracted only 12.[43] Both houses experienced internal dissension during the decade which resulted in fewer postulants, and the departure of dissidents to new cloisters. In 1624, four dissatisfied Benedictines began a convent in Ghent, and, in 1629, 22 estranged Poor Clares removed themselves to Aire.[44] Three members of the Brussels house were also sent to assist an independently founded English cloister in Cambrai.[45]

The success of the first cloisters encouraged restoration of other contemplative orders. In 1621, two widows, Lucy (Lucy Angela) Sleford Davis and Petronilla (Petronilla Clare) Kemp Browne, began a community of Franciscan nuns of the Third Order Regular in Brussels.[46] Helen (Gertrude) More and eight companions founded the Benedictine abbey at Cambrai in 1623, which was allied to the male English Benedictine congregation.[47] Letitia (Mary) Tredway, with the assistance of the English secular clergy, located an Augustinian convent in Paris in 1634. The Canonesses of the Holy Sepulchre were revived in 1642 by Susan (Mary of the Conception) Hawley. In addition to these restored orders, 1619 saw English members of the reformed Carmelites establish themselves in Antwerp. With the exception of the Dominicans who were founded in 1661, the remaining seventeenth-century foundations were all offshoots from the cloisters begun during the first half of the century.[48] Table 1.1 lists the order, location and date of establishment for each cloister. It shows that foundations peaked in the 1620s, dipped sharply during the 1630s, rose again in the 1640s, then levelled in the 1650s and 1660s, declining into the 1670s.[49] A comparison with Elizabeth Rapley's study of Ursuline foundations in seventeenth-century France reveals a similar pattern, despite the vast discrepancy in the overall number of convents, the apostolic nature of the early Company of St Ursula, and the multiplicity of English orders versus the single French congregation.

Table 1.1 The post-Reformation English contemplative cloisters, 1591–1710*

Order	Location	Date founded
Bridgettine	Lisbon	1594
Benedictine	Brussels	1598
Poor Clare	St Omer / Gravelines**	1608/1609
Augustinian	Louvain	1609
Carmelite	Antwerp	1619
Franciscan, Third Order Regular	Brussels / Nieuport / Bruges	1621/1637/1662
Benedictine	Cambrai	1623
Benedictine	Ghent	1624
Augustinian	Bruges	1629
Poor Clare	Aire	1629
Augustinian	Paris	1634
Sepulchrine	Liège	1642
Poor Clare	Rouen	1644
Carmelite	Lierre	1648
Benedictine	Paris	1650
Poor Clare	Dunkirk	1652
Benedictine	Boulogne / Pontoise	1652/1658
Conceptionists ('Blue Nuns')	Paris	1658
Dominican	Vilvorde / Brussels	1661/1669
Benedictine	Dunkirk	1662
Benedictine	Ypres	1665
Carmelite	Hoogstraeten	1678

*Includes only the contemplative cloisters which survived the seventeenth century.
**Locations and dates separated by oblique strokes indicate original foundation and subsequent relocation.
Source: Guilday, *Catholic Refugees*.

Significantly, Ursuline growth commenced in the aftermath of the order's initial acceptance of strict enclosure in 1610. However, the majority of the 320 houses were founded between 1629 and 1640.[50] The 10 cloisters founded by various religious orders in Venice and Torcello were spread more evenly across the century, with the 1600s, 1610s and 1640s accounting for two new houses apiece, with none in the 1630s, or any after 1672.[51] Although a viable comparison is impossible, both the French and Italian experiences contrast with the English decades of expansion – 1620s and 1640–70. The divergences suggest that regional factors were central in determining monastic expansion and contraction. In the case of the English cloisters, the political situation in their homeland seems to have been decisive.

The slow growth during the early years of the 1600s can be attributed to the relative novelty of the convents, exacerbated by the negative impact of the 1605 Gunpowder Plot. Conversely, the rapid expansion between 1619 and 1629 attested to the rising confidence of Catholics as marriage negotiations with Spain, and then France, for James I's heir promised suspension of the penal laws. The accession of Charles I in 1625, and his marriage to the devoutly Catholic Henrietta Maria, seemingly ushered in a new age of toleration, which should have been matched by exuberant development. However, despite a diminution in physical persecution, the Crown continued to exact the financial penalties of recusancy, particularly after 1629 when Charles' personal rule necessitated alternative sources of revenue.[52] The heavy financial burden this placed upon recusants might explain the trough in foundations with only a single house set up in the 1630s. However, the dearth of new convents was also attributable to wars and plague on the Continent which caused the existing houses considerable hardship. The strife continued into the 1640s which nonetheless gave rise to three cloisters. Although a direct consequence of successful recruitment in the 1620s, they were also the product of difficult political and economic times. Apart from the Sepulchrine foundation in 1642, the other cloisters were filiations deemed necessary to relieve the crippling financial burden experienced by the mother-houses of Gravelines and Antwerp. The four new convents of the 1650s were founded for similar reasons.

Although beneficial in alleviating pressure on their parent house's resources, many filiations simply replicated the insolvency they had sought to eliminate. The story of the Third Order Regular Franciscans graphically illustrates the shortcomings of poverty-induced foundations. After moving in 1637 to Nieuport from Brussels to escape the high cost of living, and the impact of the plague which was blamed for a downturn in recruitment, the community faced ruin 20 years later. Nieuport's unhealthy climate and its position in the midst of a war zone, combined with events in England, brought the house to the brink of total collapse. The destruction by soldiers of the cloister's farm ultimately made their position untenable, and in 1658 the convent divided. Sickly nuns returned to their families across the Channel, part of the community was sent into France to set up a filiation, and half the remaining nuns temporarily relocated to Bruges. In 1662, those who had stayed in Nieuport abandoned it permanently for Bruges. Although the move improved the mother-house's desperate fortunes, it remained in debt until the 1700 election of the astute Abbess Margaret Clare Roper, who had restored solvency by the time of her death in 1719. The sisters who went to France from Nieuport set up a new convent in Paris in 1558. In 1661, they were forced to adopt the rule of the Immaculate Conception, after the archbishop of Paris refused permission for them to remain under Franciscan jurisdiction. The 'Blue Nuns', as they came to be known, because of the blue cloak they wore, likewise struggled to make ends meet, and relied heavily upon the charity of both English exiles and pious French gentlewomen. They remained numerically weak, professing only 27 choir nuns between 1661 and 1710. Yet, like their mother-house, the 'Blue Nuns' engineered a revival of their dwindling fortunes in the 1700s to run a fashionable school for girls during the eighteenth century.[53]

In spite of the Franciscan upheavals, by the 1660s, foundations of convents were made for less desperate reasons. In 1665, the bishop of Ypres, who reputedly admired the talented Marina Beaumont, sponsored a Benedictine filiation in his diocese.[54] But the English political scene continued to be decisive in the emergence of other houses. After the Civil War of the 1640s, and the uncertainties (albeit with relative toleration for nonconformists) of the Interregnum in the 1650s, the 1660 restoration of Charles II ushered in an era of extreme optimism, celebrated in the creation of additional cloisters. The Dominican nuns of Vilvorde were established in 1661, largely through the efforts of Philip (Thomas) Howard (later Cardinal Howard) who was prominent at the royal Court, becoming grand almoner to Queen Catherine of Braganza.[55] The Ghent Benedictine filiation to Dunkirk in 1662 was financed in part by the king, in gratitude for the assistance Abbess Mary Knatchbull of Ghent had rendered to the royalists in the 1650s, although Charles always denied any involvement.[56] Yet, despite the king's leaning towards Catholic toleration, constant Parliamentary fears of a papist insurgency and a backlash of anti-Catholicism unleashed by the Popish Plot in 1678 were reflected in the contraction of new houses to a single Carmelite filiation in the 1670s. This proved to be the final cloister established abroad. Although the nuns greeted the accession of the Catholic James II in 1685 with jubilation, and dispatched various filiations to England and Ireland, none survived.[57] The despair engendered by the events of 1688 was reflected by the absence of new houses from the 1690s into the eighteenth century.

The foundation of the 22 English contemplative houses therefore occurred for a range of spiritual, political and economic reasons. The convents' emergence was grounded in the aspirations and fortunes of England's Catholic minority, but it was subject to events in both England and the regions where the cloisters were situated. The next section will discuss a factor instrumental in the beginning of many new houses – recruitment. By analysing overall trends and their exceptions in specific houses, the impact of English and local political and economic influences becomes more apparent. However, there were broader logistical issues at stake in the acquisition of English women to populate the expatriate cloisters. The significance of clerical and lay networks in monastic expansion and their impact on the convents' social composition will also be examined.

Choir nuns, lay sisters and factors affecting recruitment

Overall recruitment included in my statistical analysis of nine religious communities is shown in Table 1.2. It shows that the 1620s marked the highpoint for monastic professions. The sum of new nuns dropped dramatically during the 1630s and 1640s, intimating the grave difficulty of receiving women and, more importantly, obtaining their dowry money during times of political turmoil. Professions began to increase again in the 1650s, peaking in the 1680s. The final decade of the century saw a return to Civil War figures, and in the 1700s this decline con-

Table 1.2   Total professions, 1591–1710*

	Number	Percentage
1591–1600	35	3.3
1601–1610	26	2.5
1611–1620	94	8.9
1621–1630	155	14.7
1631–1640	70	6.6
1641–1650	71	6.7
1651–1660	108	10.2
1661–1670	121	11.4
1671–1680	102	9.7
1681–1690	124	11.7
1691–1700	83	7.9
1701–1710	68	6.4
Total	1057	100.0

*Sample includes data for Brussels Benedictines, Gravelines Poor Clares, Louvain Augustinians, Third Order Franciscans, Cambrai Benedictines, Bruges Augustinians, Sepulchrines, Pontoise Benedictines, 'Blue Nuns'.
Sources: 'Brussels Benedictine Registers'; 'Poor Clare Registers'; Forster, 'Poor Clares of Rouen – 2'; *Chronicle of St Monica's*, vols 1 and 2; Priory, MSS C2, J8, M1; Foley, *Records*; *Franciscana*; 'Cambrai Records'; Priory, Bruges List; Durrant, *Flemish Mystics*; 'Sepulchrine Records'; 'Pontoise Registers'; Birt, *Obit Book*; Versailles, 68 H 3, 68 H 4; Nichols, *Herald and Genealogist*; *Diary of the 'Blue Nuns'*.

tinued.[58] Recruitment therefore reflects the broad trends uncovered in the foundation movement. However, by compartmentalising the picture, separating choir nuns from lay sisters, and looking at individual cloisters, different patterns emerge. Table 1.3 shows professions each decade, according to type – choir nun, lay sister or white sister.[59] The recruitment pattern for choir nuns mirrors the model in Table 1.2, largely because there were considerably more nuns professed than lay sisters. Only the Augustinian registers distinguished the white sisters – disabled or elderly women who were unable to adhere completely to the rigours of the rule. The Sepulchrines also admitted infirm sisters, but their records did not identify them separately.[60] Other orders did not officially accept women who could not maintain monastic observances, but when expedient they made exceptions. White sisters contributed a hefty dowry to compensate for their physical shortcomings, and some houses were prepared to undertake the extra work an incapacitated member generated in order to reap the financial benefit of admitting her. However, as the figures illustrate,

Table 1.3 Professions by type of nun, 1591–1710*

	Choir nuns	Lay sisters	White sisters**	Total
1591–1600	21	2		23
1601–1610	2	1		3
1611–1620	17	7	3	27
1621–1630	90	16	4	110
1631–1640	32	17	1	50
1641–1650	47	11	1	59
1651–1660	70	16		86
1661–1670	66	25		91
1671–1680	71	15		86
1681–1690	77	14		91
1691–1700	45	15		60
1701–1710	42	11		53
Total	580	150	9	739

*Sample includes data for Louvain Augustinians, Third Order Franciscans, Cambrai Benedictines, Bruges Augustinians, Sepulchrines, Pontoise Benedictines, 'Blue Nuns'. The registers for the Brussels Benedictines and Gravelines Poor Clares did not distinguish between type of nun.
**Note that only the Augustinian houses professed white sisters.
Sources: 'Brussels Benedictine Registers'; 'Poor Clare Registers'; *Chronicle of St Monica's*, vols 1 and 2; Priory, MSS C2, J8, M1; Foley, *Records*; *Franciscana*; 'Cambrai Records'; Priory, Bruges List; Durrant, *Flemish Mystics*; 'Sepulchrine Records'; 'Pontoise Registers'; Birt, *Obit Book*; Versailles, 68 H 3, 68 H 4; Nichols, *Herald and Genealogist*; *Diary of the 'Blue Nuns'*.

they constituted a minority, even in those cloisters which endorsed their inclusion. Alternately, the number of lay sisters, who brought a meagre portion in return for undertaking the manual labour of the household, was proportionate to a house's complement of choir nuns. The Cambrai Benedictines' constitutions (or statutes) which adapted the rule of St Benedict for use in the convent, advised the nuns not to take any lay sisters without adequate provision.[61] The Louvain Augustinians' confessor explained the rationale for such a restriction. He claimed that lay sisters consumed more of the convent's resources, incurring 'a greater charge for cloaths, eating and drinking more by reason of their labour, and breeding, and occasioning more work, by reason they have much more to wash then an equal number of Nuns', and he warned the prioress to

> be careful not to receive more sisters then are necessary for the Convents service: who otherwise will undoe each other with idlenes; gossipp and prate away their time, medle with the Monasteries affayres and eat up your temporal means like a consumption.

He accordingly recommended a ratio of one lay sister to every five choir nuns.[62] With the exception of the Third Order Regular Franciscans, cloisters averaged a ratio of one fifth to a quarter of lay sisters to choir nuns. The correlation between numbers of choir and lay sisters caused a different recruitment pattern for the latter – the number of lay sisters peaked during the decade following a high intake of choir nuns. Hence the nuns adjusted their intake of lay sisters in accordance with the overall size of the community.

The anomalous situation among the Franciscans where the mean proportion of lay sisters was only 16 per cent is worth examining. The best explanation appears to lie in the nuns' extreme poverty in both Brussels and Nieuport. Although the convent had some of the strongest choir nun recruitment during the 1640s, it obviously avoided accepting women with inadequate dowries. Once the nuns were established in Bruges the ratio expanded, reaching an extraordinary 33 per cent of lay sisters in the 1690s and 1700s.[63] This phenomenal increase can be explained principally by improved prosperity, but also by the fact that in the 1660s members of the convent were ageing and less able to conduct some of the heavier tasks they had carried out during the lean years. Indeed the house's annals noted that during the Franciscan provincial's visit of 1664, 'it was ordained, that more Lay Sisters – for the service of the Community should in the future be received'.[64] The data shows that at times of financial crisis, lay sisters were sacrificed, and the choir nuns forced to carry out more of the mundane household tasks than they would otherwise undertake. There was a comparable situation in the Flemish Augustinian cloister during the 1590s and early 1600s. The house was impoverished and survived principally through its intake of English postulants. Only two lay sisters were professed in the 1590s, in contrast to 21 choir nuns. The gentlewomen of the choir were engaged in many menial tasks, such as washing, weeding and sweeping. Furthermore, because of the advanced age of most of the Flemish sisters, the English also tended their cells, making their beds and cleaning the rooms.[65] Once the separate foundation of St Monica's was on a reasonably firm footing, the intake of lay sisters rose.

Choir nuns, primarily responsible for singing the canonical hours, provided a dowry, and women whose financial status was questionable could not be admitted to profession until their portion was secure. As a consequence, they were particularly vulnerable to English political unrest which disrupted their capacity to procure the money. Nowhere was this illustrated more graphically than in the Bruges Augustinian house. Founded in 1629, it suffered low recruitment in the 1630s and 1640s with only two professions for the choir per decade. The flood of 19 professions in the 1650s was in part a result of the backlog of novices from the 1640s whose dowries fell victim to the Civil War. But the Bruges convent's failure to grow did not rest solely upon events in their homeland. In its early years the cloister suffered the dual perils of local warfare and plague. Moreover, the poverty stemming from few professions and a lack of alms from England, left the nuns suffering what was described as 'some sort of Famine'.[66] The effects of destitution, disease, and war, along with reports of disunity, disaster and corruption, wrought similar patterns of poor recruitment in other cloisters.

The Gravelines Poor Clares suffered repeated adversity during their first 50 years which did much to reverse the house's phenomenal success of the first two decades when over 70 women had taken their vows.[67] Before experiencing the vicissitudes of warfare, the convent survived a fire in 1626 which destroyed its refectory, dormitories, granaries and novitiate. This disaster occurred in the midst of an internal dispute over the cloister's jurisdiction in which the abbess had been deposed and the nuns divided.[68] It was resolved in 1629 by the filiation to Aire, but not before the damaging affair had been debated widely from London to Rome. Gravelines then became enmeshed in the war between France and Spain, which saw it fall first in 1644 to the French (who celebrated their victory with a *Te Deum* in the nuns' chapel), then returned to the

Spanish in 1652, and finally back to the French in the 1659 Treaty of the Pyrenees. However, the greatest catastrophe occurred in 1654 when the powder arsenal in Gravelines exploded, destroying a large part of the town, including the castle, ramparts and parish church. The English Poor Clare convent suffered considerable damage, described by one of the nuns, who reported

> The strong Gaites of our Inclosure the Doors and windows of the house the whole Top of the Quire Carry'd of in one Clap beames and rafters with other Timber all hoysted up burst a Sunder and disjointed all the Bricks tyles and eaves of the Gutters round the Quire and Church all fallen about our heads and the whole House shatter'd in Pieces.[69]

With the assistance of grants from Louis XIV, the cloister was again rebuilt, and it survived the remainder of the century relatively unscathed. However, the diminishing recruitment of the 1620s and 1630s points to the impact of the dispute and the fire. Its virtual collapse in the 1640s and 1650s was in part the consequence of the Civil War and Interregnum, but the local military conflict and the arsenal explosion exacerbated the English factors. Although the numbers of women taking the veil at Gravelines never again reached the heady days of the 1610s, the 23 professions in the 1660s and 28 in the 1680s were evidence that a reputation tarnished by disaster could be resurrected.[70]

This was not always the case. The Brussels Benedictine house, which had prospered in the 1610s, began its inexorable decline in the 1620s during an acrimonious dispute between Abbess Mary Percy and several nuns who criticised her leadership, particularly her changed attitude to Jesuit involvement in the convent. The appointment of a new chaplain who was strongly opposed to the Society of Jesus in 1628 escalated the tensions. Split into factions and openly warring, the cloister's problems became common knowledge – a fact reflected by the absence of professions in the 1630s and a single one in the 1640s. The eventual resolution of the dissension in 1652 was rewarded by the addition of 13 new nuns. But the revival was short-lived with only 20 women joining the house during the remaining four decades of the century, which contrasted sharply with Gravelines' 72 choir nuns, the Louvain Augustinians' 44, and the relatively new Pontoise Benedictine house's 52 professions.[71] The economic and health concerns which led the Third Order Franciscans to depart Brussels for Nieuport probably added to the Benedictines' internal difficulties in the 1630s and 1640s. However, there is no doubt that its recruitment woes were caused chiefly by the domestic strife. Other cloisters also declined when their reputations were similarly blighted. In 1675, among the 'Blue Nuns', Mary (Gabriel) Huddlestone, a young choir nun, and Elizabeth (Agnes Didacus) Lathom, a lay sister, challenged the authority of Abbess Anne (Elizabeth) Timperley and the confessor, Henry Browne, in an apparent quest to secure Jesuit direction. Rumours of the disturbance were soon circulating in Paris, and the earl of Castlemaine threatened to remove his two nieces, Jane and Christina Darell, who were due to be professed there. The incident was apparently resolved and the Darells took their vows in 1677. However, in 1681, ongoing tension, intensified by the house's considerable debts, led to the departure of Anne Timperley to a French cloister, accompanied, somewhat surprisingly, by Gabriel Huddlestone. Their abrupt exit signalled that all was not well in the house. The two professions in the 1680s and a single one in the 1690s reflected people's wariness of a cloister so obviously divided.[72]

The Cambrai Benedictines were damaged by recurring doubts regarding the orthodoxy of their spiritual teacher, Augustine Baker. Relatively strong growth in the 1620s was followed by a decline in the 1630s, 40s and 50s to a low point which saw only three professions in the 1660s. Numbers then stabilised at the 1640s level for the remainder of the century.[73] While subject to the same pressures as many other houses which also experienced recession in the 1630s, Cambrai's fortunes began to slide in the aftermath of Baker's removal in 1633. Although his writings were examined and cleared of heretical leanings at the time, they were questioned again in 1655, and the nuns were ordered to hand them over for correction. When they refused, the convent incurred the Benedictine president's displeasure. Abbess Catherine Gascoigne won the altercation, but at a price. With the exception of the abbess's niece, Frances Gascoigne, no choir nuns were professed between 1656 and 1662 when Mary (Agnes) Errington made her vows, and there was a further drought until 1668 and 1669 when two more women joined the community. Other factors compounded the spirituality problems. The cloister was located in the disputed region of Artois, and suffered during the protracted war between the French and the Spanish. The military disturbances devalued the currency, rendering food and fuel prohibitively expensive. The nuns' situation was made worse by the fact that the cloister's English investments lay in royalist hands. The victory of the parliamentary forces over Charles I left them virtually bankrupt. Amidst the controversy in 1655, the abbess and her supporters blamed the house's penury on the monks who, as its procurators, had mismanaged the finances.[74] However, in the eyes of prospective postulants and their parents, evidence of incompetence tarnished the nuns' reputation, regardless of who was actually to blame. The Paris Augustinians learned this to their peril in the 1660s, when their agent purchased property on the convent's behalf using fictitious rents. Despite the nuns' protestations of ignorance (and thus innocence) regarding his fraudulent dealings, doubts were raised about their financial acumen. After professing 20 women between 1656 and 1665, during the next ten years there were only six new nuns.[75]

Convents were acutely conscious of just how devastating negative reports could prove in recruitment terms. Some houses did all in their power to prevent unfavourable news leaking beyond their walls to dissuade potential postulants. Incidences of plague were especially disabling and struck most of the cloisters, particularly during the 1630s. The Augustinians in Bruges were afflicted in 1634, losing Sister Elizabeth Lovel and a boarder.[76] Mary Trevelyan of the Ghent Benedictines died of plague during the same year.[77] In 1635, two lay sisters at St Monica's contracted the disease, but recovered. Mary Worthington was not so fortunate in 1636, dying soon after a lay servant of the cloister had succumbed.[78] The Brussels Franciscans buried four of their nuns and their confessor in 1635, all of whom had acquired the fatal illness.[79] Although subject to the stringent public health laws which governed their towns, the nuns tried hard not to publicise their misfortune. The Louvain Augustinians went into a self-imposed quarantine upon the death of Mary Worthington, not writing to anyone in England.[80] But it was often hard for houses of women, dependent upon the sacramental services of priests, to avoid notification. The Rouen Poor Clare abbess, Margaret (Margaret Ignatius) Bedingfield faced a difficult dilemma when two children in the school contracted plague in 1667. In an effort to stave off the inevitable damage public knowledge of the outbreak would inflict upon recruitment to both the novitiate and school, she remained silent. However, when one of the nuns contracted the disease and was in danger of dying without the last rites, Bedingfield capitulated and informed the civic authorities. The house was accordingly sealed for two months, depriving it of contact with England, postulants, and its new confessor. During her agony of indecision over whether or not to divulge the infection, various people confided that their cloisters had not disclosed plague for fear of negative impact.[81]

The ability of events on the Continent, like warfare, plague or internal dissension, to constrict the flow of choir nuns to individual cloisters suggests that the recusant families who patronised them were informed about their circumstances. Open channels of communication between the convents and England was an integral aspect of the recruitment process and, although such publicity proved something of a liability when convents experienced problems, the contact more commonly worked in the cloisters' favour. By 1620 the majority of nuns was drawn from England. Monasteries therefore depended upon the formal and informal networks of family, friends and clergy who acted as procurators in their homeland. These allies remained in touch with the religious communities, and informed prospective postulants about available options and potential difficulties. Hence, they were highly influential in a woman's choice of house, and they facilitated her journey across the Channel.

Formally each house was allied with priests working in England. Recruitment for the Paris Augustinians was in the hands of the English secular clergy. Organised through the network of local vicariates and archdeaconries, the cloister's register reveals that many choir nuns came from families closely associated with leaders of the secular clergy.[82] Other houses depended on Jesuit procurators. Individual stories suggest that priests were influential in choosing which religious order women would adopt, often sending postulants to houses with which they were associated. Mary Thoresby, professed a lay sister in Louvain in 1619, had wanted to join Mary Ward's Institute. However, the priest accompanying her to the Low Countries took her to the Augustinian house which she finally agreed to enter, so long as she did not have to labour too hard.[83] The four Clopton sisters who made their final vows there in 1622 had consulted the priests who serviced their recusant household as to which order to join, and Louvain 'was judged and thought the fittest for them'.[84] Some clerics achieved notoriety for their enthusiastic dispatch of English children abroad. In 1599, two years after the Jesuit, Henry Floyd, became chaplain to the Southcott family of Bulmer on the border of Essex and Suffolk, their eldest daughter, Elizabeth, went overseas to the Benedictine cloister in Brussels, where she was professed in 1600.[85] Floyd became well known as a procurator for Jesuit associated colleges and cloisters throughout his career. In 1633–34 he reputedly converted young boys and sent them to St Omer, and conveyed the daughters of Henry Yaxley of Suffolk to convents.[86] His efforts were not limited to these individuals' immediate families. Many of Elizabeth Southcott's relations entered the religious life during the early decades of the seventeenth century. Mary Welch, a cousin, was professed at St Ursula's in 1599. Elizabeth (Clare) and Margaret Curzon, her cousins, made their vows at Brussels in 1605 and 1612 respectively. Other cousins,

Appolonia and Jeronima Waldegrave, entered her own cloister and the Ghent Benedictine house in the 1620s. In 1627, Elizabeth's niece, Mary Southcott, made her vows at Ghent, along with her cousin, Margaret Roper.[87] While Floyd's role in these subsequent vocations is unclear, the majority of Southcott's kin did enter houses with ties to the Society of Jesus, suggesting his influence.

It is possible, however, that Elizabeth Southcott's relations sought information about the convents from one another. While priests provided the initial contact, the laity rapidly established their own links with the cloisters through their nun relatives and clerical associates, and they procured postulants from within family ranks and wider recusant networks. Groupings of family members within specific houses attest to kin's importance as informal agents. Among the Louvain Augustinians, Mary and Helen Copley, professed in 1612, were the nieces of Prioress Margaret Clement. In 1624, their cousin Elizabeth (Clare) Copley took her vows in the cloister.[88] Correspondence shows that the nuns' families actively worked towards the convents' expansion.[89] Letters from Thomas Worthington and Jane Plumpton Worthington to their four daughters at Louvain during the 1690s discussed relatives who were keen to settle their daughters in the house. Mary (Mary Genevieve) Worthington, the eldest sister, was procuratrix at the time, so family business was directed through her.[90] Monastic registers record several generations of some clans taking the veil. The diarist, Nicholas Blundell of Little Crosby in Lancashire, had great-aunts, aunts, sisters and cousins in the Poor Clare cloisters at Gravelines and Rouen, the Benedictine house at Ghent, and with the Augustinians in Louvain. His mother, Mary Eyre Blundell, joined her daughters at Ghent in 1706.[91] Stalwart supporters of the monasteries like the Blundells even recruited from beyond their immediate family circle. Between 1709 and 1711, Nicholas collected alms money for the Poor Clares from Edmund Tristram, a yeoman of Ince Blundell, whose daughter Ann (Ann Joseph) Tristram subsequently took her vows at Gravelines in 1712.[92]

The prominence of families, like the Southcotts and Blundells, in directing their daughters, kin, and sometimes neighbours, across the Channel is reflected in an analysis of the nuns' geographical origins, which shows that the cloisters drew most of their inhabitants from the populous Catholic counties, or those with pockets of recusancy centred around gentry estates. Of the 793 women whose region of origin was listed in the registers, the greatest proportion came from Lancashire (9.6 per cent) and Yorkshire (8 per cent). However, there was solid representation from Suffolk (3.3 per cent), Kent (3.1 per cent), Essex and Oxfordshire (both with 2.7 per cent), Hampshire and London (2.6 per cent each) Staffordshire (2.3 per cent), Northumberland and Sussex (2.2 per cent apiece).[93] Although the sample is very small, it illustrates the significance of local recusant networks, particularly with respect to those counties on the eastern seaboard with ready links across the Channel. It also confirms the important role played by the priests who serviced these regions and households, inspired vocations and, crucially, provided the means by which women could safely embark overseas to realise their ambition. The process of reaching the Continent was complicated by the requirement of a travel pass, and the English authorities became increasingly suspicious of young women making the journey. Various nuns related harrowing tales of being stopped and searched at the port and, in some cases, imprisoned upon the suspicion that they were destined for a convent.[94] Thus, the routes and guises employed by the missionary priests, whose own safety depended upon secure passage, likewise served the cloisters. Women commonly related their passage in the company of clerics or their assistants who, upon arrival, deposited them safely in their appointed religious house.[95]

The nuns' social status further reflected the importance of priests and the gentry in recruitment. Given the seigneurial leadership of the English Catholic community, and the concentration of clergy in their midst, it is not surprising that over 92 per cent of religious women were daughters of gentlemen, esquires, baronets, knights and peers. Table 1.4 depicts the rank of the 530 women whose worldly standing was recorded. It shows that although plebeian recusants vastly outnumbered their elite co-religionists in England, they evidently lacked the connections and financial means to dower their offspring for the exiled convents, even as lay sisters. The data from such a small sample may well be misleading, particularly with respect to the lay sisters for whom there is little information. Yet the choir nuns' social status mirrored their European counterparts in houses adhering to the ancient monastic rules, which were similarly populated by the daughters from the upper echelons of society.[96] Moreover, the concentration of nuns from gentry households concurs with the picture now emerging of English convents in the late middle ages.[97] While the timing of the convents' re-establishment and their recruitment patterns point strongly to their spiritual and political importance for English Catholics, their distinctive social make-up implies that there might well have been more pragmatic reasons for their resurrection and patronage by the recusant elites. Rising secular dowry prices, evidence of child oblates and coerced vocations imply that family strategies were often behind a woman's adoption of the religious life.

Table 1.4   Social origins by type of nun, 1591–1710

	Choir	Lay	White	All	Percentage
Peer	29		1	30	5.7
Knt/Bart	128		3	131	24.7
Esquire	297	6	2	305	57.5
Gentleman	20	5		25	4.7
Bourgeois	7			7	1.3
Professional	10	5		15	2.8
Yeoman	3	7		10	1.9
Soldier	1			1	0.2
Artisan	1	1		2	0.4
Servant		4		4	0.8
Total	496	28	6	530	100.0

Definition of categories of social origin: Peer: daughters of lords; Knt/Bart: daughters of knights and baronets; Esquire: daughters of those described as esquires; Gentleman: daughters of those described as 'gentlemen'; Bourgeois; daughters of merchants and civic officials; Professional: daughters of doctors of medicine and lawyers; Yeoman: daughters of rural small landholders and farmers; Soldier: daughters of soldiers; Artisan: daughters of tradesmen; Servant; daughters of domestic servants.

Sources: 'Brussels Benedictine Registers'; 'Poor Clare Registers'; Forster, 'Poor Clares of Rouen – 2'; *Chronicle of St Monica's*, vols 1 and 2; Priory, MSS C2, J8, M1; Foley, *Records*; *Franciscana*; 'Cambrai Records'; Priory, Bruges List; Durrant, *Flemish Mystics*; 'Sepulchrine Records'; 'Pontoise Registers'; Birt, *Obit Book*; Versailles, 68 H 3, 68 H 4; Nichols, *Herald and Genealogist*; *Diary of the 'Blue Nuns'*; 'Ghent Obituary Notices'.

Vocations

Although the Council of Trent's review of female monasticism purport-edly addressed the centuries-old abuse of the cloister, studies of early modern convents have detailed the continued forced monachisation of elite women. Spiralling dowry prices and the need for refuges for un-marriageable or unwanted female kin meant that no amount of clerical coercion could break the elite's attitude towards the convent as the only acceptable repository for women outside marriage. Indeed Gabriella Zarri has suggested that churchmen, who hailed from similar social backgrounds, often viewed convents in the same way as their secular kin, preferring to make nuns of female relatives than permit them to marry below their rank.[98] Hence, although officially Church reform aimed to break the ruling order's influence which rendered monasteries instruments of lay political, social and economic power, its success was limited. In the confessional era, the cloister became an integral marker of civic identity and state formation. Jutta Sperling's study of Renaissance Venice has shown how certain prestigious cloisters not only preserved

the patrimonies and honour of the patriciate, but also the political
integrity of the republic itself, visually represented in the ritual marriage
of one cloister's abbess to the doge.[99] In France, where state regulation of
marriage disempowered the Church, and accordingly advanced the
social and economic interests of France's governing classes and the
absolutist ambitions of the crown, convents were important as alternative prisons where rebellious women and children could be incarcerated.[100] Religious houses were thus vital secular institutions in which
spiritual goals were often sacrificed (along with daughters) to the interests of family and state.

In post-Reformation England where Catholics were effectively separated from the Protestant Church and State, the cloisters did not possess
quite the same economic, social and political resonance. Yet for a religious minority which paid highly for its nonconformity in financial
terms, and which aspired to reproduce itself by avoiding intermarriage
wherever possible, convents theoretically offered financial relief in the
form of cheaper dowries and a refuge for daughters without a recusant
husband. However, despite clerical discouragement of interfaith marriages and evidence of religious endogamy in elite circles, some parents'
willingness to marry their daughters to Protestants if the match was
advantageous suggests that secular ambitions could outweigh spiritual.[101] Moreover, current research on the English Catholic community
dispels previous assertions of its exclusivity and detachment from mainstream society and politics.[102] Some adherents to Rome most certainly
did all they could to preserve their confessional identity, marrying co-
religionists and dispatching daughters across the Channel, but there was
no coherent policy or practice which would support an assertion that
the cloisters were designed and patronised to maintain Catholic purity.
The more probable secular motivation lay in the economic benefit of the
cloister for parents suffering the fiscal penalties of recusancy during a
period of rising marriage portions.

As in Europe, English dowries increased in value throughout the seventeenth century. Among the peerage, average portions increased from
about 2,000 pounds in the final quarter of the sixteenth century to
roughly 9,500 pounds between 1675–1729.[103] Given the social composition of the cloisters, it was patently cheaper for the daughters of aristocratic families and those in the upper echelons of the gentry, who paid
1,000–5,000 pounds, to marry Christ rather than seek a secular groom.[104]
Yet the gentry was a somewhat amorphous group, and the large number
of nuns who identified their parents as esquires or gentlemen suggests
that many would have belonged to the minor (or county) gentry, whose

portions lay between 500 and 1,000 pounds.[105] The disparity between this sum and official monastic dowries, which ranged between 300 and 500 pounds, would have made the cloister less attractive to this broader group. The sum requested varied among orders, with the Benedictines in the upper price bracket, and it rose during the course of the century, but stipulated amounts did not exceed 500 pounds. The Third Order Franciscans required no less than 300 pounds in 1640, but by 1698, they were demanding 400 pounds.[106] In 1631 the Cambrai Benedictine constitutions decreed that no novice should be accepted with less than 400 pounds.[107] In the 1670s the Dunkirk Benedictines sought 500 pounds, although 400 pounds was the lower limit for the choir.[108] Other cloisters capitalised on their lower fees. In 1652 the Sepulchrines set their price at 300 pounds, declaring 'portions...are no where more moderate than here'.[109] The Poor Clares most likely demanded even less. In the early years of the Gravelines house's existence, Abbess Mary Gough unsuccessfully strove to dispense with dowries and to subsist on alms alone.[110]

Moreover, data relating to dowry payments reveals that the convents did not always adhere to the stipulated fees. In 1676, Abbess Mary Caryll of Dunkirk admitted in the midst of her endeavours to extract 500 pounds from a reluctant parent that, during the early years of the Benedictine house's existence, she had accepted novices for only 300 pounds.[111] The first Poor Clares at Gravelines contributed 100 pounds, although two sisters gave 400 pounds and some were accepted with nothing.[112] Discrepancies occurred because during the early years of their foundation, cloisters required ready funds to pay for their residence and its furnishings, and many were tempted to discount their prices to attract postulants whose portions would cover these expenses. The same strategy was employed if a house later suffered financially or in terms of recruitment. Thus, parents who sought the cloister as a cheaper alternative might well have negotiated a sum to suit their circumstances. Between 1677 and 1710, 16 Sepulchrines professed at Liège contributed an average of 333 pounds, with only three women bestowing in excess of 350 pounds.[113] Even successful convents did not demand much more. The 52 choir nuns who joined the Louvain Augustinians between 1671 and 1710, brought an average of 358 pounds. Prior to 1700, 21 per cent of these portions were over 400 pounds, with the figure rising to 57 per cent thereafter.[114]

The dowry figures illustrate the cloister's attraction for recusant parents who had been impoverished by fines, or who did not want to pay a marriage dowry commensurate with their social status. Some drove a hard bargain in their quest to settle a daughter cheaply. The protracted negotiation between the Benedictine abbess, Mary Caryll, of Dunkirk and Sir Thomas Clifton of Lytham in Lancashire over the portion of Ann (Benedict) Clifton demonstrated his reluctance to pay more than he deemed acceptable. Sir Thomas had four sisters who were Poor Clares, and he was evidently expecting similar rates in the Benedictine cloister. When Caryll requested 500 pounds up front, in addition to an annuity during Ann's novitiate and the cost of her entrance, clothing and profession, he grumbled that other cloisters sought much less. Ann sided with the abbess, begging her father to contribute a sum which would reflect her rank, desperately pointing out that some of the nuns had given 600 or 700 pounds, others 1,000 pounds. However, Sir Thomas was deaf to her pleas and Mary Caryll eventually settled for 500 pounds paid in instalments.[115] The baronet's apparent intransigence suggested that he intended to dispose of Ann as cheaply as possible. Indeed Ann's eldest sister, Mary, subsequently received the handsome dowry of 5,000 pounds upon her marriage to Thomas, Lord Petre in 1685, implying that Sir Thomas had been reserving his resources for her good match.[116] Yet, the situation was not that simple. Another sister, Bridget also married. Moreover, Ann's annuity was raised from 10 to 16 pounds per annum in 1677, and upon her father's death, she was to receive a further 500 pounds.[117] Nonetheless, he still settled her for a considerably lesser sum than her worldly marriage would have demanded; a point not lost on Ann who reminded him as much.

Other parents likewise viewed the convent from a worldly perspective. Disabled women, or those who were unmarriageable for other reasons, often became brides of Christ. Although white sisters came with a substantial dowry to compensate for the burden their illness placed upon the cloister, their portions were still below lay expectations. In 1626, Frances Parker, the daughter of Baron Mounteagle, was professed at Louvain 'in respect that she was crooked, and therefore not so fit for the world', contributing 900 pounds. However, Parker was apparently not compelled to be an Augustinian. She had wanted to be a nun from the age of 12, and had originally joined the more aristocratic Brussels Benedictines on the advice of her mother, but her experiences there had not been happy. In their critique of Mary Percy's leadership, the abbess's opponents cited the clothing of Parker as further evidence of Percy's disregard for the house's statutes, which did not allow for nuns 'notably defective in bodye'. After a furore surrounding her acceptance for profession in 1625, the novice left to become a white sister in Louvain.[118] Although her mother had obviously influenced the vocation, Frances was apparently happy at St Monica's, keeping the rule to the best of her ability until forced to spend the final 18 years of her life bedridden.[119] Other crippled women were not so fortunate. Mary Fortescue, who was professed a white sister at Louvain in 1617 because she was 'crooked' had wanted to remain in England with her married sisters. Her parents were insistent that she should take the veil, so she decided to join Mary Ward's Institute to pursue an active vocation. Despite yielding to their wishes, Fortescue's parents would not agree to her chosen order, deeming the contemplative life at St Monica's more suitable for their disabled child.[120] Illegitimate women also found their way into a nun's habit. Elizabeth Smith, professed upon her deathbed at Cambrai in 1635, was the natural daughter of a baronet, who had made the mistake of falling in love with her half-brother, and was dispatched hastily to the Continent to be 'educated' by the nuns.[121] However unwilling her choice of the religious life might have been, she was in good company. In 1690, Dame Ignatia Fitzjames, the daughter of James II and Arabella Churchill, became a Benedictine nun at Pontoise. Dame Benedict Fitzroy, a child of Charles II's mistress, Barbara Palmer, duchess of Cleveland, was professed there the following year.[122]

Although they lacked the social stigma which directed Mary Fortescue and Elizabeth Smith unwillingly into the cloister, many other women did not choose to be nuns. Lady Anne (Anne Dominic) Howard, who joined the Bruges Augustinians in 1692, later revealed that she had taken the veil not from choice but in obedience to the will of her mother, whom she feared.[123] The Carmelite, Gertrude Aston, professed in 1672, had entered and left two cloisters before settling at Lierre. The daughter of Lord Aston, Gertrude wanted to marry, but her parents were determined that she would take the veil. For 14 years she fought their wishes, but finally capitulated.[124] Other women had lived in their cloisters since they were children. Placed in convent schools at a tender age, such girls were more or less destined to become nuns, with what Elizabeth Rapley has termed 'conditioned vocations'.[125] In 1648, aged eight, Lucy (Lucy Laurentia) Hamilton was sent to be educated by the Bruges Augustinians, 'and afterwards to be a religious amongst us, if it please God to call her, the child herself being very much inclined to it'. She was professed in 1656, aged 16.[126] An analysis of the age at which 458 women entered convents suggests that over 18 per cent were admitted aged less than 15, the year in which they would have begun their 12-month novitiate.[127] Indeed over five per cent of these girls were under 10 years old. The scholars were received on the understanding that they would become nuns only if they 'had a mind to be a religious'.[128] In some instances they exercised their right of choice and left the cloister in which they had been placed. However, it is likely that several women who took the veil after many years in the school did so because of a lack of worldly experience, rather than out of any deep-seated religious compulsion.

In early modern society it was extremely difficult for young women to resist their parents' will, and just as many were contracted in unhappy marriages, others became unwilling brides of Christ. In most instances it is impossible to establish parental motivation, leading to the inevitable conclusion that fathers and mothers were lured by economic and social considerations. Once the cloisters were in existence and a steady stream of women was crossing the Channel, it more or less became customary in some families for at least one daughter to take the veil. The presence of several generations of nuns from clans, like the Blundells, implies that the cloister was considered a respectable course of life for recusant gentlewomen. But not only parents viewed it in this light. In the absence of alternatives, women who were reluctant to marry chose the religious life as their only viable option. At the age of 10, the Augustinian, Mary Worthington, had decided to become a nun, after witnessing the unhappy marriage of a friend.[129] Less dramatically, the Benedictine mystic, Helen (Gertrude) More, was persuaded by her religious director to ✓ become a nun when she expressed little desire for the married state.[130] Even some Protestant women were attracted by the prospect of a female refuge. Catherine Holland, who defied her Protestant father by converting to Catholicism, did so to join a convent. She explained:

> By this means I was settled, after a great deal of trouble, in the State of Life I had so long desired: In the which I live truly content, and no little satisfaction of Mind it was to me; I was out of danger of ever being in the Slavery of Marriage for which I had so great an aversion and there was no other way to avoid it, but in embracing the State of Religion.[131]

Another convert from Protestantism, Elizabeth Shirley, one of the founders of St Monica's, also opted for the cloister 'for she had never had any mind to marry'.[132] Although most women lacked the freedom to enact their desire for religious retirement, the idea of the convent as a female haven persisted, and it crossed confessional boundaries.[133] Thus, after 1598, for Catholic parents, and for a handful of gentlewomen who exercised their own will, monasticism once again became a feasible alternative in a society which offered women of their status little choice beyond marriage and motherhood.

But it would be wrong to assume that women took the veil solely for worldly reasons. Winefrid Thimelby who was professed at Louvain in 1635 and unanimously elected prioress in 1668 had, according to her brother, desired to be a nun since childhood.[134] Thimelby consistently expressed deep spiritual satisfaction in her religious profession. So much so that she tried hard to persuade other members of her family to partake of her happiness.[135] She was delighted when her niece, Katherine Aston, and her widowed sister-in-law, Gertrude Aston Thimelby, were at St Monica's in the late 1650s with the intention of becoming nuns, writing:

> I have but won desyre between them, yet wholl to both which is continuance of that peace the world cannot give, oh may ther soules glide in this soft streame, till thay arive [at] that torrent of delights which heaven prepares for them.[136]

Other women also described the spiritual attraction of the cloister. The widowed Lady Mary Roper Lovel left her young children to join the Brussels Benedictines in 1608, informing her patron, the earl of Salisbury, that she was called to the cloister by something 'more powerfull then the love of any mortall creture'. Certain that Robert Cecil would disapprove of her action, she nonetheless explained:

> I have thought it fitt to signifie to yor Lordship the Retired course I have undertaken which happily will seeme straing[e] and I fere distastfull to yor opinnion, but as my eand is only to seeke the glorye of god and the securitie of my soule in [that] state of life seperated from the miseries and dangers of the world soe my hope is that it shall be noe occasion to devert yor honorable favor from me or mine.[137]

Lovel left Brussels and eventually founded a Carmelite house in Antwerp well before the outbreak of hostilities in the Benedictine convent, but her passionate articulation of the cloister's place in her personal salvation was echoed by many of her former sisters during their struggle against Abbess Percy. Among many strong assertions of a desire to serve God in accordance with the rule and statutes, the voice of Anne Healey stands out. Healey had opted to become a lay sister at Brussels, rather than a choir nun elsewhere, because of the cloister's reputation for 'perfection and spirituallity', so she despaired of its descent into 'disunion, unquietnes and Insecurity'. Fearing for her soul, she requested a transfer to another monastery, assuring the archbishop:

Speaking the truth in the presence of almighty God: My hart shall sooner Loose its heat, and Change its place, then this resolution of serving our Lord according to the vocation he gave me, and the practis and intention wherin I vowed.[138]

Other nuns' spiritual diaries and letters, and convent annals and obituaries articulate similar commitments to the religious life. Thus, although undeniably useful to parents and children alike for secular reasons, the convent was also a place where many women believed they could best achieve salvation. Parents too expressed their piety through patronising the convents. There were spiritual benefits in having a monastic child, and it is possible that some reluctant or conditioned vocations were the product of recusant devotion. The Augustinian lay sisters, Ann and Mary Stonehouse, had been dedicated to God at birth by their devout father, who had vowed 'if our Lord did send him two daughters he would name one Ann and the other Mary, and give them both to God'. Ann willingly sought a place at Louvain after several years in service in Catholic gentry households, and made her vows in 1618. Mary did not join her until 1632, after their father had died, when their brother, 'asked her if she would be a religious, that then he would seek to get her a place. She answered, Yes, although she knew not what religion was'.[139] Likewise, Frances Fortescue, professed for the choir at Louvain in 1622, 'was by her mother offered unto God in her childhood, and from the age of seven years had a mind to be a religious'.[140] Other parents were not quite so interventionist, but nevertheless derived pious satisfaction from their daughters' choice. Mary Lamb, another Augustinian, had wanted to be a nun when a child, but her resolve subsequently lapsed until a cousin, who also joined St Monica's, persuaded her that it was not such a hard life, and she made her vows in 1623. Her 'very constant and zealous Catholic' parents were supportive and reputedly 'very glad that their eldest daughter would give herself to God'.[141] The Augustinian chronicle, like other houses' annals, was replete with similar stories of juvenile religiosity and parental encouragement. It described deeply pietistic households where children were instilled with the tenets of their faith and a corresponding reverence for the monastic estate. The didactic purpose of such literature has been discussed by Isobel Grundy and others.[142] Yet taking its obvious bias into account, the convents' journals reflected something of the pious recusant tradition they sought to document and revere. They informed future generations of nuns about the laity's heroic struggle to preserve the faith, and its translation into the exiled cloisters abroad. Vocations, like the stories behind them, were thus inimical to the post-Reformation Catholic tradition.

Indeed, attaining heaven as a Catholic in seventeenth-century England was not simply a matter of devotion, particularly for members of religious orders. Like the recusancy of their lay co-religionists, taking vows in an expatriate house constituted an act of religious and political disobedience against the English Church and State. Moreover, the convents directed their prayers towards the overthrow of those 'heretical' establishments, which would presage their return to their homeland. Therefore caught up in the myriad economic, social and spiritual motives for monachisation, lay the political ambitions of both the nuns and their parents regarding the future of their faith in England. The cloisters' significance as sites of recusant solidarity and resistance was reflected in their composition, with nationality figuring as prominently as social status in defining their character. The next section will discuss how the overwhelming recruitment of English women both reflected and determined the monastic institutions' sense of identity and destiny.

National character

The cloisters were strikingly, even stridently, English in both orientation and composition. Although many houses included residents of other countries, such women were a distinct minority. Only 3 per cent of all nuns claimed Welsh, Scottish or Irish paternity, in contrast to almost 94 per cent registering their English origins. There were similarly limited numbers of Continental women, with locally recruited nuns forming just over 3 per cent of convent populations.[143] The paucity of women from other parts of the British Isles reflects the separate Catholic communities in each country, represented on the Continent by distinct colleges, seminaries and convents. Despite common traditions of Protestant persecution, therefore, Rome's adherents in the British Isles maintained discrete identities. The bias against so-called 'foreign' entrants was formally inscribed in the statutes of some houses which articulated their intention to profess English women only. When in 1633 Mary Tredway secured the approbation of Louis XIII to found the Paris Augustinian convent, it was stipulated that the cloister would accept English subjects alone.[144] However, even without such an embargo, many houses were reluctant to admit locals. The 'Blue Nuns' of Paris twice rejected the application of a Frenchwoman, Anne Veauquet, finally permitting her to take the veil in 1668. Justifying their wariness, the nuns said Veauquet would be the only foreigner in the exclusively

Table 1.5 National origins by type of nun, 1591–1710*

	Choir	Lay	White	All	Percentage
English	859	130	9	998	93.7
Irish	18	1		19	1.8
Scottish	5			5	0.5
Welsh	8			8	0.7
French	1	1		2	0.4
Low Countries	10	21		31	2.9
Total	901	153	9	1063	100.0

*Determined by paternal origin.

Sources: 'Brussels Benedictine Registers'; 'Poor Clare Registers'; Forster, 'Poor Clares of Rouen – 2'; *Chronicle of St Monica's*, vols 1 and 2; Priory, MSS C2, J8, M1; Foley, *Records*; *Franciscana*; 'Cambrai Records'; Priory, Bruges List; Durrant, *Flemish Mystics*; 'Sepulchrine Records'; 'Pontoise Registers'; Birt, *Obit Book*; Versailles, 68 H 3, 68 H 4; Nichols, *Herald and Genealogist*; *Diary of the 'Blue Nuns'*; 'Ghent Obituary Notices'.

English cloister, and they feared she might regret not joining a house of her own country.[145] Their reasoning would have been well understood by the majority of other convents.

Anne Veauquet subsequently left the 'Blue Nuns' for a French house, vindicating her sisters' initial reservations, and they did not profess any more French women.[146] But two other cloisters accepted local entrants for the choir, and they fared better than the Paris nuns. The Third Order Franciscans recruited two Flemish women during their time at Nieuport. The dowry of a farm provided by Catherine (Mary Catherine) Detill Valant in 1652 reveals the tangible benefits indigenous women could bring. Valant also served as assistant procuratrix at Bruges when the cloister was suffering the ill effects of the Popish Plot.[147] Such advantages were recognised by the Sepulchrines at Liège, who professed seven local choir nuns. The pragmatism behind this move is clear from the chronology – four came within the first seven years of the cloister's beginning in 1642, and another was accepted in the aftermath of the Glorious Revolution.[148] One of the early entrants, Anne-Barbe (Anne Francis of the Seraphins) Plenevaux, was related to the burgomaster, and the convent soon appointed her procuratrix, and then subprioress, in recognition of her capacity to enlist local patronage.[149] Marie-Catherine (Mary Susan) de Roveroit, the daughter of a local aristocrat, professed in 1690, was elected prioress in 1721, presumably in an effort to assist the convent's diminishing fortunes after 1715.[150] However, almost 68 per cent of the English convents' foreign members took the vows of a lay sister. The houses could not be so particular about their recruitment of these sisters because the cost of travelling to the Continent, and the contacts necessary to make the journey, were well beyond the means of most Englishwomen socially appropriate for the position. Indeed the majority of English converse sisters (albeit in a very small sample) were drawn apparently from the ranks of the impoverished gentry.[151] They often accompanied their wealthier kin or mistresses to the Continent, and occasionally they served exiled recusants abroad before scraping together sufficient funds to gain acceptance as a lay sister.[152] But there were finite numbers of English women with even these resources, so the cloisters turned to locals. Their willingness to do so was pragmatic in other respects, as the indigenous sisters spoke the regional dialect, and they often had contacts among the artisans and merchants with whom the nuns did business.[153] Yet it also points to the lowly status of the lay sister who was not deemed so crucial as the choir nun in the struggle for English Catholicism.

The cloisters' insular recruitment strategies encapsulated the spirit within which the monasteries were founded and which they maintained throughout the seventeenth century. Certain that they would return to their homeland, the nuns were reluctant to accept foreigners. Although it is difficult to gauge the policies of French and Spanish convents, the presence of English women in Continental cloisters in the late sixteenth and into the seventeenth century suggests that they were more flexible when it came to accepting foreign women. Margaret Clement, English prioress of the Flemish house in Louvain, had 'many sorts of nations under her goverment as, Duch, french, Inglish, spane-ish, garmons, all in one house'.[154] The cosmopolitan nature of institutions such as this was possibly a feature of the Spanish Netherlands. Yet many English cloisters were not willing to extend similar hospitality to their former hosts. Lady Mary Roper Lovel was so incensed by the infiltration of several Flemish women into the Carmelite community she had founded at Antwerp that, in 1624, the Flemish and their English supporters removed themselves to Bois-le-Duc.[155] Lovel's attitude confirms that many women saw themselves primarily as members of the English Catholic community, and only secondly as members of the universal Catholic Church. Within their enclosures they maintained scrupulous records of the sufferings of missionary priests and their kin for the faith, and they directed all their actions towards its restoration in their homeland. The contemplative cloisters set their sights on preserving the monastic tradition for *English* Catholics, and as a consequence, there was no place for outsiders who had little understanding of the recusant experience.

This was where the contemplative nuns differed markedly from Mary Ward's sisters. During the heady years of the first Institute, Mary Ward's goals encompassed areas of need across Europe, and this comprehensive vision was preserved in the order's reincarnation in the 1630s. Although Ward focused her attention on missionary work in her homeland, the scope of her organisation moved beyond the Spanish Netherlands into the territory of the Holy Roman Empire and beyond. She opened convents and provided free education for poor children in several German and Italian towns and cities. The speed at which the Institute grew necessitated recruitment from all areas, and the English sisters welcomed locally born women. Even when Mary Ward directed her personal energy in the latter years of her life towards the apostolate in England, the broad base from which members were drawn ensured the survival and growth of the Institute on the Continent. The communities established in England during the 1640s, 1660s and 1680s were offshoots of the European organisation. Moreover, the difference in outlook between Ward's Institute and the other English religious orders was exacerbated by another significant factor – strict monastic enclosure. Mary Ward fought clausura because she believed that her sisters had important educative and missionary work to do among Europe's urban communities as well as in England. The traditional monastic houses, conversely, accepted enclosure as an inevitable condition of their contemplative apostolate. As a consequence, the nuns were physically removed from the local population by their house's walls and grilles, and this encouraged a sense of isolation which was not part of the Institute's experience. The dislocation from their immediate neighbours was enhanced by the very nature of the contemplative apostolate which encouraged introspection. Thus, the convents' inward focus, combined with their identification with England's persecuted religious minority, made them somewhat insular establishments.

Yet the cloisters' primary focus upon the needs of their co-religionists in their homeland did not preclude engagement with the wider Catholic Church, nor with those in their locale who sympathised with their plight and assisted them. As subsequent chapters will explain, the English nuns were subject to the same religious and secular imperatives faced by Continental religious houses. Clausura, episcopal supervision, poverty, strict spiritual surveillance, and an abiding need to procure patrons who would ameliorate the problems resulting from these conditions, were not exclusive to the expatriate foundations. However, the exigencies of exile, most notably the nuns' geographic removal from the community they served and which supported them, invariably increased these difficulties and lessened the cloisters' ability to solve them. Their peculiar situation accordingly encouraged pragmatic and occasionally innovative responses to the challenges facing abbesses and their nuns. This led some women to redefine the parameters of their vocation to encompass much broader economic, spiritual and political issues than those envisaged in their house's rule and statutes. The remaining chapters explore the delicate balance between Church regulation and the vagaries of daily life and survival, which intersected with the nuns' abiding sense of English identity and mission, to evaluate the degree to which their experience was unique. The next chapter discusses the ecclesiastical and secular ideologies about governance which structured the monastic household, and provided the framework within which the nuns negotiated their relationships among themselves and with their clerical superiors.

2
The Monastic Family: Order and Disorder in the Cloister

In conclusion he made a speech, and told them, that he had been in their monastery 3 days, and cou'd find nothing to reprehend them for, for they kept their rule so exactly, that he had never found so much perfection in any Visit he had ever made of that order, and he did believe that if Saint Clare herself were to come from heaven upon earth, she wou'd make choice of that house, before any other of her order, nevertheless, said he, I must say what I know will displease you, yet so it is, you must necessarily change your Abbess, and choose another in her place; at this word the Religious were amaz'd; but he charg'd them with the thundring words of obedience, and excommunication to proceed presently to a new Election... they said resolutly they wou'd give no voices, upon which he said, that he wou'd himself supply... which he did, and gave all for Sister Margaret of Saint Paul, and made her Abbess, and bid Sister Clare Mary Anna goe and rest in her cell... the poor afflicted sisters againe perus'd their rule, where they find they cannot change their Abbess, unless she violates the rule, or is not able to perform it, with out either of these the change is a mortall sin, and all knew no Abbess did or cou'd perform that office better then she had done.

(Poor Clares of Gravelines Chronicles)[1]

On 27 October 1626 two friars deputed by the commissary of the Franciscan order arrived at the Poor Clare convent in Gravelines to 'visit', or inspect, the house, ostensibly to ensure that it was economically and spiritually healthy. However, as the chronicler recounted, despite the seemingly model government of Elizabeth (Clare Mary Ann) Tyldesley,

43

she was deposed and Margaret (Margaret of St Paul) Radcliffe appointed abbess. The visitor's arbitrary action precipitated a period of civil war, which divided the cloister until 1629 when Margaret Radcliffe and her supporters established a new Poor Clare community in Aire. The Gravelines dispute was only one of several incidents in the English cloisters which centred upon political and spiritual alliances between convents and male religious orders. During the course of the century, the Benedictines at both Brussels and Pontoise, and the 'Blue Nuns' of Paris all experienced similar ruptures. The Gravelines house had been founded under the authority of the bishop of St Omer and was served spiritually by the Jesuits. However, the first abbess, Mary Gough, had initiated a transfer of jurisdiction to the friars, believing their governance and spirituality would prove 'more conformable in the spirit of the [Franciscan] rule'. Following the establishment of the English Franciscan monastery of St Bonaventure at Douai at 1618, the convent was placed under its administration.[2] However, some of the nuns were evidently unhappy about their changed allegiance. Thus, the 1626 visitation, which was a peremptory move on the part of the friars to overcome resistance, brought the factional tensions which had hitherto simmered quietly within the enclosure to public notice.

Like its better-known counterpart in the Brussels Benedictine cloister, which occurred at roughly the same time, the Gravelines incident has been explained as a sideshow to the wider conflict between the English secular and regular clergy.[3] Political tensions within the post-Reformation English Catholic community clearly played some part in forming the dissenting nuns' opinions. However, as subsequent discussions of the Brussels affair will explain, disunity within cloisters was rarely simple and cannot be attributed to a single cause.[4] What is interesting about the disputes from the perspective of this chapter is what they reveal about the formal and informal processes of monastic government. In the light of the Council of Trent's reform of the regular life, houses of religious women were supposedly subject to rigid ecclesiastical regulation. Strict enclosure was meant to remove nuns from the influence and distraction of society beyond convent walls, and tighter episcopal supervision aimed to impose conformity and unity. Yet, as the events in Gravelines suggest, governance was often a contested issue, even in cloisters founded in the aftermath of Trent. Scholarship on the reforms, particularly those pertaining to clausura, commonly gives the impression that religious women became the (often unwilling) victims of unremitting patriarchal control in the wake of the council, and more specifically, its corollary, Pope Pius V's bull, *Circa Pastoralis*

(1566).[5] Katherine Gill has cogently argued that its thirteenth-century antecedent, *Periculoso*, did not result in strict claustration for many, perhaps the majority, of late medieval female religious communities. Yet she accepts that, conversely, the sixteenth-century regulation 'did have far-reaching and lasting effects', principally because its sentiments reflected broader social values.[6] An examination of the Tridentine legislation and its application in the English cloisters suggests that early modern nuns ignored, opposed, assimilated, or modified it in much the same way as their medieval forebears had dealt with *Periculoso*.[7] Various theological, historical, political and social principles underpinned the Catholic Church's policy with respect to convent government, but a similarly diverse array of factors fashioned its interpretation and practice – by both the women and their clerical supervisors. I will begin with a discussion of the sixteenth-century reforms and what they meant for religious women, before addressing the ideologies which influenced the ordering of cloisters, their translation into the English convents and, finally, the realities of governance for prelates, abbesses and their nuns.

Nuns in the post-Tridentine church

The convent has traditionally been considered a site for women's independence from patriarchal authority; a place where talented women organised their political, economic and spiritual affairs, occasionally even ruling men in the instance of medieval double monasteries. In reality, the power of abbesses and convents varied considerably.[8] One only need contrast the enormous wealth and public authority of the German prince-abbesses who wielded great proprietorial and seigneurial rights, and sat on the prelates' bench in the Reichstag, with the modest revenues and marginal political influence of pre-Reformation English cloisters to see this.[9] The Reformation highlighted the vastly differing sovereignty among women's communities with various houses quickly capitulating to reformers' demands and disbanding, others adeptly transforming themselves into Protestant establishments, and some managing to resist the occasionally violent efforts to convert them to remain defiantly Catholic.[10] The sixteenth-century onslaught was nothing new. Over several hundred years clerical reformers had tried to remedy the religious life. *Periculoso* in 1298 constituted one such attempt. In the fifteenth century, the Observant movement had imposed encloisterment, common property, and uniform observance of their monastic rule on female communities.[11] This revision proved a precursor to

Rome's response to the Protestant attack on monasticism. In its twenty-fifth session, the Council of Trent laid down the conditions to which all houses of women, regardless of order and rule, had to adhere. Although the decrees were implemented somewhat unevenly across Europe and greeted with mixed reactions, they were to have significant consequences for convent government.

The Tridentine reform aimed to regulate religious institutions by returning them to what the Church defined as traditional monastic discipline. Clausura, or strict enclosure, constituted the central pillar of reform. No professed nuns were permitted to leave their cloister, nor could anyone enter it, without episcopal sanction. Not only were women immured within their convents, their houses were confined inside city and town walls, ostensibly for the women's protection from 'the rapacity and other crimes of evil men'. Significantly the responsibility for ensuring compliance lay with the bishop. All religious communities, unless subject to a religious congregation, were placed under the direct jurisdiction of the diocesan bishop, who was charged with their regular visitation to ensure conformity with the rule and Trent's decrees.[12] The power of abbesses was curtailed by an insistence upon triennial elections by secret ballot, and a requirement that female superiors had to be 40 years of age and eight years professed.[13] This restriction aimed to limit the influence of the nuns' families and powerful friends to orchestrate election of kin. A decree that all property should be held in common further limited the opportunities for individual nuns or their relatives to wield power contrary to the prescribed order of authority. Moreover, there was an attempt to stamp out unwilling vocations by setting the minimum age for nuns' profession at 16, and a stipulation that all women prior to making their vows had to be interviewed by the bishop to ensure they did so voluntarily.[14] Church reformers therefore aimed to wrest influence over convents' human, economic and spiritual resources from nuns' families and friends to reconfigure monasticism according to ecclesiastical imperatives for order and surveillance.

Strict enclosure was the vehicle facilitating this agenda, and it was unequivocally gendered. Gabriella Zarri's influential research on Italian nuns has noted that while monks were expected to be celibate (and there were many complaints about male sexual misdemeanours), their chastity had a different meaning. They had to reside in a specific house and obtain permission to attend their duties outside it, but they were not rigorously cloistered like religious women.[15] The gendering of sexual continence reveals the degree to which worldly concerns drove the reforms. Chastity's equation with feminine virtue was common in secular discourse, so the policy reflected lay imperatives to protect women's honour, an issue of particular concern in Italy and other parts of southern Europe. Indeed confinement was a common early modern phenomenon for single women of all estates. Holy women who shunned the cloister to become lay mystics, prophets, and social reformers were propelled into organised religious bodies under ecclesiastical control. Individual *beatas* in Spain and *pinzochere* in Italy, as well as *beguines* in northern Europe and other 'open' communities of lay women, who pursued charitable apostolates unencumbered by enclosure and solemn vows, found it difficult to maintain their worldly activities.[16] Secular women deemed problematic received similar attention. Repentant prostitutes, unhappily married wives and the poor were incarcerated across Catholic Europe in asylums which resembled monasteries.[17] Even married women might be considered to have been institutionalised. Writers of Spanish prescriptive literature urged husbands to enclose their wives within the domestic realm to prevent the gossiping and sexual scandals inevitable if they were free to roam abroad.[18] Studies of Italy confirm that, like the convent, marriage was viewed by both church and state as a safe repository for the 'disruptive potential of female sexuality'.[19] Moreover, even Protestants who had rejected the cloister used the household to contain women's sexual, economic and political activity. Lyndal Roper's analysis of sixteenth-century Augsburg argued that the reformed insistence upon marriage constituted 'a politics of reinscribing women within the "family"', and confined Protestant women within their homes under patriarchal authority.[20] The Tridentine effort to protect the chastity of Christ's brides via clausura therefore reflected a process of social disciplining which crossed confessional boundaries.

While the rhetoric of enclosure emphasised its moral imperative, it had far-reaching implications for nuns' status in Church and society. Most obviously it limited their apostolate to prayer at the very moment the Church was embracing a missionary and social activist agenda.[21] Women who reacted to the momentous religious and economic changes of the sixteenth and seventeenth centuries by founding communities which addressed their confessional and social consequences, often came up against ecclesiastical and secular authorities determined to uphold Trent's gendered division of spiritual labour. Mary Ward's 1609 vision of a teaching and missionary order modelled on the Society of Jesus responded to the educational needs of European women and the perilous position of Catholicism in England. Yet, despite her Institute's remarkable success and rapid expansion, she was unable to convince the

Church that 'Jesuitesses' could perform the same tasks as men whilst preserving their virtue and obedience to the hierarchy. Censured as 'galloping girls' and 'wandering nuns', Ward's sisters attracted the disapprobation of Rome which led to the Institute's suppression in 1631.[22] Likewise, even with the support of the bishop of Geneva, François de Sales, Jeanne Françoise de Chantal's combination of prayer with charitable visits to the sick and poor in the Visitation of Holy Mary, established at Annecy in 1610, was destined to be constrained by the imposition of clausura in 1618.[23] Angela Merici's Company of St Ursula, founded before Trent, was more successful in overcoming the council's strictures and conducted an apostolate among the sick and disadvantaged. Yet ultimately its French houses had to bow to claustration.[24] Louise de Marillac's Daughters of Charity and Alix Le Clerc's Congregation of Notre Dame which further challenged the bounds of reform, however, escaped enclosure to pioneer the religious orders which were to transform women's religious life in the modern era.[25] The mixed success of these attempts to circumvent the Church's limited notion of organised female religiosity depended upon a combination of factors. The support of powerful patrons, especially churchmen, was decisive in most cases. Similarly the social status of the orders' membership often determined their capacity to resist clausura and remain living under simple rather than the solemn vows required in monastic orders. Moreover, the institutes and their founders had to be flexible enough in their objectives and *modus operandi* to alternately sidestep and accommodate their opponents' efforts to recast them in the Church's preferred mould of the traditional contemplative congregations.

For the convents which accepted Trent's reforms, strict enclosure conferred various economic, spiritual and political problems. Confinement constricted these cloisters' financial capacity to attract benefactors, their public performance of commemorative prayers for the dead, and the small-scale businesses supplementing regular (and often insufficient) income.[26] There were even more serious consequences for religious women's autonomy. Claustration interrupted a convent's ability to connect with the very society it served spiritually, and upon which it depended economically and politically. The reformers' determination to curtail the influence of lay patrons further diminished the capacity of nuns' traditional allies to step into the breach and assist them. Instead networks of clerical supervisors and mediators regulated a convent's relations with the world outside. As Gabriella Zarri explained, 'with the obligation of cloister, dependence upon male authority became complete'.[27] Jo Ann McNamara phrased it even more bluntly, writing 'the real issue was not cloistering but clerical control'.[28] The fear of diminished freedom clausura represented no doubt inspired the Tuscan nuns who reputedly defended their convent gates with sticks and stones against clerics intent upon imposing the new discipline.[29] Yet within this seemingly bleak outlook for female monastic independence, there were opportunities to bypass rigorous patriarchal interventions. Zarri noted the multi-layered ecclesiastical and lay hierarchies responsible for convent discipline which allowed the nuns to mitigate the censure of one supervisor by appealing to another.[30] Certain women even turned the architecture of strict enclosure against their regulators. When in 1662 the Bavarian provincial of the reformed Franciscans demanded the Pütrich nuns in Munich relinquish their newly acquired corpse of St Dorothea intended for public veneration in their church, to his indignation they refused, securing the saint's body inside the convent beyond his reach.[31] In 1628 the Gravelines Poor Clares likewise locked their walls and gates against Margaret Radcliffe to block the friars' efforts to restore her as abbess.[32] Others, like the canonesses of Remiremont, mustered traditional networks to withstand efforts to reform them, appealing to their relatives, the estates general and Marie de Medici against enclosure, and conducting charivaris against their opponents.[33] Thus, in even the bleakest interpretation of the Tridentine decrees implementation, it is clear that the nuns were not simply passive recipients of unpopular reform from their ecclesiastical masters.

In fact, some women willingly embraced Trent's measures. Teresa of Avila insisted upon strict enclosure as an essential tenet of her Carmelite reform. She argued that spiritual autonomy was nigh impossible without the freedom from worldly discourse and obligations it provided.[34] In 1609, Angélique Arnauld of the famed Port-Royal convent in Paris signalled her convent's espousal of a more austere rule in the 'day of the grille' when she barred her visiting parents entry.[35] In the seventeenth century, numerous convents in the archdiocese of Mechelen embraced encloisterment; some petitioned the bishop seeking its 'privilege', others raised the funds necessary to erect its architectural requirements, and many wrote proudly of their stringent regimes.[36] They and other women saw clausura as liberation from secular distractions, rather than a mechanism for patriarchal domination. Numerous cloistered nuns exploited the barrier between them and the world to pursue intense spiritual regimes which occasionally led them into mysticism and other supernatural phenomena. Reputed holiness within a convent inevitably encouraged public veneration and support for its saintly inhabitants. Thus, far from separating nuns from their worldly kin, enclosure's benefits united such holy women and their convent with the surrounding citizenry. The well-ordered convent accordingly constituted a vital civic resource – its holiness, chastity and prayer protecting and benefiting the wider lay community.[37] Successfully cloistered women could symbolise the purity and power of their elite families who had sequestered them rather than diminish patrician bloodlines through socially inferior marriages. In Venice the metaphor extended to include the body politic and the city itself which was often depicted as virginal and immaculate.[38] The Tridentine incarceration of nuns therefore reflected a complex political, spiritual, economic and moral agenda which acknowledged that the virtue of the cloister represented the honour and integrity of both the Catholic Church and the secular institutions which supported it. Thus, the convent's potency as a symbol of Catholicism was behind the clerical and civic administrators' insistence upon more intense surveillance of female religious communities. As prominent emblems in the confessional struggle, it was essential that convents advertised not only moral rectitude, but also patriarchal governance.

The English cloisters' spiritual and political significance was not lost on the Roman Church, the nuns, their families or indeed the Protestant authorities in their homeland. Thus, clausura constituted an integral part of their existence. Mostly established after the decrees of 1563, all the houses were subject to strict enclosure and their statutes and constitutions detailed its architectural and behavioural norms. The Ghent Benedictines' statutes were typical in requiring high walls around the nuns' buildings and gardens, with only one door to the outside world for authorised movements of people and a 'turn' (revolving cupboard) for the exchange of sanctioned goods. Legitimate face-to-face meetings occurred at a grate (occasionally curtained to preclude visual contact) in the parlour, while a covered grille separated penitents from their confessors. All interaction between the religious women and those outside was mediated by these physical limits, but also by strictly defined codes of conduct. In dealings with secular folk and clergy alike the nuns were commanded to show 'all modesty and humilitie in their wordes, Countenances, gestures, and Actions'. Thus, in the Ghent cloister chastity, defined as 'the integritie of their bodyes and myndes', was to be preserved literally by stone and mesh and figuratively by bodily comportment, or *disciplina corporis*.[39] Other cloisters and their inhabitants were similarly confined. The design of the Paris Augustinians' convent buildings had to facilitate 'the conservation of religious discipline', with particular attention given to constructing 'all things so stro[n]g and high, that none may be invited by any occasion to enter in or goe out'. In the event of meeting visitors in the parlour, the nuns' conduct 'ought to be an expression of the goodness of their profession', and they were exhorted to 'shew modestie and a virginall bashfulnes ... in their lookes, gates and expressions'.[40] The Third Order Regular Franciscans were likewise reminded that in addition to the physical restraints upon such occasions 'let them all wayes have religious modestie before their eies and be circumspect in their wordes and manner of speaking'.[41]

The nuns seemingly accepted clausura's structural and postural confinement. Indeed some positively welcomed it. In the 1570s, the English prioress of St Ursula's in Louvain, Margaret Clement, established strict enclosure in her Flemish cloister, to the dismay of several locally born women, while others purportedly appreciated the freedom 'from distraction' it provided.[42] Decades later, Elizabeth Shirley, the subprioress of St Ursula's English filiation, St Monica's, proudly affirmed that during Clement's governance, 'there was not any lyk unto us in strictnes of inclosior, so great was her care therein'.[43] The founding nuns of the Rouen Poor Clare monastery, journeying from Gravelines to their new abode in 1644, evidently felt uncomfortable about venturing forth from the safety of their cloister into the world. The sisters were accommodated in various religious houses en route, but they were also forced to put up at inns when more suitable lodgings were unavailable. At one popular hostel they locked their chamber's door against the noisy revelry outside thereby creating their own 'cloister'. The next day they sheltered in the local parish church until they could resume their journey, shunning the inn where 'being full day we should have bin exposed to the sight of all'.[44] Perhaps the habit of sequestration made such women shy of public attention, but they clearly displayed a preference for withdrawal from the world, which the walls and grilles facilitated. In 1623 Anne Ingleby explained her desire for claustration was grounded in spiritual considerations. She had joined the Brussels Benedictines in 1610 because of the house's reputation for strict enclosure. She admitted, 'I must confesse I find my selfe more inclined to follow secularity and vanity then perfecti[on]', therefore she deemed that seclusion was essential in order to forswear worldly ties and behaviour.[45]

Anne Ingleby's comments were sparked by her concern that standards at Brussels were becoming lax, and the convent's hospitality to guests was having a deleterious effect upon many nuns who evidently did not subscribe to clausura's behavioural norms. But not all women allowed worldliness to permeate their conduct. Abbess Margaret (Margaret Clare) West of the Third Order Regular Franciscans, impressed her chastity upon visitors through 'Modest; grave; and gratious Comportment'.[46]

The Catholic, and therefore perhaps somewhat partisan, earl of Perth wrote effusively of the virtuous women whom he encountered in convent parlours during his travels in the 1690s.[47] Indeed, the observations of travellers, although invariably tainted by their religious persuasion, reveal much about the practice of clausura in the English cloisters. The diarist, John Evelyn's, 1641 visit to the Brussels Benedictine cloister where he 'sat discoursing most part of the afternoon' suggests that Anne Ingleby's fears 18 years previously had been realised.[48] Sir Philip Skippon's 1663 itinerary apparently missed the Brussels cloister, but his meticulous descriptions of both the architecture of convent parlours and the freedom with which he conversed with his hosts implied that the Benedictine houses were more liberal than others. At Ghent he was able to talk freely with the nuns, although separated from them by a grate. In Dunkirk he was entertained by five or six nuns whom he 'had freedom to see' because the curtain was drawn at the iron grille. This contrasted starkly with his meeting with the Poor Clares in the town, who could be seen through the wooden grate, but they 'would not discover their faces'. At Gravelines, the Poor Clares were more severe, and he was informed 'they never see the face of any man'. The Louvain Augustinians were less strict, and he was able to describe Prioress Magdalen Throckmorton's habit because she had opened the curtain to chat with him.[49] Skippon's observations, and those of other tourists, suggest that the terms of clausura varied among communities, even those of the same order. Yet, despite these subtle variations, the houses he visited were patently enclosed. This was in stark contrast to his encounter with members of Mary Ward's Institute in Munich with whom he was able to socialise 'without any grate between them and some of our company'. Moreover, he noted that 'these nuns are called by some the galloping nuns, because they go abroad'.[50]

Episcopal visitations confirmed that the principal threat to clausura in the English cloisters lay in the nuns' proclivity for hospitality in their parlours, and occasionally within the enclosure itself. The archbishop of Mechelen's 1620 visitation of the Brussels Benedictines had cautioned that socialising with clerical and lay friends at the grate and allowing them to dine at the convent was a source of distraction and potentially damaging to the convent's reputation.[51] Anne Ingleby's complaints in 1623 that guests in the enclosure had brought 'much vanity and distraction in to our house: for ther wordes and carrage is very unfitting for us to see which hath left the world alltogether' suggest his recommendation went unheeded.[52] Indeed, despite regular chiding, the issue remained a perennial problem in many houses. When in 1698 the archbishop of Paris's representative, Benedict Nelson, evaluated the state of the city's English Augustinian cloister, he warned the sisters against entertaining visiting priests in the enclosure.[53] They had been cautioned in 1694 about their conduct in the parlour and told to cover their faces as their constitutions decreed.[54] Moreover, when some nuns left their enclosures on convent business or to escape wars and natural disasters, they clearly enjoyed the freedom. For all Prioress Margaret Clement's efforts to acculturate her nuns to clausura, when in 1635 half the Louvain Augustinian convent fled their besieged town to seek shelter among their sisters at Bruges, they apparently had no qualms whatsoever about the social whirl they experienced there. Although when they dined at neighbouring convents, their hosts courteously provided transport in coaches, 'it being not fit for nuns to walk the streets', the nuns evidently made the most of their liberation from the security of walls and grilles.[55] In 1668, the confessor bemoaned the 'great breaches of cloister' still evident in the house.[56] Likewise, individuals who obtained permission to return to England to conduct convent business, seemingly relished the opportunity to escape the monastic routine. Various 'Blue Nuns' removed themselves from their Paris convent for several months on such errands. Abbess Anne (Elizabeth) Timperley went to England 'about some business for the good of the hous' three times during her 20 years in office, and was absent for 18 months on one such occasion. In 1698–99 Abbess Susanna Joseph Hawkins was away for 12 months.[57] Apart from a few episodes in which nuns neglected to return from such forays, or attracted too much public attention, or even escaped from the confines over walls, these breaches could be justified as falling within Tridentine regulations.[58] In the majority of circumstances they occurred with the clerical authorities' tacit approval. Thus, scandals centred upon clausura were not a prominent part of the English nuns' experience.

This was not the impression that readers of Protestant literature on the religious houses abroad would have received. Anti-Catholic polemic resounded with titillating accounts of the monastic dens of iniquity situated across the Channel. In *The Anatomy of the English Nunnery at Lisbon*, reputedly an eyewitness account by an erstwhile lay brother, the Bridgettine convent was portrayed as little better than a bordello where the naive nuns were bullied and seduced by their priestly supervisors. Amidst salacious details about the nightly bawdy revelry taking place in the confessor's chamber, accessed via a removable grate in the confessional, it detailed the senior nuns' petty jealousies, incompetence and venality; and, moreover, their subjection to the friars and the Jesuits.[59]

References to other convents recounted similar tales of debauchery, accompanied by clerical greed and tyranny.[60] The pamphlets' litany of sexual peccadilloes echoed earlier Reformation propaganda in which lusty clerics and incontinent nuns represented the corruption and hypocrisy of the Catholic Church. However, the persistent image of the unchaste and disorderly nun not only struck at Rome's theology and reformist endeavours, it also reflected the English Protestants' discomfort with the notion of female autonomy. From the ancient Assyrian queen, Semiramis, to Pope Joan, women had supposedly proven incapable of controlling their own passions, thereby disqualifying their claims to self-determination.[61] By narrating tales of the nuns' sexual promiscuity and their subservience to priests, the polemical tracts not only undermined the convents' symbolism as repositories of Catholic virginal sanctity, they also reflected wider debates about women and governance.

Women's power in early modern society

During the half century before the re-establishment of women's monasticism, the reigns of Mary Tudor and Elizabeth I had forced theologians, political polemicists, and other commentators to consider the legitimacy of women rulers. The prospect of a reigning queen was confronting for a number of historical, legal and practical reasons, but it also entailed an ideological shift. Female sovereignty was anomalous with contemporary concepts of authority which drew upon centuries of medical and theological scholarship to rationalise women's subservience to men as natural and God-given. This prescribed gender order structured the domestic household where the benevolent *paterfamilias* was expected to govern his obedient wife, children and servants. William Gouge's popular domestic advice manual explained that because nature had endowed the male of the species with a greater eminence, 'he should governe, she obey'. Moreover, scripture dictated that the terms of their relationship paralleled that of Christ (the husband) ruling the Church (the wife).[62] The religious and institutional analogies implicit in the familial metaphor extended its utility to define other hierarchies of authority, most significantly the state. Monarchs used patriarchal imagery to characterise their power over their subjects. For example, James I described himself as both husband and father of the realm in his treatises on kingship and statements to Parliament.[63] Hence the language of governance was masculine in early modern England, and family, Church and state were structured in line with contemporary gender considerations.

Women were not completely powerless within this idealised patriarchal order. A wife's permissible jurisdiction lay over the other members of the household – children and servants – whom she ruled in accordance with her husband's will.[64] This concept of maternal power tempered by wifely obedience constituted the archetype for female authority, and it was articulated in sermons, domestic conduct books, and political pamphlets. Yet it was deeply ambiguous. William Gouge termed the family 'a little church, a little commonwealth', which implied parents' obligation to educate their sons and daughters in the values underpinning Church and state.[65] Hence, women's domestic duties were invested with religious and political significance. Moreover, the lived experience of patriarchal family life rarely matched the prescription. Instead there was a variety of power relationships which stretched on a continuum from marriages in which wives were dominated by husbands who permitted them little or no freedom, to relationships in which spouses addressed one another as equals and women exercised considerable sway, even control, in family matters.[66] Women's influence even spread beyond their households to infiltrate circles of kin, neighbours, patrons, and, occasionally, spaces of institutional authority.[67] Thus, there was a dichotomy between the feminine ideal of the obedient wife and mother, and the realities of women's participation in the governance of household and state. Contemporaries recognised women's active involvement, yet continued to pay lip service to the ideal of wifely subservience.

However, there were certain female incursions into ostensibly male preserves which could not so easily be ignored. In Elizabeth's reign and throughout the seventeenth century, religious and civic officials grappled with the problem of how to restrain what they perceived were veritable hoards of papist amazons in the counties of England. As early as 1581 the House of Commons debated measures to control recusant wives. By 1592 the Privy Council was arguing that ineffective laws against such intractable women encouraged Catholic nonconformity because through the wives' example 'whole families refuse to resort to Church and continue in recusance'.[68] Some women's religious influence surpassed the boundaries of the household. The actions of stalwart Elizabethan recusants, like Margaret Clitherow, Dorothy Lawson, Viscountess Montague, and Jane Wiseman are well documented, but their proselytising was not unique. In 1585 the bishop of Winchester recommended the continuing imprisonment of Nicolas Sanders' sister who if released 'would do more harm than ten sermons do good'.[69] The penalties of recusancy were such that to protect the family from crippling fines, husbands commonly outwardly conformed to the Church of England,

leaving the direction of religious dissent to their wives. Historians continue to debate the extent to which Catholic nonconformity took this
form.[70] However, there is ample evidence in recusancy presentments,
hagiographies, and seminarians' and nuns' accounts of maternal influence to confirm that many Catholic families colluded in what Alexandra
Walsham has called 'a natural division of labour in the management of
dissent'.[71] Frances Dolan's invigorating study of anti-Catholic rhetoric
has argued that spousal collaboration to devise survival strategies for the
practice of their faith and the preservation of their estates realised the
authorities' worst apprehensions – Catholic subversion of the patriarchal
family.[72]

   After 1626, a succession of Catholic queens consort, of whom Henrietta Maria was the most contentious, aroused concern that this micro-
cosmic disorder would engulf the macrocosm. Like other recusant wives,
Henrietta Maria was feared for her capacity to pervert her husband, and
particularly their children, in religious matters. From 1593 Parliament
had warily considered removing children from recusant parents, and
legislation to this effect was unsuccessfully proposed in 1605, 1610,
1621, 1624, 1625, 1641, 1642, 1646, 1649 and 1677. Such laws struck
too closely at paternal authority for them to be passed, but their regular
reappraisal pointed to the widely held opinion that Catholic mothers
played a pivotal role in forming their offspring's nonconformity. Significantly a watered down version of the 1605 penal legislation barred
husbands of recusant women from office, unless their children were
educated as Protestants and conformed.[73] Catherine Holland, who was
professed among the Bruges Augustinians in 1664, recalled that her
parliamentarian father, Sir John Holland, forbade his Catholic wife to
speak of religious matters with the children for fear she would persuade
them into her faith. Yet she secretly taught Catherine and her siblings
Catholic prayers and affirmed Rome's veracity in their presence, thereby
securing her daughter's subsequent conversion and vocation.[74] Other
children provided similar testaments to maternal influence.[75] Henrietta
Maria's actual sway over her husband and sons are much debated by
modern scholars, but her contemporaries were convinced of her persua-
siveness. As Dolan has explained, 'In a period when Catholic mothers
were thought to be dangerously influential... she came to stand as a
symbolic figurehead for Catholicism's generativity and motherhood's
ascendancy'.[76]

   The English nuns, although important symbols of recusant survival,
did not generate quite the same hysteria.[77] Legislation tried to prevent
parents sending their offspring abroad to monasteries for education and

religious profession, but mothers were always considered far more threatening than nuns, whose celibacy denied them children of their own over whom they could assert maternal influence. The convents' distance from England's shores further lessened their danger. Moreover, the Catholic Church had effectively curtailed the nuns' disruptive potential by cloistering them. Clausura meant that, unlike their male counterparts, the nuns remained confined on the Continent and they were unlikely to return to England to proselytise in the way that their lay mothers and grandmothers had done in the households and neighbourhoods of their childhood. The fate of Mary Ward's Institute demonstrated graphically how intolerant Rome was of religious women who aspired to work on the English mission. Thus, while the Church had applauded the recusant militancy of Margaret Clitherow and Dorothy Lawson who defied husbands and the Protestant authorities to promote their faith, their daughters who had taken the veil were sequestered under strict clerical regulation. Rome accordingly applied a double standard to England's Catholic women, encouraging those in the counties and at the Court to usurp the gender hierarchy and establish authority, while insisting that those in convents submit to patriarchal governance.[78]

Indeed, the conjugal metaphor which ordered secular families was common currency among the compilers of monastic statutes and conduct literature. Like the Protestant divine, William Gouge, they enlisted scriptural references to husbands ruling their wives like Christ commanded the Church, to describe monastic relationships and power structures. Nuns exchanged secular marriage for a spiritual union in which they were deemed to become brides of Christ. Clothing and profession ceremonies were often called 'bride days' and the novices were dressed in costly and elaborate gowns reminiscent of secular brides. However, unlike worldly wives, their spouse was physically absent and consummation of the union was deferred until death, which was described in the obituaries of the Benedictine house at Ghent as the 'eternall nuptialls'.[79] In the interim, nuns were to be subject to Christ's priestly representatives who assumed the status of the *paterfamilias*. Thus, as Gabriella Zarri has observed:

> The marital metaphor, with everything it meant in terms of relationships and submission to men, constituted the unifying status of woman, whatever her condition of life. If virginity continued to be considered the state of greatest perfection, marriage was the exemplary model for relations. Although she was a virgin, the *sponsa*

Christi was subject to male authority: her father, her bishop, her spiritual father.[80]

Abbesses and nuns accordingly owed an alternately filial and wifely obedience to their convent's clerical overseers, in conjunction with the maternal, daughterly and sisterly respect due to one another.

This gendering of the monastic hierarchy in line with lay concepts of authority suggests that nuns could only ever exercise limited power. Hence, the patriarchal ideal of maternal jurisdiction, tempered by wifely (or filial) compliance was seemingly just as applicable in the convent as in the secular household. Yet, as in the worldly family, relationships in the cloister could be ambiguous. Susan O'Brien commented of the nineteenth-century convent (where the marital metaphor persisted), 'although the vocabulary they used was familial, an all-female community could not reproduce the dynamics of the patriarchal family'. Instead, the monastery's composition encouraged a perception that the abbess was all-powerful, and her authority was described in the language of both sovereignty and motherhood.[81] 'Queen' and 'mother' were titles accorded that most potent symbol of Catholic femininity – the Virgin Mary, who remained a significant figure in post-Tridentine piety. Already armed with memories of powerful mothers and influential queens from their earlier lives in England, the nuns therefore did not necessarily interpret the conjugal imagery as absolute submission to male dominion. However, the very multivalency of maternal symbolism was to have significant consequences for the relationship between abbesses and bishops, and indeed between the female superiors and their nuns. Although, as the next section explains, the nuns accepted and used the familial discourse within the cloister, its meaning changed according to circumstance. This had both positive and negative implications for female governance.

The well-ordered monastic family

Richard White (alias Johnson), confessor to the Louvain Augustinians from 1630 to 1687, was one of the clearest proponents of the familial archetype's utility in the convent. In 1668 he presented the newly elected prioress, Winefrid Thimelby, with a treatise titled 'Instructions for a Religious Superior'. Bemoaning the 'want of government' in the convent, he explained that 'as a father I present you with these instructions' to remedy its manifold ills.[82] White urged Thimelby to structure her religious household according to the familial model, admonishing:

Wherefore you being the Mother of the familie, ought to esteem and treat the Nuns as your Children, the [lay] sisters, as yours and their servants...so that as the Nuns must be in all things, times, and places be dutifull and respectfull to you as their mother; so must the sisters much more be dutifull, respectfull and servisable both to you and them, as their Mistresses.[83]

Thus, within the cloister the prioress (or abbess) was 'mother', the nuns were her spiritual 'daughters', and the lay sisters became 'domestic servants'. True to the model, White further declared that paternal authority resided in the house's clerical supervisors. Yet, while he acknowledged that the prioress's 'imediate and chief Superiour is the Bishop', he cast the convent's confessor more definitively in the position of *paterfamilias*, advising

As no greater disorder can happen to a secular familie then for the wife to govern and the husband to be subject, which is as if the head should be governed by tongue, or reason by some sense or passion; so nothing can begett a greater traine of miseries and disorder in a Cloister, then the superiours ruling the gostly father, or labouring to bring him to her judgement and follow her advice.[84]

Hence, in White's opinion, the monastic household ideally replicated the early modern gender order where the abbess certainly held the highest position among women, but ultimately was compelled to submit to a man.

The 'Instructions for a Religious Superior' further affirmed that, in addition to gender, social status also determined the monastic hierarchy. As 'servants', the lay sisters were 'such as have been bred up and used to labor' and they were to be reminded regularly of their servile status.[85] A woman's worldly origins therefore accompanied her into the cloister. The choir nuns who brought the full dowry (or part thereof) formed the premier group, and the lay sisters who came with insubstantial means constituted the lowest division among the professed. In certain religious orders, there was an intermediate caste of elderly or infirm women who were of similar status to the choir nuns (often having contributed a considerable dowry to compensate for their disability), but exempt from the more rigorous aspects of the rule by virtue of their weak health. The 'white sisters' or 'donates', as they were called in Augustinian houses, did not participate in decision-making or daily governance, so their position in the monastic family, although between the ranks of choir nuns and lay sister, was marginal. Novices for each estate were positioned after its professed sisters, but those for the choir were ranked above the donates.[86]

Within the categories of choir nun and lay sister, there was further stratification, based upon age – of religious profession, not physical years – and office. The more senior women in a house therefore obtained the privileges of professed experience, and they were more likely to hold administrative positions. In some instances, chronological years were a factor; for example, with respect to the election of abbesses who, according to Tridentine law, were to be over 40 years old and eight years professed. The council of older nuns who assisted the abbess with decision-making, was also required to have the experience of both natural age and profession. Stratification by office depended upon the importance of the administrative position. The abbess held the supreme position, closely followed by her deputy, alternately known as the prioress, sub-prioress or vicaress, depending upon the religious order. The third most significant figure was the procuratrix, who was responsible for the finances, property and provisions of the house. Below her ranged a series of other household officers and their deputies who managed specific religious and temporal portfolios.[87] However, if both the abbess and prioress were absent, the eldest professed nun, almost certainly a discreet, filled their place.

The ranking of the monastic household was exemplified in a variety of images and rituals. The familial analogy provided just one point of reference. Corporeal imagery offered another. Richard White invoked the popular metaphor of society as an organism when he explained that if 'the Superiour is head ordering, and governing all; the Nuns the bodie subject to the head; and the Lay-sisters hands and feet subject to both to bear their burthens, and labour to serve them, there is order: which if constant produces peace'.[88] But, in addition to the hierarchy expounded in prescriptive texts, the nuns encountered its manifestations in their daily activities. In the choir, chapter house, refectory, and every other corner of the monastery, the nuns acted in accordance with its dictates. Most noticeably, they were seated during formal observances according to seniority. A Benedictine ceremonial manual from Brussels detailed how at the conclusion of her profession rite, the new nun was placed 'in the last seate of al the professed' by her abbess, signifying her status vis-à-vis existing members of the house.[89] This position was preserved in all household rituals. During convent elections votes were cast in order from the youngest to the eldest. Likewise, in the chapter of faults, a forum for communal discipline, those admitting misdemeanours did so according to their age.[90] The significance of a nun's seat in establishing her communal status was evident in the Third Order Franciscans' statutes, where women who acted without the abbess's permission had to sit in the 'Last place in the Communitie and acknowledge their faultes with the Novices'.[91] The shame of being ranked with the unprofessed would have been palpable. Other Franciscan rituals and privileges reinforced the hierarchy. On special occasions the eldest nuns were given precedence at recreations and banquets, and they headed festive processions. Jubilarians – women who had attained 50 years of profession – obtained extraordinary privileges, including the allocation of a young nun to make their bed, clean their cell and perform whatever other tasks they required.[92] Seniority even prevailed in the execution of household duties. Among those appointed to wash the dishes each week, the youngest sister was obliged to scrub the pots and pans.[93] Although death ultimately proved the great leveller for old and young alike, the principal distinctions between choir nuns and lay sisters were preserved in the number of masses said for the repose of their souls. The 'Blue Nuns' of Paris accorded their abbesses 'thrice thirty Masses', while the choir nuns were entitled to 30, and the lay sisters received 15.[94] Thus, in the hierarchical religious household everyone was well aware of her place.

Documents written by the nuns confirm that the language and ritual of monastic order entered their consciousness and vocabulary. They regularly used the familial metaphor to characterise relationships among one another. The death in 1654 of Elizabeth Tyldesley, the 'old deare Mother' who the Gravelines Poor Clares had defended in 1626, unleashed a torrent of grief among her 'afflicted Children', who despaired that they had been 'left Orphelines by the deprivation of so worthy a Mother'.[95] The Louvain Augustinians extended the analogy beyond the cloister, claiming kinship with Margaret Giggs, adopted daughter of Sir Thomas More, and mother to their acclaimed prioress, Margaret Clement. Elizabeth Shirley described Giggs as the nuns' 'grandmother', claiming that her natural relationship with Clement who was their 'moste holy Mother' justified this title.[96] Priests were similarly incorporated into the monastic household. In the 1670s, Abbess Marina Beaumont begged the English secular clergy to assume jurisdiction of her Ypres Benedictine community, asking the clerics to 'make us your childrin'.[97] When Barbara (Melchiora) Campbell of the Brussels Benedictines petitioned the archbishop of Mechelen in 1683, she identified two father figures – the prelate, approached for his 'paternal care', and the convent's confessor, praised for his 'fatherly affection for everyone'.[98]

Margaret Radcliffe, who was at the centre of the Gravelines Poor Clare dispute, appealed to the hierarchy of age when recommending that 'in all Religious families well ordred the younger are allwayes taught and instructed to shew all respect to their elders'.[99]

However, the facility with which the nuns appropriated the secular terminology to describe associations within and outside the cloister does not necessarily reflect their acquiescence with its message about order and authority. Raised on the whole in the recusant households of the English gentry and among exiled Catholics abroad, they understood only too well the ambiguities of gender and social hierarchies. Moreover, within the cloister, the language and structure of governance was sufficiently ambivalent about patriarchal control, maternal sovereignty and filial obedience to encourage different understandings of just where power resided in the monastic family. The status of the abbess was the most contentious. In rules and statutes, she was responsible for both the spiritual and temporal welfare of her community, and held jurisdiction over its religiosity, personnel, order and discipline, assets, business ventures, and day-to-day functioning. Although she was assisted by the nuns who took charge of specific areas of household management, such as the finances, novitiate, chapel, choir, kitchen, furnishings, infirmary and school, they were answerable to her, and she conducted regular audits of her officers' affairs.[100] Should the convent fall upon hard times as a consequence of mismanagement, the blame lay squarely upon her shoulders for failing to govern effectively.[101] In other words, as the Paris Augustinians' constitutions declared, her 'full administration of the temporalities and spiritualities of the house' meant that 'none hath authoritie to command or compelle her'.[102] Indeed the nuns were bound to her by a vow of obedience.[103] The extent of her authority, and the degree to which it contrasted with secular and ecclesiastical paradigms of female sovereignty, is evident in the 'Blue Nuns' constitutions which demanded obedience to the abbess 'who holds the place of God' within the cloister.[104] Thus, formally, the abbess's position in the monastic household was analogous with that of an abbot, and indeed it echoed the Christological characteristics conferred upon the father/king in the secular household/state.[105] Although a woman, she wielded masculine authority.

However, the abbess's mandate to govern was complicated by her relationship with other members of the monastic hierarchy. Most obviously, as the Tridentine reform stipulated, she was subject to episcopal supervision. This anomalous position of power and subjection was exemplified in the Louvain Augustinian convent where, upon election, the prioress received her community's vows of obedience, but then pledged her own submission to the archbishop of Mechelen.[106] The bishop, or 'ordinary', was authorised to intervene in a cloister's domestic affairs. He or his deputy regularly audited the abbess's rule during the visitation, when they inspected the convent's books and interviewed the nuns to ascertain that the house was functioning in accordance with Trent's decrees.[107] In the event of serious irregularities a superior might even be deposed. The other 'paternal' figure who seemingly compromised her authority was the confessor. Although ostensibly in charge of spiritual affairs, he was at hand to offer advice on all matters of household government. Yet his position was often contradictory in official documents. While the Louvain Augustinians were reminded that 'to theyr Ghostly Father theye shalbe also obedient in all thinges that are decent and lawfull', a point reiterated by Richard White's conduct book for the prioress, other confessors were sidelined.[108] The Paris Augustinians' confessor was 'not to medle with the administration of the temporalities of the Monasterie' unless commanded by the abbess.[109] The fact that he was appointed to his position by the abbess actually indebted him to her patronage.[110] Moreover, his subordinate status was reinforced symbolically in the requisite number of masses offered upon death. At Paris, the 'Blue Nuns' procured 30 for their deceased confessor, the same number as for the choir nuns, and well below the abbess's stipulated 90.[111] Thus, unlike the bishop, a confessor formally lacked direct jurisdiction in household matters.

Surprisingly, some of the most regular checks to abbatial power actually came from within rather than outside the enclosure. Despite the nuns' vows of obedience to their leader and her undisputed primacy in all internal affairs, the structure of monastic government empowered them to monitor and, in some instances, to challenge her administration. The greatest anomaly in her sovereignty lay in her election to office by all professed choir nuns. The Council of Trent strengthened a community's moderating influence over their superior by insisting upon triennial elections. Although not all the English cloisters adhered to Tridentine law in this respect, with some houses maintaining life terms, the nuns' election of their governor clearly complicated power dynamics within the enclosure where an abbess's authority was conferred by her subjects.[112] If they were dissatisfied with her conduct, they could also depose her – either in the triennial election, or by appealing to the bishop. There were additional procedural limits upon the abbess's powers. She had to take the advice of a select clique of senior nuns, the council or 'discreets', on sensitive matters relating to convent property and personnel. Although ostensibly chosen to support their ruler, the 'discreets' were intermediaries to whom dissatisfied nuns could address grievances. The Franciscan statutes acknowledged the discreets' potential to challenge their leader's primacy, reminding them that they were not her critics. Instead they were to assist her 'by their Counsell in the Governement of the Monasterie; for the Abbesse is not to doe any great matter of moment without their Counsell, and advice'.[113] She also had to consult the convent's chapter before acting upon other important household business, most significantly the acceptance of postulants for clothing and novices for profession. Chapter comprised all the professed nuns of the choir who were of sufficient maturity, wit and reputation to vote on such matters. It acted as a vital regulatory body which not only assuaged the abbess's power, but also enabled other members of the community who did not hold office to participate in the preservation of the rule and monastic discipline.[114] Thus, although 'by almightie God appoynted Governesse over the spowses of Jesus-Christ, to direct and confirme them in the way of his holy Commandments', the abbess's dominion was tempered by the very subordinates she ruled.[115]

The conflicting messages about abbatial authority in the monastic power structure was reflected in the nuns' ambivalence about it. Even when they asserted their legitimate dominion over others, most abbesses chose to cloak it within the language of the familial metaphor. During the Brussels Benedictine dispute, which centred in part upon the abbess's right to make decisions on behalf of her community, Mary Percy repeatedly termed herself the 'mother' of her 'children'.[116] As we have seen, a mother's power could be extremely potent. Thus, Percy invoked the full weight of a compelling maternal authority in her efforts to command her nuns' obedience. Other women appropriated masculine imagery to describe their ascendancy. The Augustinian prioress, Margaret Clement, who was acclaimed by her nuns, ecclesiastical superiors and lay folk alike for strong and effective leadership, alternated between maternal and Christological symbols. When there were few vocations during the early years of her rule, she was said to have 'accounted herself a barren Mother'.[117] However, once her cloister was thriving, she likened herself to the 'good shepherd', who guarded her flock 'lest the ravening wolf should do any hurt to her little lambs'.[118] Clement's representation of successful governance in masculine imagery and weaker rule with feminine suggests she accepted a gendered differentiation of power. Yet the good shepherd symbolism bespoke parental solicitude for her charges, which was in line with the common exhortation that abbesses should rule with 'a Mothers heart and the tender love of a superiour'.[119] It was best illustrated by the Ghent Benedictines who acknowledged Abbess Jane (Eugenia) Poulton's strenuous efforts to guide their cloister through difficult financial times by likening her to 'a hen feeding and clocking them all to-gether under the wings of her tender solitude [sic], brooding and warming them with the fervent zeal of common order and disciplin'.[120] This was a reference to the maternal Christ, who had equated his care for Jerusalem with a hen's protection for her chicks.[121] Thus, the Ghent nuns acknowledged that their abbess had considerable, even Christ-like, authority but she was expected to wield it with motherly affection and care.

This conception of abbatial power was not new. Caroline Bynum's influential work on maternal imagery in the writings of twelfth-century Cistercians identified its appropriation by abbots and novice masters. Bynum argued that male ambivalence about pastoral administration, which conflicted with spiritual imperatives for humility and contemplation, led to the men's attempts to temper it via a new image of authority. Abbesses, however, did not generally have recourse to the imagery, and the visionaries who did use it seemed far less anxious about their devotional leadership. Bynum attributed the women's less troubled feelings about wielding institutional power to their concurrent existence as dependents upon male confessors and supervisors which assuaged the psychological stresses of ruling over others.[122] The English nuns' appropriation of the imagery reflects their different perception of female power. Many abbesses were clearly uncomfortable about assuming office. Significantly, when the validity of Margaret Clement's election as prioress was questioned, Clement concurred and did all she could to be released from the charge of government, which she did not relish.[123] Likewise, the 1709 obituary of Bruges Augustinian prioress, Mary Wright, observed 'that in the practice of humility she seemed to abase the authority of Superior rather too much by the difficulty she had in submitting to the respect due to her in that charge'.[124] Reluctant abbesses accordingly downplayed their mandate via the maternal imagery which not only ameliorated their jurisdiction as nurturing rather than authoritarian, it also invoked the subjugated wife and mother of the domestic ideology. However, although supposedly 'emasculated' by Tridentine reform, the English nuns' experiences as members of a religious minority had highlighted the limitations of patriarchy. Although still subject to male clerics they were confident that they could negotiate a degree of autonomy. Moreover, within the all-female household where the *paterfamilias* resided at a distance, considerable authority resided in the mother. As the next section will explain, the nuns' relations with the clerical hierarchy varied enormously. On the whole the convents were able to manoeuvre their position within the religious family to their advantage, often against the sternest of patriarchs. However, the very flexibility of the monastic structure opened abbatial power to challenges not simply from external supervisors, but also from within the ranks of the cloister.

Negotiating power: the realities of government

Elizabeth Tyldesley's controversial removal from office in the Gravelines community brought into sharp focus the competing forces in convent government, with the house's clerical supervisors, Tyldesley's supporters, and the faction surrounding her rival, Margaret Radcliffe, struggling to gain the ascendancy. Although the Poor Clare chronicler recounted the furore in the language of the familial metaphor, the combatants' actions belied their acceptance of its prescribed order. First and foremost, Tyldesley's supporters were not prepared to allow the friars to ride roughshod over their privileges, detailed in the house's constitutions. Strenuous resistance to their endeavours to impose their authority over the convent followed the nuns' initial capitulation to the visitor's wishes. Secondly, the women were well informed about their processes of government and they fought their opponents with every means available, including their statutes, alternative clerical bodies, civic authorities, and other lay supporters. Thirdly, they understood how to garner the favour and assistance of their allies through their exiled status and virtuous reputation. Finally, as the division of the cloister into two rival camps suggests, there were divergent views among the nuns regarding just what and who constituted legitimate authority in the house. Thus, dissenting nuns might well be prepared to oppose their abbess and clerical overseers to implement their political or spiritual vision. The events in the Gravelines cloister, and similar episodes of family breakdown in other houses, highlighted the manifold loopholes undermining the cloisters' internal and external hierarchies, which ultimately rendered the patriarchal ideal unstable and opened the way for a more fluid concept of authority.

Indeed, despite Trent's endeavour to limit the autonomy of nuns, the whole process of superintendence in practice can be read as something other than heavy-handed clerical interference in the religious women's affairs. Craig Harline and Eddy Put have noted that bishops were often prepared to compromise on certain issues, including enclosure. They argue that visitations must be seen as a process of negotiation in which

prelates, like Mathias Hovius, the reform-minded archbishop of Mechelen from 1596 to 1620, traded concessions with the nuns on minor
points in order to secure their larger agenda of monastic renewal. Far
from being authoritarian tyrants, such men acceded to cloisters' long
held traditions and to the practicalities of balancing spiritual obligations
with temporal necessities. They also considered a house's particular
circumstances. In 1620 Hovius granted the Brussels Benedictines' request to receive the eucharist more frequently 'so as to more fervently
pray for your friends in England'.[125] He had already displayed his compassion for the cloister upon issuing its constitutions in 1612. Compiled
by him, in consultation with other learned divines, Hovius insisted that
the convent try them out for over 12 months to ensure their suitability
before he would confirm them.[126] Thus, Trent's decrees, their translation into convent constitutions, and their application in individual
houses were, like the familial metaphor, open to debate and revision.
The flexibility of monastic regulation invariably encouraged the nuns to
assert their opinions about how their cloister might best be managed,
and they were not afraid the challenge the bishop if his actions were at
odds with their interests.

One nun who consistently maintained her interpretation of Tridentine law against all odds was Prioress Margaret Clement of the Flemish
cloister in Louvain. She earned a reputation among local ecclesiastics as
a 'virago' for her determined resistance to anyone or anything which
might impugn her house's reformed credentials. On one occasion she
discharged a young priest whom she deemed 'some what Light of beha-
veour', and resisted his patrons' entreaties to restore him to his position.
Although censured by some, a leading churchman 'held it as a thing
worthy of commendations, that a woman should resist so many men,
yea and those of so great account'.[127] Clement's reforming zeal even
outstripped that of her ordinary, Mathias Hovius. When in 1603 the nun,
Helen Allen, was mortally ill, her mother sought entry into the enclosure. The prioress was loath to breach clausura, particularly in the
case of an English woman when so many of her Flemish subjects had
been denied similar visits. Not to be thwarted, the anguished mother
obtained a licence to enter the cloister from Hovius. Faced with the
archbishop's approval which contradicted her own inclination, Margaret Clement opted to incur his wrath, rather than 'the breking of the
Inclosure'. Mrs Allen, understandably unhappy, returned to Hovius to
complain about Clement's disregard for his order. The archbishop was
evidently abashed by the prioress's unswerving commitment to the very
ideals he was seeking to implement throughout his diocese. Rather than

taking offence at her insubordination, he upheld her decision, reputedly telling his frustrated petitioner 'I am sory, I have so few such superiour, I would to god I had more of them'.[128] By obtaining the respect of their supervisors, leaders like Margaret Clement were able to garner considerable bargaining power.

However, such blatant insubordination more commonly required greater justification on the nuns' part. Like the Gravelines Poor Clares who quoted their statutes when questioning the legality of Abbess Tyldesley's deposing, other convents turned to their legal documents when in conflict with their ordinary. In 1641 the Ghent Benedictines thrice refused their bishop's choice of an assistant to monitor the election of a replacement for the incapacitated abbess, Eugenia Poulton. Although the nuns deemed two of his candidates totally unsuitable, they even rejected his placatory offer of an Irish priest who was a friend of the cloister. Instead they insisted upon their right, detailed in the house's statutes, to propose prospective candidates to the bishop. The nuns convincingly argued their case, pointing out the relevant passages in a Latin copy of the statutes, and they forwarded the names of two English Jesuits to act as electoral officials in a petition signed by every member of the community. Faced with the nuns' conversance with their privileges the bishop capitulated, praising their commitment to uphold their constitutions. Commenting later on the affair, Abbess Mary (Anne) Neville insisted that it was crucial that the nuns preserve their prerogatives, warning 'This poynt of chusing thos that are to attend and assist the Bishope at visites and ellection of the Abbesse is of so great importance to be mayntayned in vigor as shold it ons come to be at the Bishops appoyntment; you wold hardly find it restord agayn to its former latitude'.[129] Her warning to future generations reveals that although confident that they could overcome further episcopal encroachment upon their entitlements, she deemed it essential that the nuns defend their freedom vigorously because authoritarian prelates would always try to whittle it away. The statutes might detail their legal position but, once a precedent had been established, custom could just as readily revise it.

Anne Neville, who was professed at Ghent in 1634, but later transferred to the abbey at Pontoise where she became abbess, was well aware of some clerics' autocratic ambitions. The controversial foundation of her own community, which was originally sited in Boulogne, would have informed her wariness of male superiours who narrowly interpreted canons and statutes to insist upon their absolute jurisdiction. In 1652 the Ghent abbess, Mary Knatchbull, had incurred the wrath of Bishop François de Perrochel over the planned daughter-house.

Although aware that episcopal approval was required for new establishments, Mary Knatchbull, who had become frustrated at delays caused by her reliance upon messengers to conduct the business, dispatched the six founders before receiving formal permission. When the nuns arrived in Boulogne, Perrochel ordered them home within 48 hours under pain of excommunication.[130] He chided the Ghent abbess for disregarding legitimate procedure, sternly noting that

> folks have not proceeded with me in so good maner as they ought... You neither ought to have sent them with out knowing first whither I would like it, and whither I were satisfied with those condissions under which you pretend to establish them heer. Yea and after all that you ought to have demanded my permission and that in writing.[131]

Clearly annoyed by Knatchbull's disrespect for his authority and a stickler for due process, Perrochel had also heard reports of the Ghent cloister's penury which led him to assume that she had 'sent out those Religious as the Scum of their Cloyster to shift for them selves in his Dioces'.[132] The abbess worked tirelessly to secure the revenues he insisted the house must have to obtain his sanction, but still could not meet his exacting terms, principally because she lacked sufficient local connections to raise the funds.

The impasse was eventually resolved when the case went before a council of learned divines in Paris which ruled in the nuns' favour, noting that the situation of English Catholicism permitted a looser interpretation of Tridentine law than Perrochel had allowed.[133] Thus, the nuns' exiled status, formerly an obstacle to securing the stipulated financial support, ultimately reaped the sympathy necessary to bypass normal regulations. The clerics' attitude was no doubt swayed also by the virtuous reputations of both Mary Knatchbull and the Boulogne founders, which subsequently persuaded even Perrochel to relent and do all he could to assist the new establishment. So much so that when in 1658, to his great dismay, Abbess Christina Forster decided to relocate the community to Pontoise, he wrote commendatory letters on the nuns' behalf to Church officials in Paris, and reputedly mourned the departure of 'such pyous deserving children'.[134] Therefore, although a determined patriarch who adopted a stern paternal posture in his initial dealings with the nuns, the bishop subsequently recast himself as the kind father of the cloister.[135] However, in the disputed Boulogne foundation the crucial factor appears to have been the ecclesiastical authorities who overturned the bishop's objections. The presence of bodies beyond the cloister's immediate supervisors to whom the nuns might appeal significantly enhanced their ability to circumvent problematic decisions and relations when their own resources failed.

Indeed, it might be argued that the existence of external arbitrators, including the bishop, was a positive element of internal monastic government. Should an abbess prove incompetent or tyrannical, or law and order break down inside the cloister, these mediators could resolve the problem. It is evident that many nuns viewed the hierarchy in this way. At times of disputed internal authority the protagonists sought the assistance of the ordinary, and higher ecclesiastical bodies, in their quest for justice. The collapse of authority in the Brussels Benedictine abbey during the 1620s and 1630s offers a case in point. In 1620 Mathias Hovius's visitation report, which noted a developing rift between the abbess and senior nuns, intimated the troubles that lay ahead. Abbess Mary Percy was advised accordingly to stem the disquiet by heeding the advice of the elder nuns and not so readily listening to the opinions of the younger women and lay sisters.[136] However, as the daughter of a martyred peer and a leader with a strict sense of her sovereignty, Percy was unwilling to concede power to those who opposed her opinion. Numerous letters written by the disaffected nuns to Hovius's successor, Jacob Boonen, accused the abbess of authoritarianism, favouritism, and persecution of her critics.[137] Although differences of opinion regarding the house's spiritual allegiance were at the root of the conflict, the aggrieved sisters sought remedy for several other alleged irregularities. Complaints ranged from unequal spiritual rights for those who were not of Mary Percy's camp, through disregard for the rule and statutes in various aspects of household government, to hints of sexual impropriety between some nuns and their confessor, and the possibility that certain novices had dabbled in witchcraft.[138]

The rebels clearly looked upon Archbishop Boonen as a mediator who could mitigate the dictatorial actions of Mary Percy. Indeed combatants from both sides asked him to intervene in the escalating breakdown of order. Alexia Blanchard requested a visitation in 1622 which he duly conducted, but it failed to resolve the mounting crisis.[139] Indeed in its aftermath various nuns complained that the abbess had sought to learn who had complained about her and the confessor, Fr. Ward.[140] By December, Potentiana Deacon was writing of the cloister's impending demise unless Boonen 'undertake the busines, and with your powerfull hand, reduce us under due Religious peace and discipline, from which we are fallen, but by you may be raysed agayne'.[141] Likewise, in April

1623, Elizabeth Southcott, one of the 'discreets', begged him 'to shew your selfe a most compassionate father unto us... [for] if you proseede with my Ladye and the Convent by your poure and acthoritye I verily thinke you will reforme what is amis with fasilitye'.[142] Frances Gawen also confidently informed the ordinary that 'by your authoritie matters that are amisse wilbe amended'.[143] Jacob Boonen did make further efforts to ease the tensions. Responding to ongoing allegations that the abbess harassed her adversaries, in 1623 he sanctioned a secret ballot for the convent chapter's vote on a contentious novice's acceptance for profession.[144] However, despite the nuns' optimism regarding his capacity to restore unity, the archbishop failed to do so. In fact, far from being an impartial judge, he sympathised with Mary Percy's stance and did more to fan the flames than extinguish them.

Boonen's appointment in 1628 of a new anti-Jesuit confessor, Anthony Champney, fuelled the tensions to the point at which they exploded into anarchy. A third of the cloister opposed the newcomer and, when their pleas for assistance went unheeded, they purportedly attacked their abbess and blockaded parts of the convent against her. The archbishop could not countenance, nor it seemed control, such insubordination, and the most he could do in 1632 was to expel six of the ringleaders. Others left to found their own monastery. Disillusioned with him, the dissidents had sought assistance elsewhere, and obtained the support of the papal nuncios, Fabio de Lagonissa and Richard Pauli-Stravius. Through their efforts Rome entered the fray. In fact, Mary Percy had already lobbied her contacts there, as well as enlisting the aid of various civic officials in the Spanish Netherlands, including the Infanta Isabella. The involvement of these external patrons merely widened the ever-increasing circles of combatants, and further broadcast the scandalous events in the abbey. All attempts by the pro-Jesuit faction's supporters to dismiss Champney failed. His eventual departure in 1637 eased the situation, and heralded the return of the estranged rebels. However, dissatisfaction in the convent simmered beyond even the death of Mary Percy in 1642.[145] What finally united the opposing factions was Boonen's peremptory intervention in 1651, when he imposed his own candidate, Alexia Blanchard, as abbess. After fighting against the authoritarianism of Mary Percy, the rebels would not countenance such a blatant intrusion into their privileges. Even their opponents within the cloister agreed, and the nuns collaborated to overturn the decision, publishing a 14-page Latin pamphlet which condemned the archbishop's action, amidst a torrent of letters and other strategies designed to enlist the support of patrons and canonists.[146] The death of Abbess

Blanchard in 1652 and the election of a former rebel, Mary Vavasour, finally healed the 30-year fissure.

The events in the Benedictine abbey at Brussels illustrate graphically the problems inherent in the structure of monastic government. The familial model, no matter how conveniently it ordered the cloister's internal and external hierarchies, simply did not work when challenged so conclusively. Within the enclosure the various ranks of women were invested with substantial influence in governance issues. Like their abbesses who stood up to episcopal erosion of their prerogatives, the household officers, council and senior choir nuns were careful to preserve their privileges. During regular visitations they would draw attention to any breaches of the statutes by their abbess. Outside these formal occasions they were able to write to the ordinary about her infelicities. The overflowing files relating to the Brussels affair in Mechelen and Rome testify to their preparedness to do this when they felt it was necessary. Correspondence to Jacob Boonen further suggests that the stratification of the sisters by age of profession was not always accepted. Invariably some women of elite social background, and those who had invested substantial dowries in a house, ignored the conventional hierarchy, thereby incurring the censure of their elders. For their part, abbesses had to be scrupulously attentive to both the constitutions and customs of their community, and they had to maintain a tight grasp on internal discipline. No matter how potently their authority was expressed in official documents, they were always open to challenge from inside as well as outside the enclosure. Mary Percy survived the mutiny against her rule, but others were not so fortunate. A breakdown in relations between Abbess Elizabeth Timperley and the 'Blue Nuns' in Paris, over the convent's confessor, led eventually to her resignation and departure from the house.[147] Yet, as the conclusion to the Brussels dispute reveals, internal dissent invariably dissipated when the convent's autonomy was threatened by an overbearing bishop.

The dominant discourse of monastic authority most certainly belied the realities of power within the cloister. Beneath the veneer of the familial terminology lay a complex web of contested relationships between 'mothers' and their 'children', as well as 'daughters' with their 'fathers'. Entering the cloister with knowledge of the secular ideology, its reality in recusant households, and stories of its inversion at the royal Court, the English nuns then encountered its translation into Tridentine canons, monastic constitutions and cloistered relationships. Under normal circumstances these relationships would be negotiated in an orderly fashion. Like Catholic wives who were empowered by their religious nonconformity to redefine domestic roles with their Church Papist husbands, the nuns similarly gained concessions and privileges from superiors using an astute grasp of their legal situation, their virtuous reputations and their exiled status as bargaining chips. However, the secular and ecclesiastical paradigms for an ordered convent were sufficiently ambiguous to countenance overt challenges. Mary Percy might well berate her nuns for not heeding her, 'whose judgment you should somewhat esteem as being your mother'.[148] But they were well versed in the limitations of maternal power within the secular patriarchal household to acknowledge the existence of other, possibly more potent, alternatives to female authority. Thus, the women who deemed her government problematic were deaf to her strident claims of motherly command and chose instead to approach the alternative masculine jurisdiction. Yet the Church authorities could not be assured that they held ultimate sovereignty over convents. While they mediated during disputes and proposed compromises which were often accepted by opposing convent factions; as Brussels showed, they were not always heeded.

Ultimately, however, it was not within a convent's interests to challenge the *status quo* and wrest power from their superiors. The porous nature of the enclosure which allowed secular ideologies to infiltrate the convent, just as readily channelled reports of disorder to the world outside. In 1675, reports of dissension among the 'Blue Nuns', prompted the earl of Castlemaine to consider removing his nieces from the house, noting 'I perceive ther are factions among yu a misfortun which of it self is able to ruine any Hous'.[149] The abbess enlisted the epistolary support of the cloister's clerical allies in an effort to avert his action, and sent him a detailed account of the dispute to allay his fears that the house was about to descend into Brussels-like anarchy.[150] The English religious communities knew only too well the consequences of the Benedictine furore. At Brussels in 1622, Potentiana Deacon had heard 'that there was so ill an opinion held of us abroad, that we weare compared to the ruins of Troy', leading her to 'feare this monasterie wilbe much disgraced and impoverished therby, and we shalbe in daunger to Loose our best friends'.[151] As she predicted, the house which had flourished to the point of severe overcrowding prior to 1620, suffered a severe falling off in recruitment and revenues during the dispute and in its aftermath. As the next chapter will explain, this was potentially fatal.

3
The Monastic Economy: Prayer and Manual Labour

Being humbly to expose unto the charity of the citty the distress of our Community wee desire it may be in the first place understood and considered that this great poverty hath occurred through no excess of ours, but from the common calamnity of o[u]r Nation or rather in way of suffering for justice as being Religious and the children of Catholikes from whom the unjust lawes of England now violently executed takes all their temporall fortunes.

(Mary Knatchbull, 'An account of the necessitys of the Community', c.1650)[1]

Soon after assuming office in 1650 Abbess Mary Knatchbull was forced to appeal to Ghent's citizens for charitable assistance. Her poignant petition detailed the Benedictines' inability to pay creditors for previous years' debts and their lack of subsistence for the year to come. Abbess Knatchbull was at great pains to exonerate the cloister from any blame for this parlous financial position. It was, she said, the outcome of the Civil War and the victory of the Parliamentarians which had disrupted the flow of rents and dowry monies from England and, worse still, impoverished the nuns' families and other Catholics who had provided the cloister's regular income. The Ghent Benedictines were not alone in their plight. None of the English communities survived the 1640s unscathed, and the situation of several monasteries worsened in the 1650s. In 1644, when the pecuniary impact of the first Civil War was felt in the over-populated Poor Clare house at Gravelines, its abbess sent 15 women to begin a new convent at Rouen.[2] Continuing financial stress resulted in a further purge of the community in 1652, with another daughter-house established in Dunkirk. The loss of their English investments in the 1640s likewise forced the Cambrai Benedictines to send a group of nuns to Paris in 1650 to relieve pressure on the mother-house.[3] The Civil War period thus highlighted the inherent weakness in the exiled monastic movement – the nuns' economic situation.

Poverty was not peculiar to the English religious communities. However, as studies of early modern female monasticism have shown, Continental contemplative houses were populated by the daughters of local elites, and they often comprised an important thread in the social and spiritual fabric of many cities and towns. Families supported them as a civic resource where their unmarried daughters could live honourably.[4] Although most parents were reluctant to dower their religious daughters overly generously, they acknowledged the importance of their cloisters' reputations, so financially embarrassed houses could often rely upon their kin for assistance. Likewise municipal and ecclesiastical authorities aided convents in times of need. Jutta Sperling's study of late Renaissance Venetian nunneries found that 15 of the 40 convents were in debt, but only a few seemed to have serious difficulties. Between 1564 and 1769 all establishments, bar one, had increased their yearly taxable revenues by between 27 and a phenomenal 4,662 per cent.[5] Generous endowments and patronage seem to have been the crucial factors. Houses which boasted both of these criteria, and professed the daughters of the local nobility, were most likely to succeed. In the fifteenth and early sixteenth centuries the Benedictine convent of Le Murate in Florence acquired well-connected novices with large dowries, and exceptional patrons, including the Medici and Pope Paul III, who bestowed money, property and privileges upon the house.[6] Likewise, most houses founded for noblewomen in Seville were able to exist comfortably upon income from dowries and bequests.[7] Property and patronage could however create a serious conflict of interest between the spiritual and temporal interests of a religious community, particularly in the aftermath of Trent with efforts to impose strict clausura. Reformers, like Teresa of Avila, eschewed dowries and endowments in an effort to avoid the corruption they represented. Yet even Teresa was forced to concede that nuns required access to reliable support, in her final years allowing her cloisters to accept dowries and fixed incomes.[8]

Those houses which lacked secure income from property, relied upon civic and familial support in the form of dowries, alms and subsidies, and upon what they could earn through handicrafts and services. Poorer communities were often those more recently founded. Jutta Sperling found that the wealthiest Venetian convents were long-established

Benedictine, Cistercian and Augustinian houses, while many of the poorest dated from the fifteenth and sixteenth centuries, caught by government prohibitions against large endowments.[9] In Spain and France female houses ultimately fell victim to the popularity of the religious life during the sixteenth and early seventeenth centuries, which had given rise to so many new communities. In the latter decades of the seventeenth century, waning enthusiasm for monasticism, characterised by dwindling vocations and alms, saw the livelihoods of several convents collapse. Those with wealthy endowments were able to weather the storm, but for those close to the subsistence level, which depended upon recruitment and charity, prospects were bleak. Elizabeth Rapley noted that by the eighteenth century about 500 of the 2,000 women's houses in France were 'miserably poor'.[10] Many monasteries had to eke out an existence via the fruits of their members' labour. To survive, Spanish nuns in Seville engaged in silk weaving and embroidery.[11] Similarly, some French Ursulines manufactured secular and religious furnishings with their needles; other orders produced sweets, preserves and herbal remedies.[12] The practice of taking in boarders and pupils was also common across Continental communities.[13] In addition to these tasks, the Flemish Third Order Franciscan sisters in Louvain also washed the local Jesuits' 'church-linen'.[14] A broad spectrum of economic capacity therefore existed among the European religious houses. They were not immune to poverty, but strong endowments, good recruitment, and access to patrons and kin, enabled the majority to survive the seventeenth century with some modicum of security.

With those criteria in mind, the English foundations were at a distinct disadvantage. They were often established upon the slenderest endowment, and they drew most of their income from the dowries of their members, the charitable assistance of families and friends, and from both landed and paper investments. Indeed the greater part of most houses' revenue originated in their homeland. As evidenced by the impact of the Civil War on the Benedictine and Poor Clare cloisters, the nuns were particularly susceptible to England's religious and political upheavals. Yet they were also subject to the economic and political vagaries of their adopted location. Their foundation dates, and their location in France and the Low Countries, allocated them to that vulnerable category of recently established houses which had to compete for increasingly meagre resources as the seventeenth century drew to a close. To survive the English nuns fell to the usual combination of handiwork and services. This chapter focuses upon the financial situation of the convents and the money-making ventures they adopted to remain solvent, but it locates the nuns' economic activity within the conflicting ideological imperatives governing religious women's work in post-Tridentine Church and society.

Financial position of the cloisters

The post-Reformation English convents were in a unique position. Unlike cloisters in Italy, Spain and France, which were founded by local women for the benefit of their fellow citizens, and therefore drew their financial support, the English houses were at a distance from the community they aimed to assist and were thus removed from their chief benefactors. Although there were English Catholics living on the Continent, few had possession of sufficient local property and incomes to offer the nuns the kind of generous endowment necessary for complete security. Economic survival accordingly entailed a complex mix of good recruitment, sizeable dowries, sound investments, reliable financial advisers and generous patrons.

Initial sponsorship, however, remained a key factor, and one of the better-endowed communities was the Brussels Benedictine abbey, which had attracted the patronage of the archdukes, Albert and Isabella. Mary Percy and her friends began with 22,400 florins in pensions and alms. After buying their residence, furnishing it and clothing themselves, the four founders placed the remaining 10,400 florins in the bank. Steady recruitment over the next 15 years brought 128,300 florins in dowry payments, but it also necessitated expansion of the monastic buildings.[15] Brussels was fortunate in that its relatively secure foundation enabled it to save enough to cover such costs. When in 1614 the household expenditure for the 30–odd choir nuns and novices, plus lay sisters and servants began to outweigh income, the nuns could rely upon their savings.[16] Other convents were not so well placed. The Augustinian foundation of St Monica's proceeded largely upon the strength of a 500-pound bequest from a pious English Catholic gentleman. To this sum were added the various pensions scraped together by the founding nuns, plus promises of charitable assistance from the exiled English Catholics in Louvain.[17] With such a small and unstable endowment, the Augustinian nuns purchased their house and set up the monastic regimen of prayer. Financial hardship was inevitable and, a few months into the venture, the procuratrix was convinced that the archbishop would dissolve the cloister upon the grounds that it was not a viable foundation.[18]

The principal difference between the Brussels Benedictines and Louvain Augustinians was that the latter was a filiation from the town's

Flemish cloister, St Ursula's. In such circumstances, the founding nuns often had to leave their own dowries in the mother-house. When in 1624 the archbishop of Mechelen approved the departure of four nuns and two novices from Brussels to begin a new establishment in Ghent, he did so 'on the express condition ... that the said Religious shall take out of the said Monastery nothing whatsoever, either in pensions and annuities brought by them, ... except what the Rev. Lady Abbess ... may be willing to grant them'.[19] The founders left accordingly 'without on[e] penny in theyr pockets', but Abbess Mary Percy ceded their religious habits, furniture from their cells, and a few household items and church ornaments.[20] Likewise St Ursula's did not provide the seven founders of St Monica's with any money or food, although they too were given certain household goods, church furnishings and prayer books, which were considered surplus to the needs of the remaining nuns.[21] 13 of the 22 English cloisters were filiations, and at least half of these were established by nuns from overcrowded and poverty-stricken mother-houses.[22] Therefore it is hardly surprising that they lacked adequate endowments.

To survive such new establishments had to recruit rapidly. Both St Monica's and the Ghent Benedictine house were successful in this respect.[23] The Benedictines, who began with insufficient money to purchase their initial premises, pinned their survival upon the vicarious prospect of a novice's 3,000-pound portion. By the death of its first abbess, Lucy Knatchbull, in 1629, the cloister had professed 12 choir nuns. Their dowries had enabled Abbess Knatchbull to purchase the land upon which the nuns built their own convent in 1628.[24] However, successful recruitment could prove a double-edged sword for communities which expanded beyond the capacity of their accommodation. The popularity of the Louvain cloister eventually led to severe overcrowding, which had to be relieved by the filiation to Bruges in 1629. At Ghent the deaths of several nuns in the 1630s from consumption, attributed to their cramped quarters, persuaded Abbess Eugenia Poulton to embark upon an ambitious extension in 1639. She allocated 2,000 pounds of dowry money for the scheme, but this barely covered the cost of the new building's foundations. With several women in the novitiate, and the security of over 5,000 pounds invested in England and Ireland, the abbess borrowed money at a high rate of interest from a Dutch merchant to complete the project. Her folly only became apparent in 1642 when the onset of civil war in England saw the cessation of all income from money invested there. Moreover, many of the novices were forced to leave because their families could not afford to dower them. The strain was too much for the abbess, who lost her senses and had to be replaced at the end of 1642 with Mary Roper.[25] Solvency was not achieved until Mary Knatchbull became abbess in 1650. Initially she was overwhelmed by the enormity of the 68,100 florin debt, and it was within this context that she appealed to Ghent's citizens for charity. However, by 1655, she had more than halved the amount by renegotiating the terms of the crippling merchant's loan, managing to collect 9,000 florins from her own creditors, and carefully investing the portions of the nuns she had professed.[26] She had also relieved pressure on the house's strained resources by dispatching a filiation to Boulogne in 1652. Steady recruitment in the 1650s and 1660s assisted Knatchbull's programme of debt reduction. However, after 1670 so few women joined the convent that by the time of her death in 1696, the nuns were again in such a desperate position that the new abbess, Justina Petre, was authorised by the bishop to leave the cloister to obtain relief from family and friends.[27]

Dowries, derived from regular recruitment, therefore represented economic security. Their importance explains the set fees for entry to specific cloisters, and abbesses' determination to achieve the highest price possible in their negotiations with parents. In heated correspondence with Sir Thomas Clifton in 1675 over the sum he would settle on his daughter, the Dunkirk Benedictine abbess, Mary Caryll, insisted that she was not permitted to accept anyone for less than 400 pounds.[28] In reality Dunkirk's dowries fluctuated from as little as 350 pounds up to 1,000 pounds.[29] Such discrepancies were common. Settlements among the Brussels Benedictines ranged from Lucy (Winifrid) Tresham's 10,000 florins in 1615, to Alice (Placida) Brooke, professed in 1619 with no portion. However, of the 55 dowries negotiated as lump sums from 1600 to 1632, most stood between 3,000 and 5,000 florins, with a mean of 3,940 florins.[30] The problem for superiors was that in difficult times, when there was competition among cloisters for novices, they were usually forced to accept women for significantly lower sums. Between 1652 and 1672 the mean price at Brussels plummeted to 2,147 florins.[31] Yet for many houses a lesser amount paid up front upon the nun's profession was more acceptable than the alternatives. Some portions were paid as rents from family estates. For example, the dowry of Anne Constable, professed at St Monica's in 1672, was left in the hands of her father 'att Rent, and lande bounde for itt'.[32] Abbess Caryll of Dunkirk, who would accept up to 100 pounds of a portion as a life rent if assured of good security, was far more reluctant regarding annuities. The terms for these varied from the convent receiving the interest upon money invested on the nun's behalf, often claiming the principal at her death, to an annual payment of a predetermined sum. Mary Caryll observed that she often lost the principal in such deals.[33] Moreover, most families were not as conscientious as Sir Thomas Gascoigne whose account book annually recorded the 15-pound pension paid to the Paris Benedictines for his daughter Catherine (Justina) Gascoigne in the 1660s and 1670s.[34] Columba Gage had made her vows at Brussels in 1617 with a discounted dowry of 2,000 florins, and an annuity of 100 florins for her life. In 1631 the account book noted that the payment was two and a half years overdue.[35] The problem was perennial. In 1717 Prioress Lucy Herbert of the Bruges Augustinians complained that she had received nothing of Barbara Caryll's annuity since her profession, and that the arrears was nearing 1,200 livres.[36] Beyond sending the nun to her family to collect the money outstanding (which was an expense in itself), superiors could do little other than write reminders and urge their procurators in England to bring in the debt.[37]

Non-payment of portions highlights the vulnerability of abbesses and prioresses when it came to business dealings. As member of enclosed orders, the nuns could not pursue their creditors personally, so they had a series of agents both locally and abroad, who were empowered to conduct certain transactions. Called the steward, agent or procurator, these men were responsible for collecting money and forwarding it to the convent. They also acted as investment advisers, and often conducted many of the financial affairs of the house. Their assistance was invaluable to abbesses and prioresses faced with decisions regarding where to invest dowry capital. The most common practice among houses in the southern Netherlands was to purchase perpetual or life annuities. A cloister would invest capital and in exchange receive periodic rent payments, which were either permanent or tied to the life of a few annuitants. The Brussels Benedictines had initially invested in annuities, which were permanent loans secured against wealthy religious financiers and the public credit institution, the *Mont de Piété* in Brussels. In 1622 they had 50,000 florins located among the English College at Douai, the English Jesuits, the Dutch Jesuits and the *Mont de Piété*, for which they received 3,125 florins in annual rent. By 1639 they were transforming this capital into life rents. In September, the 33,600 florins in the *Mont de Piété* were renegotiated as life rents, tied to the lives of 43 nuns. Other life annuities were arranged through the States of Hainault and the *Hôtel de Ville* at Brussels. By 1676 the cloister had resorted to converting part of each nun's portion to a life rent within a range of credit institutions.[38]

The French houses relied principally upon annuities, which were permanent loans guaranteed through the *Hôtel de Ville*. In 1699, Mary Caryll of Dunkirk placed 5,000 livres in the *Hôtel de Ville* at Paris.[39] When the Benedictine community considered investing smaller amounts in Dunkirk's *Hôtel de Ville*, she sought advice regarding its security.[40] Abbess Caryll had a reliable adviser in John Caryll, her brother, who was attached to the exiled Jacobite court at St Germain-en-Laye. He helped her to invest her cloister's assets prudently in secure institutions. Other nuns, however, were not so fortunate in their choice of financial assistants, sometimes placing their trust and their cloister's assets in unscrupulous hands. The Brussels Benedictines were left with 2,150 florins of debts when their steward ran away in 1616.[41] More seriously, in the mid-1660s, the Paris Augustinians found themselves in debt after their banker dishonestly invested funds on their behalf. The nuns not only lost considerable money, but the cloister's reputation also suffered greatly.[42]

The experience of the Paris convent shows graphically the English houses' vulnerability. Should their financial administrators fail them, convents were forced to rely upon kin and friends. Mary Caryll regularly complained of the failure of Dunkirk's various agents to collect debts, and wished that they were as competent as her brother in the business of her convent.[43] Ultimately, the nuns leant increasingly upon such supporters, who ensured that despite bouts of severe poverty during the seventeenth century, none of the houses was forced to disband, although some came close to it.[44] The story of the Benedictines of Pontoise provides clear evidence of how, almost miraculously, some houses were able to survive in spite of crippling economic liabilities, and the importance of patrons in such circumstances.

From the outset, this community was beset with difficulties. It began as a filiation to Boulogne from Ghent in 1652, when Mary Knatchbull was attacking that cloister's enormous debts. Hence, as discussed in Chapter 2, the venture was vehemently opposed by the bishop of Boulogne, who recognised its impecunious financial grounding. The prelate's eventual acquiescence was based more upon his perception of the nuns' virtue than satisfaction that they could support themselves.[45] Mary Knatchbull had solicited the support of English merchants in Antwerp to provide Boulogne with annual pensions. However, the expectations of the house were vested principally in the dowries of prospective novices.[46] When permission was finally granted for the Benedictines to set up their cloister, the nuns were well aware of their inadequate funding. Christina Forster, later the second abbess of the community, wrote constantly to her father requesting that he 'take seriously to hart this Foundation'.[47] Although Sir Richard Forster, who was treasurer to Henrietta Maria, had already invested greatly in the Poor Clare cloister at Rouen, his daughter persuaded him to endow her convent also.[48]

Soon after she became abbess, Christina Forster decided that the climate of Boulogne was too unhealthy for the English nuns, so they moved to Pontoise in 1658. The Benedictines purchased their new house with money given by Sir Richard Forster, and the dowries of several novices awaiting profession. Unfortunately, the premises were too small and required extending. Ignoring the Ghent precedent, the nuns borrowed money at a high rate of interest. This initial foray into debt began the interminable cycle of borrowing on future expectations, which led to decades of debt.[49] Furthermore, the Pontoise nuns had limited land and could produce very little for their own needs because their convent was located close to the river which regularly overflowed its banks, sweeping away their enclosure wall and vegetable garden.[50] The account book which recorded annual income and expenditure reveals that even when the nuns broke even, they never accumulated enough capital to carry them through bad years. For example, in 1659, the procuratrix recorded a loss of 3,049 livres. The following year's profit of a few hundred livres could not cover the 1659 debacle.[51] This pattern of high debits which could not be covered by ordinary income continued for the remainder of the century. Between 1680 and 1702 expenditure constantly outweighed income.[52] In the 1680s and 1690s, the Pontoise annual debt fluctuated, occasionally rising above 10,000 livres. Somehow the cloister struggled through much of the eighteenth century, until a final chapter meeting in 1786 when the community voted to disband. The abbess reportedly commented that 'the frightful list of our enormous debts on the one hand and the hopeless sight of our scanty income, so inadequate to meet our expenses on the other, seem not to leave us any option'.[53] Given the perilous state of finances in 1702, the survival of the house until this juncture is amazing. Prior to the eighteenth century, it seems most likely that it was the alms and influence wielded by powerful patrons which protected the convent from closure.

Pontoise's principal benefactors in the seventeenth century were the aforementioned Sir Richard Forster, and Abbot Montague. Walter Montague had been almoner to Henrietta Maria, and he was commendatory abbot of St Martin, near Pontoise. He befriended the town's new English cloister, and proved a constant source of charity, paying debts, donating money for living expenses, and even providing dowries for two nuns.[54] Writing to the marquis of Ormonde in 1660, Abbess Knatchbull of Ghent acknowledged Montague's generous care for her filiation, and she declared her intention to press him for more aid.[55] He needed little prompting. In 1672, he invested 10,000 livres on the nuns' behalf, which would earn them 500 livres per annum. However, given the ever-accumulating debts, this amount did little to return the convent to solvency. Nevertheless, for the remaining five years of his life, Montague did all he could to sustain the cloister. Abbess Anne Neville noted that while the nuns were unsuccessful in their endeavours to generate extra income, 'ether by work or address to frends all our supplys were from my lord who never seemed weary of releeving his poore children'.[56] The Pontoise sisters greatly lamented his death in 1677. Significantly, the demise of Montague saw the cloister slide into the decades of almost permanent annual deficit.

Thus, when recruitment, dowries, investments and servants faltered, benefactors bailed the nuns out of their budgetary predicaments. Yet even they could not provide convents with sufficient means. Nuns were forced to exploit other sources of revenue to supplement their customary income and aid from patrons. Like Continental women religious, the English engaged in the small-scale craft and service ventures. These piecemeal activities enabled their houses to generate enough money to survive the worst crises, yet it never enabled them to rise above their precarious economic footing. The issue of work in early modern monasticism was enveloped within a complex web of ideological, cultural and economic values, which mitigated against the cloisters' opportunity to support themselves adequately. Some understanding of these factors explicates the modes of revenue raising chosen by the English nuns.

The ideology of work[57]

Work in monasteries fell into two apparently disparate categories, which were invested with radically divergent merit. First and foremost, monastics performed their spiritual duty of the divine office, the *Opus Dei*. Manual labour ran a distant second. The differing value of the two pursuits was typified by the status of those undertaking them. The contemplative vocation was the province of the choir monks and nuns, who were men and women of respectable, often noble, social status. By contrast, the physical toil of the cloister, carried out by the lay brothers and sisters, fell to men and women from the lower social orders. However, this simple dichotomy which classified cenobitic work in accordance with the prejudices of the ruling orders, was a corruption of the original spirit of monasticism, established most successfully by St Benedict in the sixth century. Benedict had reconciled the conflict between prayer and those necessary jobs which interfered with it by imbuing the latter chores with a spiritual meaning. In the Benedictine rule physical labour prevented idleness and hence limited the opportunity to lapse into sinful behaviour. Moreover, for the sons of the aristocracy, toil in the fields, which belonged to lowly and servile groups, became an exercise in humility. Thus, in monasticism, work had a spiritual rather than a material meaning.[58]

Inevitably, work in monasteries was practised more in tune with cultural norms than with St Benedict's original ideals. Manual labour was rejected as unsuitable by the elites who comprised the choir monks and nuns, and the rank of the lay brother and sister was cemented within the cloister. However, work in religious houses was not coloured simply by social status, it was also gender specific. To accommodate Benedict's concerns regarding the moral turpitude of idleness, monks engaged their hands and minds in the advancement of knowledge. From the twelfth and thirteenth centuries, when learning moved into the universities from which they were barred, religious women increasingly pursued feminine occupations with their distaffs and needles to keep the devil at bay.[59] The disparity was clearest in the Dominican order where the men engaged in academic studies, while the nuns sewed and embroidered.[60] So while the Church could offer men an alternative scholastic career, nuns' occupations differed little from their sisters in the world. This monastic gender divide widened spiritually too in the thirteenth century, upon the arrival of the mendicant orders, with their insistence upon evangelical poverty. The rejection of financial security proved contentious enough among the Franciscan friars, but for Clare of Assisi and her followers the issue was even more complex. The ideal of poverty for religious women, which required begging for alms and ministering to the needy beyond the cloister, was abhorrent to a Church hierarchy eager to enclose all nuns, so Clare's efforts to have her rule confirmed for all houses failed.[61]

Ironically, although determined to preserve nuns from the perils of ideologically inspired poverty, ecclesiastics did little to alleviate real poverty, which was a common experience among nunneries. Studies of medieval women's religious houses have revealed that patrons were more generous in their endowment of male institutions, making women's cloisters especially vulnerable.[62] The thirteenth-century Norman visitation register of Archbishop Eudes Rigaud suggests that although women's houses were generally larger than men's, the resources of nunneries stood at 15 per cent of their male counterparts.[63] Roberta Gilchrist's archaeological analysis of English cloisters has concluded that a similarly gendered poverty existed across the Channel.[64] However, neither the moral, social or spiritual considerations which underpinned nuns' ability to earn their living took account of a convent's financial needs. Piecemeal embroidery would not fill the empty coffers, but religious houses were castigated by monitoring bishops if they embarked on more realistic attempts to earn their keep.[65] Yet, in the light of the mendicant orders' rejection of property and wealth, the nunneries' actual poverty might not have been perceived as negative by their inmates. Recent research has suggested their marginal geographic and economic position actually enabled the religious women to embrace the stricter ascetic ideals denied them by the Church hierarchy. Marilyn Oliva's study of monastic establishments in the diocese of Norwich has shown that the poorer and more isolated female houses were less entangled in worldly politics, business and corruption than their male counterparts, thereby permitting the pursuit of an eremitic spirituality which 'embraced poverty as an active ideal'.[66]

The medieval ideologies which underpinned nuns' labour were maintained in the early modern Church. Despite evidence of convents' poor economic infrastructure, the Tridentine reformers seemed unprepared to make concessions. References to manual labour in the constitutions of women's communities implied that nuns would be employed with their needles.[67] That such work had a higher symbolic value than economic utility was evident in injunctions against the sale of needlework in some houses.[68] Indeed the Council of Trent actually worsened nuns' financial plight by its insistence upon strict monastic enclosure. The terms of clausura forbade work in the community beyond the convent walls, and any activity which involved secular folk entering the enclosure. Hence the possibility of gaining alms through the performance of valuable community work was closed to female houses, and their participation in the urban market for textiles and other goods was limited, if not forbidden.[69] Similarly, although schools were permitted within the cloister, enclosure requirements for students and nuns alike meant that convent schools were never large enough to offer complete economic security. Claustration even threatened the relationship between monastic families and their kin in the world. The close interaction between them which saw female relatives entering the enclosure at will, and the nuns offering their patrons services and gifts in return for support, was declared dangerous to the nuns' spiritual purity. The

severing of these ties severely disrupted the symbiotic relationship between the cloister and the world which secured the patrons and alms so
essential in the convent economy.

Clausura further eliminated the mendicant concessions snatched by
women in the preceding 200 years through the explosion of tertiary
orders, the reforms of women like Colette of Corbie, and the phenomenal success of the *beguine* movement in northern Europe. For example,
Colettine Poor Clares who had formerly maintained themselves on alms
alone were no longer permitted to do so. When Mary Ward established
the Poor Clare cloister at St Omer in 1609, the house adopted the rule of
St Clare promulgated by Urban IV in 1263, which allowed the owner-
ship of property and goods, rather than St Colette's stricter revision.[70]
Even more serious was the Catholic Reformation's gendering of spiritual
labour which denied women the active apostolate. Monks were able to
perform missionary work; nuns could only pray for the conversion of
the heathen and heretic. Yet at the very moment that the Church
restricted nuns to the spiritual labour of prayer, it promoted salvation
through regular attendance at the sacraments, especially the mass.
Nuns, who had always been barred from conducting the eucharist,
accordingly had to pay priests to say increasing numbers of masses for
benefactors who believed in the primacy of the sacraments over the
prayers of nuns. Catholic reform therefore realigned the status of spiritual labour in a way that had severe economic implications for houses of
religious women.

The Church did recognise the financial problems it had created for
nuns, and its solution flouted centuries of ecclesiastical law. In the
aftermath of Trent, ecclesiastical authorities sanctioned the dowry
system for religious women to compensate for any monetary shortfalls
caused by claustration. In previous centuries, the payment of a monastic

dowry had been tarnished by hints of simony. Pragmatic early modern
bishops reinterpreted Tridentine law, which permitted houses to accept
boarding fees for women in the novitiate, to allow the payment of a sum
of money upon profession.[71] Settlement of a dowry upon making their
final vows ultimately became mandatory for nuns, and formally convents were not permitted to profess anyone whose portion was in doubt.
This requirement meant that a nun, like a secular woman, was dependent for her future upon securing a sum of money that reflected her social
status.

Yet, in spite of the difficulties imposed by the reforming Church
which added to the historical precedent of poverty for many women
religious, nuns largely survived the harsh economic climate of the

seventeenth century. They did so by manipulating the spiritual and temporal dimensions of monastic work to generate income, while remaining within the ideological and spiritual parameters set over the centuries. The English cloisters' strategies for solvency will now be examined.

Spiritual work for profit

The primary function of the contemplative monastery was the *Opus Dei*. Spiritual duties in the choir accordingly dominated a day comprised of formal and private prayer, manual labour, recreation and other religious observances. Given its centrality in the daily routine, the divine office played an important role in many houses' financial concerns. In feudal society nuns and monks had prayed for those founders who endowed their communities with lands and goods, and for the patrons who continued to provide alms. The monastics became intercessors for their benefactors who were too busy with secular concerns to undertake the hours of prayer necessary for salvation. In her study of medieval English nuns, Sally Thompson argued that the desire to enlist the spiritual assistance of nuns for family members, alive and deceased, was a significant motivation for the establishment of numerous post-Conquest cloisters.[72] Ludo Milis has termed this relationship between medieval cloisters and their patrons 'functional reciprocity'. According to Milis, the way in which the partnership operated was simple: 'We look after you on earth, you look after us in heaven'.[73] Therefore the 'spiritual labour' of the religious person repaid the material assistance of the benefactor.

The endowment of the English cloisters in the seventeenth century was conducted on similar terms. Although the feudal exchange of land for service was not possible, prayers were accorded benefactors in recompense for rents, icons, household goods, or whatever the nuns received from their supporters. For example, in 1658 when the filiation of Franciscans from Nieuport (later the 'Blue Nuns') arrived in Paris, they rented a baker's house in the suburb of St Jacques. The nuns' poverty became known throughout the area and they survived largely through the charity of a few devout French gentlewomen who provided them with food and fuel. In order to repay the kindness of these benefactors, Abbess Angela Jerningham established the practice of saying a *Te Deum* and *Salve Regina* for the charitable person, no matter how small the gift. Subsequent superiors continued this spiritual recompense.[74] Practices and payments varied from house to house, but all cloisters acknowledged their debt to helpers, both ordinary and extraordinary. Although the aid provided by Sir Richard Forster and Abbot Walter Montague never lifted the Pontoise Benedictine convent entirely out of the financial mire into which it had fallen at its outset, the nuns gratefully acknowledged their endowments. Forster was recognised as a founder of the community, which bestowed upon him all the entitlements due to a founding benefactor: once a year the convent would say or sing a dirge on his behalf and offer a mass for his soul. Montague, described as 'both our frend, father and benefactor', received the same anniversary dirge and mass. However, in recognition of his more significant financial contributions, there were also monthly masses said on his behalf which were to be attended by all members of the community.[75] The additional devotions offered for Montague, who had provided a greater financial contribution than Forster, suggest that functional reciprocity in English convents operated on a carefully graduated scale.

Documents detailing the complex rules and regulations governing the receipt of temporal assistance and repayment to benefactors indicate that this was indeed the case. The Pontoise Benedictine community had memoranda which detailed the criteria for repaying temporal assistance with spiritual mediation. The religious women were reminded that it was their duty to render 'a just return agayn of spirituall Almes, of prayers pious labours and austerities' to those who blessed the community with 'temporall almes'.[76] In fact, the convent was scrupulous in determining the spiritual payment necessary for each gift, believing that their livelihood depended upon the goodwill of the giver and God. A summary of obligations noted that

> as almes is on[e] of the greatest benefits and advauntages that we can give or receave, soe ther must be singular care taken that thos that gives almes to us may not be frustrated of theyr expectation by it, but that according to the measure of the charity wee receave, wee endeavour to render a competent return, of prayers and other pyous good works by which we shall both pay the duty of gratitude, which wee owe to o[u]r Benefactors and take the best cource we can in o[u]r powre to oblige All mighty God, to inspire his Servants in the world to be bountifull to his Servants in Religion, to assist them to support and carry on a Religious state by theyr liberallity.[77]

The status of a benefactor was judged according to the amount of money or goods he or she donated. The Pontoise nuns then calculated what spiritual recompense was necessary for the gift.

In 1682, George Slaughter and his wife, Bridget Fielding, made their will, citing the Pontoise community as beneficiaries of 6,000 livres. In gratitude, the abbess and nuns offered prayers for the couple's longevity and prosperity. Each nun was required to hear mass, communicate and recite the rosary twice, once for George Slaughter and once for Bridget Fielding. Upon the death of each benefactor a solemn mass would be sung for them after the office of the dead. These memorial masses would be repeated on the third, seventh and thirtieth day. Additional devotions in memory of the pair would be left to the discretion of the abbess of the day.[78] This agreement was drawn up by a notary as a contract between the cloister and its benefactors, and signed by all parties. Similarly, in 1708, the mayor of Calais gave the English Poor Clares of Gravelines a grant for which they were required to fulfil two conditions. Firstly, the nuns were to have a solemn requiem mass on the anniversary of his death. Secondly, the convent was to receive, without dowries, two poor girls from England, Scotland, or Ireland who would invoke prayers for the conversion of England. The conditions were written into a contract between the nuns and the mayor.[79] It and other documents like it show clearly how the nuns adapted the traditional framework of monastic functional reciprocity to repay the generosity of friends. Such spiritual recompense was not always formalised. From 1696, the Paris Augustinian nuns, overwhelmed by the abundant generosity of 'our special good friend and Benfactrix', Mme de Fontenais, offered an annual requiem mass for her long deceased husband 'in some small acknowledgment of the many favors, kindnesses, and charitys received from her'. Upon her death in 1701, they rendered her the same annual memorial in honour of her incomparable generosity.[80]

However, nuns did not merely proffer prayers in exchange for charitable bequests. The process could be extended to include payment for goods and services provided by local tradesmen and merchants. In 1690, the French architect who had built the 'Blue Nuns' church and extended part of their cloister waived the debt of 10,000 livres due to him, provided that the nuns would say a weekly *De Profundis* for deceased members of his family and a yearly requiem mass.[81] For the 'Blue Nuns' in a time of financial difficulty this deal was vital, as they were able to pay for services rendered with spiritual alms. The use of a notary made the arrangement between the nuns and architect legally binding. Likewise, in 1700 Abbess Magdalen Lucy of Ghent and her council signed a contract with Livine Baesbanck, an elderly local tradesman. Under its terms Baesbanck became a 'perpetuall domesticq' in the cloister who would do odd jobs for the nuns. In return the convent would feed and clothe him, pay for his health care, give him one shilling a week, and upon his death, it would procure and fund 30 masses for his soul. Although the nuns agreed to pay their handyman more than simply spiritual alms, Baesbanck's 30 memorial masses were far more than he could have hoped to secure ordinarily. The Benedictines deliberated over the terms of the deal, but eventually they agreed that Baesbanck's services would save them time and money.[82] The English nuns therefore in various ways exploited 'functional reciprocity' to survive the pecuniary vagaries of their exile.

Closer examination of the feudal scheme reveals its utility as a framework for explaining monastic economic strategies. Ludo Milis argued that in medieval Europe patronage of cloisters represented a survival strategy on the part of the elite feudal clans. Although monasticism was imbued with feudal notions of loyalty and service, Milis argued that through the endowment of religious houses aristocratic families profited not only in heaven, but also on earth. He pointed to bargains struck between cloisters and patrons regarding the acceptance of family members, and noted that benefactors often retained some control over the financial interests of their investment.[83] Economic dependency encouraged this kind of lay interference in monastic affairs, and the situation arose more frequently in female institutions which, as I have already noted, were often poorly endowed. Poverty made cloisters susceptible to grasping financial opportunities which were contrary to their rule, such as accepting the unwanted or disabled children of patrons for large sums of money.[84]

The financial hardship experienced by the English cloisters invariably led to similarly exploitative relationships. The Paris architect, who accepted prayers in recompense for his buildings, required the 'Blue Nuns' to allow his female relatives to board at the convent whenever they wished to enter the enclosure.[85] Although this clause contravened clausura, the debt-ridden community had little choice other than to accept it. Other cloisters found themselves in a similar bind with powerful benefactors. In 1681, Abbess Anne Forster of the Brussels Benedictines asked the archbishop of Mechelen to resolve a difficult situation. The duke of Norfolk had placed his mother in the cloister as an unwilling novice. The duke was giving nothing towards her maintenance, yet the nuns were reluctant to insist upon her removal for fear of offending the influential nobleman.[86] Other houses accepted novices under conditions which were illegal in Tridentine law. In 1688, anticipating future financial benefits, the Louvain Augustinians accepted Elizabeth and Catherine Radcliffe, daughters of the newly created earl of Derwentwater. Described as 'weake' in physical capacity, the sisters received dispensations from regular attendance at the divine office and other formal religious obligations. In recompense for their inability to participate fully in the *Opus Dei*, their father dowered each with a 100-pound annuity. However, even this generous portion was accepted at a price. Under the terms of the dowry agreement the Radcliffes were each entitled to 40 pounds of the annuity for their personal use, although the private use of property had been declared unacceptable at Trent.[87]

The example of the Radcliffes indicates the extent to which penurious nuns were prepared to manipulate the terms of functional reciprocity. Apart from the generous annuity, they could expect considerable alms from the sisters' family. In fact, the convent did not have to wait long for the benefits of the dowry agreement. Elizabeth and Catherine Radcliffe's father died in 1696 leaving the house a legacy of 4,000 guilders on behalf of his daughters.[88] Although the nuns had agreed to the earl's terms when they accepted the Radcliffe sisters, they gained considerably from the transaction. What is more, the prioress ensured that Elizabeth and Catherine did not misuse their private income from the annuity, by insisting that the 80 pounds could only be used with her permission. They accordingly spent it in part on charitable works, in 1690 donating a religious habit for the novice, Barbara Constable.[89] The earl had also benefited from the deal. He had disposed of two perhaps unmarriageable daughters relatively cheaply. The Radcliffe family also obtained the prayers of their professed kin, as well as those of the convent as a whole. Weighing the advantages attained by both parties, it seems that the arrangement was of mutual benefit. The same could be said for the deal between the 'Blue Nuns' and their architect.

Thus, in the seventeenth century changing economic and religious conditions had modified the terms of functional reciprocity, but the feudal notion of spiritual returns for financial support remained. Convents were able to exploit this centuries-old relationship to their economic advantage. The terms of the Council of Trent concerning strict monastic enclosure insisted that religious women specialise in the contemplative life. Male contemplation had been largely sacrificed to the missionary ideal, leaving prayer for the conversion of England principally to the nuns. Thus, within the English Catholic community, the enclosed nuns had the monopoly on prayer. In this position they were able to attract the attention and financial assistance of their co-religionists who adhered to the traditional method of achieving salvation by using intercessors.

Domestic work for payment

Adaptation of the *Opus Dei* was only one example of the nuns' ability to earn income through daily household business. In addition to conducting their choir obligations, the nuns were also responsible for managing the cloister's temporal affairs. In the hours when they were not attending formal devotions, nuns conducted household business, received visitors, taught novices and pupils, and engaged in myriad other domestic chores. Inevitably for some women these worldly duties impinged upon time supposedly spent in the choir. Monastic rules reluctantly acknowledged that household officers might require dispensations from attendance at every canonical hour. In reality, this loophole gave nuns an opportunity to exploit their domestic chores to the economic advantage of the community. The most obvious examples of this manipulation of household activities were the convent schools and boarding facilities.

Several English cloisters established schools which taught girls the skills desirable in a Catholic gentlewoman. Pupils were recruited from among the exiled English Catholics on the Continent, as well as from Catholic families in England, and they were often very young. In 1670 the 'Blue Nuns' admitted a four-year-old child into their school. Other schools accepted similarly youthful pupils. In 1660, the Bruges Augustinians took in Ursula Babthorpe at the tender age of eight years. In 1701, Bruges acquired 'little Miss Petre', aged five; and 1710 witnessed the arrival of Mary Gifford who was only four years of age.[90] Obviously some parents sent their daughters to be educated by the nuns in the hope that they might develop a religious vocation. However, many of the girls who studied abroad left the cloisters to return to marriage and motherhood in England. The English Catholics recognised the importance of instilling firm Catholic principles in their daughters who would pass the faith on to the next generation. Hence, the convents were seen to perform a vital religious function in this respect, and parents were willing to support them financially.

Certain convents actively sought pupils by advertising their educational curriculum and fees. The Sepulchrine nuns at Liège promoted their school in a text which aimed to encourage postulants, boarders, scholars and benefactors. The sisters evidently cared for potential novices, and any young gentlewomen who desired good breeding, 'until they be ripe enough to choose some state of life. They teach them all qualities befitting their sex, as writing, reading, needle-work, French, Musick'.[91] However, the schools were generally modest in size.

Clausura demanded that pupils remain within the enclosure for their period of education, so most houses only managed to accommodate up to a dozen girls. But a few operated on a larger scale. The Augustinians in Bruges and Paris, and the 'Blue Nuns' in Paris, were popular among English and French parents, and catered for between 15 and 30 students.[92] The Franciscans in Bruges also had a prosperous school and, in 1668, the annals noted that the nuns taught 15 students.[93] One of the smaller ones was run by the Poor Clares in Rouen where, in 1652, there were only eight pupils.[94] The limited capacity of these facilities meant that cloisters did not earn much from their educational enterprises. Indeed they exacted small fees for their services. For example, in 1652, the Sepulchrines charged 15 pounds per annum if the pupil's garments were provided by parents, and 20 pounds if the cloister had to outfit the scholar.[95] However, by the mid-eighteenth century, parents would pay as much as 100 pounds per annum for a good school.[96] Indeed many cloisters, like the 'Blue Nuns' of Paris, survived in the eighteenth century, when donations and postulants were low, largely through the proceeds of their school.

However, the rewards reaped by convents for their educative work far exceeded the price they exacted for the task. Firstly, some of the pupils developed a taste for monasticism during their sojourn and subsequently entered the novitiate. If the girl was from a wealthy family, the convent stood to gain considerably. In 1697 Elizabeth Kennet, a 12-year-old heiress, was placed in the Benedictine school at Cambrai. Although later removed from the nuns' care, she returned to take her vows in 1702, bringing a 'plentifull portion'.[97] Likewise, a daughter of Lord Arundell of Wardour, became the Rouen Poor Clares' first scholar in 1646, and she remained in the school for four or five years. When, after rejecting a suitor, Cecily (Cecily Clare) Arundell was professed in 1663, she had a dowry of 1,000 pounds.[98] But the annual schooling fee and a large portion were not the only benefits such well-connected pupils could bestow upon their educators. Lord Arundell was one of the Poor Clares' principal benefactors, purchasing lavish furnishings for their chapel, including an extravagant gold monstrance and a painting of the crucifixion.[99] Similarly, Elizabeth Kennet gave Cambrai 600 pounds to build an infirmary and 100 pounds to buy silver candlesticks for the church.[100] Not surprisingly, cloisters strove to attract eligible girls like Cecily Arundel and Elizabeth Kennet. In 1680, Cardinal Philip Howard asked his brother Henry, duke of Norfolk, to send his daughters to the Dominican nuns' school in Brussels in the hope that pupils from such an illustrious family would assist the establishment's prospects.[101]

Similar financial considerations led the convents to open their boarding facilities to mature gentlewomen who had no intention of taking the veil. These women lodged within the enclosure, but in separate quarters to the nuns. They were supposed to have limited contact with the community, although they could converse with the nuns and on occasions they were permitted to dine with them. They could also attend services in the chapel. Some pensioners, like the widowed ✓ mother of Abbess Catherine Maura Hall, who moved into the Cambrai Benedictine cloister in 1674, were permanent guests. Anne Hall died in 1676 and was buried in the convent's crypt.[102] Others sought the quasi-monastic lifestyle only temporarily. The Paris Augustinians accommodated one French noblewoman for 14 years.[103] But most boarders stayed for shorter terms, like the widowed Mrs Ferrers who spent part of 1670 in the 'Blue Nuns' guesthouse, and Miss Readly who boarded there in 1687, and again in 1691.[104] At times of political crisis in England many Catholic refugees flocked to the cloisters for shelter and comfort. During the Catholic scares of the 1670s which culminated in the Popish Plot, the Pontoise Benedictines were inundated with exiles seeking shelter. The demand for beds became so great that the younger nuns and novices often had to give up their cells to the secular boarders.[105] Likewise the Poor Clares of Rouen were overwhelmed with English Catholic visitors during the Popish Plot, and after the events of 1688.[106] During the Civil War, the Louvain Augustinians had even accepted male boarders. These men were generally English exiles who lodged with the community's confessor in the priests' house.[107] The St Monica's guest facilities were maintained after the crisis, providing accommodation for English students. In 1663, Sir Philip Skippon visited Louvain and was shown around the university by some students who lodged there.[108] English visitors continued to frequent such establishments, possibly because they offered affordable hospitality. In 1711, the nephew of Abbess Mary Caryll of Dunkirk planned to stay in the Bruges Augustinians' guesthouse because it was cheap.[109]

In the face of the obvious disruption such boarding facilities entailed, the financial gains for this service did not appear to be bountiful. The enclosed gentlewomen boarders were charged an annual rent, which at the Sepulchrine cloister in the 1650s was 26 pounds.[110] However, during hard times, these paying guests at least provided convents with a steady source of revenue. For example, in 1676 the Brussels Benedictines earned 1,280 florins from their seven pensioners. Although it does not seem a great sum, it was welcomed at a time when the convent earned just 3,266 florins from its investments and recruitment was low.[111] Some pensioners reputedly saved their hosts from ruin. During the difficult years of Mary Knatchbull's abbacy, the incapacitated Lady Catherine Sedley, was sent by her husband, the playwright, Sir Charles Sedley, to reside in the guest quarters at Ghent, where she remained for 44 years. Initially the nuns were paid 400 pounds annually for her care, but her long tenure eventually reduced it to 200 pounds. The annals claimed that the nuns survived for many years largely upon the income from her pension.[112] Yet guests like the political refugees of the 1670s and 1680s and the disabled Lady Sedley surely added considerably to the housework of a community. Many gentlewomen were accompanied by their maidservants, and some even paid for their food and furnished their chambers, but their very presence disrupted the nuns from their mission of contemplation and added to the household's food, fuel and maintenance bills. In 1695 the Paris Augustinian nuns secured more money from the husband of the increasingly infirm Mrs Bailly, who required the around the clock care of two nuns.[113] As Cédoz noted, 'la grande pension' proved a great resource for the Paris Augustinians, but it was equally a source of much angst.[114]

The monasteries persisted with their boarding houses because, like the schools, they often proved to be a source of munificent patronage. In addition to paying their boarding fee, pensioners invariably proffered their hosts lucrative gifts. In 1699, the Honourable Jane Widdrington entered the Cambrai Benedictine cloister, where her sister was a nun, to lead a 'retired life'. Widdrington subsequently assisted the community by paying for the construction of the house's crypt.[115] The Paris Augustinian nuns' indefatigable patron, Mme de Fontenais, rented a chamber in the convent 'to retier her self in some times' in 1696. Her generosity to her hosts ranged from regular gifts of meat, fruit, vegetables, pastries, wine and fuel, to cash subsidies, and even a 'faire very large Turkey-Carpett' for the altar steps in the church, among other furnishings.[116] Likewise, Charles II's discarded mistress, Barbara Palmer, duchess of Cleveland, who temporarily retreated to the cloister of the 'Blue Nuns' in 1675, became one of that community's principal benefactors. During 1676, the duchess paid for alterations to the monastery, which included the erection of a new staircase and renovations to the refectory and kitchen. The following year she gave the nuns 1,000 pounds which they put towards building a new church. Her daughter, Barbara Fitzroy, entered the school in 1677, further assisting the community's reputation as a suitable place for well-connected gentlewomen.[117] Thus, by accepting gentlewomen boarders, the English convents could not only procure a source of regular income in the form of rent paid for the rooms and services required by the pensioner, they were also open to gifts and preferment from those women who lodged with them.

Although schools and guesthouses within the enclosure directly contravened clausura, the nuns justified their actions as necessitated by the desperate situation of Catholics in England. Moreover, their activities conformed with traditional roles for gentlewomen. Women had always been responsible for the care and education of young girls, just as they were in charge of hospitality within secular households. And the presence of young girls and lay boarders within the cloister was not at odds with the regular monastic routine. In most circumstances the lay women and pupils fitted into the daily schedule by following the canonical hours and leading lives of prayer. So the nuns cleverly reworked the ideological constraints which limited their economic capacity, by adapting their gentlewomanly skills to the imperatives of making ends meet.

Nowhere was this ingenuity and pragmatism more apparent than in the commercial realignment of needles and spindles. In accordance with the social and moral imperatives guiding nuns' work, the English cloisters' constitutions recommended sewing and embroidery as suitable manual labour. Such documents implied that this stitching was necessary to maintain the clothes, linen and vestments of the cloister, emphasising both the utilitarian and moral aspects of needlework. For example, the 'Blue Nuns' were advised to 'employ the time of work faithfully, profitably, and for the good of the Community, and not lose their time in frivolous Trifling'.[118] The constitutions of the Paris Augustinians were more explicit, noting that all nuns should take up the needle to avoid idleness which was 'the enemy of the soule, and mother of all vice'.[119] A large proportion of the needlework undertaken by religious communities was no doubt for their own use. The Augustinian canonesses in Louvain were adept at transforming the elaborate and costly gowns worn by women for their clothing ceremony into vestments and ornaments for the chapel.[120] Likewise, according to their confessor, the Paris Augustinians made 'ornaments for their young chapell, never for any money at all'.[121] In October 1699 the nuns completed a set of vestments and altar decorations made from Frances Constantia Molineux's fabulous scarlet velvet and lace clothing gown.[122]

The cloisters nevertheless found ways to bypass constitutional embargoes to generate income from this intrinsically moral activity. Indeed several English religious houses developed a reputation for their handicrafts. Apart from the sumptuous church furnishings, which aimed to attract the patronage of lay worshippers, and thereby comprised an indirect source of revenue, the nuns produced trinkets of a more worldly nature. Many of these ornaments were sold to visitors and friends. English tourists travelling on the Continent in the late seventeenth and early eighteenth centuries noted in their journals the purchase of souvenirs from religious houses. For example, in 1712, John Leake bought 'pictures, flowers and purses' from the Carmelites in Antwerp as well as some 'fine works' from the Benedictine nuns at Brussels. In 1707, Joseph Taylor had purchased 'a heart cut curiously in vellum with wreaths of flowers painted by herself in proper colours' from one of the Howard sisters in the Dominican house at Brussels.[123]

The Ghent Benedictines operated their craft on a more commercial footing. The convent specialised in making artificial flowers. It had shifts of weekly workers who would forgo the divine office to produce the flowers. For eight hours a day, breaking only for dinner, these nuns would labour in the work-room, saying the rosary and listening to readings from religious books. Although the community was fearful for the choir nuns' physical and spiritual health, the industry continued because it proved so lucrative. Local merchants sold the flowers in consignments which earned up to 30 pounds. Relating the success of the Ghent business, Abbess Anne Neville of Pontoise acknowledged the pitfalls of operating a convent industry, but justified it as essential for the survival of the cloister.[124] Indeed, all members of the community recognised the economic value of their flower-making. When Catherine (Teresa) Matlock, the lay sister who had initiated the industry, was dying in 1650, her religious sisters willed her to recover, saying 'we cannot Spare you Who shall Do the silk work when you'r Dead. You know what a help it is in those hard times for Supplys to the Community.'[125] Their pleas failed to save her, but the silk flower industry nevertheless survived. In 1663, during a tour of the convent, Sir Philip Skippon was shown some of the nuns' work 'which was an imitation of flowers and greens in a pot'.[126]

Other monasteries established similar industries. Ghent's mother-house at Brussels laboured in the 'making of fine regesters, working of silk flowers cutting of pictures and such like' to such a degree that in 1623 one of the nuns complained to the archbishop that 'the cheifest tymes of devotion hath been somtymes spent in those workes'.[127] Ghent's filiation to Pontoise likewise set up its own craft production. The Pontoise account book noted purchase of 'flax and things for the silke worke'.[128] And the flower-making was not simply a Benedictine industry. When the Poor Clare nuns of Aire were forced to flee the Continent in 1799, equipment for making silk flowers and some boxes of flowers were included among the belongings which followed them to London.[129] While the Pontoise Benedictine abbey was not so successful as its mother-house in using the silk flowers to stave off financial ruin, other cloisters did apply their needles effectively to make ends meet. In the *Laity's Directory* for 1796, Bishop Milner outlined the activities for which the Cambrai Benedictine nuns were renowned; notably their method of education, and 'their performances in fine needle-work and artificial flowers, and...cutting out upon vellum various ornaments and devices with the most exquisite taste and execution'. According to Milner, the nuns were able to support themselves with these and other resources and had been an asset rather than a burden to the citizens of Cambrai.[130]

Given that such industries obviously interfered with the devotional life of the cloister, applause from a bishop is rather odd. However, the economic necessity which forced convents to engage in domestic industry was acknowledged by local bishops and clergy. Clerics apparently sanctioned minor contraventions of monastic statutes, so that the cloisters would not become a burden upon the resources of the diocese. Indeed some ecclesiastics were complicit in developing monastic enterprises. Moreover, the nuns were adept at developing operations which were above question. Exhorted to wield the needle and distaff in order to keep idle hands and minds busy, religious women were merely performing tasks lying well within their province as gentlewomen and nuns. The Paris Augustinians were forced by economic necessity 'to imploye their hands to contribute to their lively hoode' which was at odds with both their monastic rule and their social status. However, the nuns' confessor insisted that the 'sweete resignation and vertue' with which they supported themselves was edifying to good Christians, thus making a positive example of their disobedience.[131] In the case of the Ghent workroom, the prayerful accompaniments to manual labour emphasised that the work was conducted not only for the well-being of the cloister, but also for the glory of God.

Yet convents had the potential to develop larger-scale enterprises than those conducted by the choir nuns. I have already noted that social status was a significant factor in monastic work. The presence of lay sisters in the English cloisters persuaded some houses to develop a variety of ambitious commercial ventures. In 1645, the Augustinians in Louvain established a laundry to bleach linen. It was operated by the lay sisters whose labours earned between 200 and 500 florins for the community.[132] Alternately, the lay sisters in the Liège Sepulchrine community operated a malt-making business. In 1680, the money they had earned helped to finance renovation of the cloister's dormitory and kitchen.[133] Other convents recognised the financial potential of brewing. In the 1620s, the Louvain canonesses planned to establish a 'brew-house' which would presumably cater for the convent's needs as well as producing a surplus for sale. The prioress wrote to the community's agents in England seeking 'some good strong maid' who would enter as a lay sister to operate the new venture. The woman chosen for the job was Elizabeth (Alexia) Hobdy who was professed in 1624, despite the fact that plans for the brewing project had by that stage fallen through.[134] The scheme was resurrected in 1672 when the prioress and her council decided to use the dowry of a deceased nun to build a 'brew-house'.[135]

While these operations could prove valuable to the financial status of a convent, they nonetheless necessitated hard physical toil. Lay sisters were taken into religious houses to conduct the drudgery of housework, and they were exempt from many monastic observances by reason of their servile vocation. Already engaged in bleaching and starching their sisters' linen, and working in the kitchens, the industries operated by lay sisters were simply commercial extensions of their daily chores. However, there was a danger that production for an external market might prove too onerous for the women. Although they were deemed more capable of heavy physical jobs than choir nuns, most communities did not have large numbers of lay sisters. Conducting a business in addition to regular household duties could well prove too much, as was the case with the Augustinians' laundry, which was eventually abandoned. The annals recorded that the toil was too great even for the sturdy lay sisters.[136]

The existence of such industries reflects not only the importance of social status in defining income-generating ventures, but also the range of skills nuns had acquired in the world prior to making their religious vows. Superiors were conscious of the pecuniary benefits which could accrue from accepting women with specific talents. The pragmatic Benedictine rule even exhorted abbesses to encourage nuns who were 'cunni[n]g in any Art' to employ their expertise for the good of the community, so long as the nun in question did not 'wax proude of her cunning'.[137] The most obvious application of this philosophy was the display of the choir nuns' musical flair during public performances of spiritual obligations. The excellence of the Paris Augustinians' choir saved the cloister from financial ruin in the 1650s and 1660s, through its capacity to attract alms from the French nobility who flocked to listen to 'their choice music'.[138] Similarly the creative talent of women like Teresa Matlock enabled other houses to produce embroidery and craft products for sale. The acumen of choristers and seamstresses merged in monastic churches where music and ornamentation not only enhanced the devotional environment for lay folk who attended mass and other religious services, but also inspired the donation of alms.

The extent to which abbesses were willing to exploit worldly accomplishments was evident in an agreement between the 'Blue Nuns' and two postulants who entered the Paris cloister in 1689. The daughters of a craftsman, Anne (Anne Teresa) and Elizabeth (Elizabeth Clare) Adamson were skilled watchmakers. Anne made the watches, and her elder sister was accomplished in the art of studding the cases. The sisters were accepted for a reduced dowry because the nuns believed Anne and Elizabeth were 'likely to be a great advantage to the hous'. However, the postulants were well aware of the nuns' intentions concerning their skills. Upon entering the monastery the Adamsons insisted that they should not be expected to work any more than the other nuns were required to labour. Nor was their craft work to interfere with their religious obligations.[139] Unfortunately, the records for the cloister do not offer any account of the success or failure of the Adamsons' work. Indeed it is unlikely that the watchmaking developed into an important form of revenue for the house, because both sisters played prominent roles in the cloister as office bearers. Nevertheless, at a time of financial hardship, the council's acceptance of the sisters for a combined portion of merely 200 pounds shows how vital their skills were deemed by the nuns. It demonstrates clearly that the application of worldly expertise was a crucial factor in the nuns' incessant quest to make ends meet.

In conclusion, the English cloisters were tied firmly to the economic, social, political and religious circumstances of their day. The nuns had to negotiate an obstacle course of financial duress, created by both the prevailing economic climate and their position as religious exiles, but intensified by ecclesiastical policy on women's role in the Church. Many convents suffered intense financial hardship, particularly during periods of political upheaval in their homeland. Some, like the Ghent and Pontoise Benedictines, seemed to be forever on the verge of collapse, and yet they somehow endured. Despite the ideological dictates governing monastic labour and the imposition of clausura, survival required the nuns to embrace rather than reject the ways of the world. Even the *Opus Dei* took on a commercial aspect as prayers earned food and paid for buildings. Daily household chores likewise contributed to the domestic economy. And the practical and artistic expertise of community members was applied to the ever-pressing need to generate income. However, in spite of nuns' resourcefulness in the choir, school-room, guesthouse and workroom, the principal sources of monastic income remained the rents and sums obtained in dowries and alms. As the example of the Pontoise cloister revealed, nuns could best achieve these things through the assistance of well-connected and wealthy patrons. The exercise of patronage provides the focus of the next chapter.

4

Beyond the Cloister: Patronage, Politics and Society

Laste weeke mr Thomson at Brussells sent me a letter which he sayd came from Dort; it was directed *For mrs Carey att the Monastery att Cambray*: I could have no cause to doubt its being not to me, there being none other of the name heere a live; but when it was opend, both my lady and my selfe did not a little wonder to find a great part of the letter, as well as the name subscribed to it and the place from whence it came, all writ in strange caracters: what was writen in ordinary letters, seemed to me, to looke as if it were some very serious matter, and I had some apprehension it might have some relation to his Majestys affaires... but after, looking upon it more seriously,... I very unexpectedly discovered the caracter... and saw the letter was concerning the Kings affaires.

(Elizabeth Cary to Colonel Grace, 10 August 1659)[1]

In 1659 Elizabeth (Augustina) Cary of the Cambrai Benedictines received a puzzling coded letter, which she duly deciphered. The contents confirmed her initial suspicion that it concerned efforts to restore Charles II to the English throne, so she sent it to a trusted Catholic family friend, urging him to convey it to the king. The mysterious letter and Elizabeth Cary's reaction to it suggest that the nuns dealt with matters well beyond their cloisters' business concerns. They obviously kept abreast of political news and in the 1650s knew of royalist activities in Flanders. Indeed, whoever sent the letter to Cambrai had assumed that Elizabeth Cary was in some way involved with the royalists. This presumption was vindicated by her ability to break the code immediately and forward the document to the king. Yet her reaction to the missive suggests that the correspondent was mistaken about the extent of Cary's royalist commitment. He or she had evidently heard about a nun who had undertaken the king's business since his removal to Flanders in 1656. Elizabeth, the sister of both Lucius, Viscount Falkland, who had died fighting for Charles I, and Anne (Clementina) Cary, a favourite ✓ of Henrietta Maria at whitehall, had the impeccable family connections to fulfil such a role. But, as her letter to Colonel Grace protests, she was not the intended recipient of the coded intelligence. It was almost certainly meant for Abbess Mary Knatchbull of the Ghent Benedictines, an indefatigable promoter of Charles's cause. Mary Knatchbull conducted a postal service for the king and his ministers, and gathered ✓ intelligence and funds on their behalf from her wide range of contacts in England and on the Continent. While the other English cloisters supported Charles's efforts with prayers, hospitality and donations, the Ghent abbess surpassed them by participating in conspiracy at the highest levels.[2] Her actions not only identify certain English nuns as political agents, they also highlight early modern women's modes of exercising power through patronage.

Recent scholarship has stressed the fluid nature of power in premodern society. Although formally most women could not exercise public authority and they were excluded from the institutions of government, studies of royal courts and elite households have revealed the extent to which they exerted influence, both at a familial level, and among a wider circle of kin, friends and acquaintances. They could do so because political business was not undertaken solely in the public space of the Court, Council or Parliament. Often negotiations occurred informally in the private space of the household. Thus, the domestic sphere was permeable and the boundaries between public and private were only loosely drawn. Moreover, in early modern society, the route to influence lay in the acquisition and maintenance of well-connected patrons who would approach others on their client's behalf. Patron–client relationships were commonly generated through social intercourse, using kin and mutual acquaintances to forge connections, which were subsequently maintained through hospitality, gift-giving and correspondence. These activities overlapped with female spaces and duties, therefore women were well-placed to secure patronage for their families. Moreover, certain women, particularly aristocratic women and those at the royal Court, could extend their operations beyond relatives and friends to wield political influence.[3]

The previous chapters have pointed to patronage's importance in the governance and business of early modern convents. As the daughters of social elites, nuns used secular skills and connections to advance their convents' economic and political interests. For example, by 1515, the Benedictine convent of Le Murate was one of the largest and most successful cloisters in Florence. It had achieved this position through the efforts of astute abbesses, in particular the formidable Scholastica Rondinelli, who adeptly courted patrons, like Lorenzo de' Medici, through strategic recruitment of novices and the practice of showering potential allies with prayers and gifts in an effort to secure their aid. Once enlisted, patrons bolstered the material well-being of the house and lobbied local secular and ecclesiastical officials on the nuns' behalf.[4] Similarly, in the sixteenth century, four prestigious Venetian cloisters invoked the assistance of their powerful kin to prevent the imposition of strict clausura; while San Lorenzo and Santa Caterina did likewise to resist the civic authorities' attempts to reduce dowry prices.[5] Conversely, reform-minded nuns enlisted their patrons to overcome those who objected to the imposition of strict enclosure. In France, the successive royal abbesses of Fontrevrault, Renée and Louise de Bourbon, sought assistance from the king and *parlement* in their efforts to reform both male and female houses of their monastic order.[6] Nuns therefore employed their worldly contacts in a range of financial and governance matters which they were unable to resolve from within their enclosure. Convents' need for powerful patrons in these instances led them to court anyone with access to the ruling elites of Church and state.

However, nuns were not simply clients. Through their own family connections, their patrons and the status of monastic office, they could offer patronage themselves. So, in the sixteenth century, Renée de Bourbon's niece, Abbess Renée de Lorraine of the abbey of St Pierre in Rheims, advanced the interests of her Guise relations in the area. She was also petitioned by the local nobility to intercede on their behalf to her powerful kin.[7] In the Holy Roman Empire, the superiors of the free imperial abbeys wielded formidable rights of patronage over clerical and lay posts within their territories. They were also benefactors to educative and welfare institutions, and commissioned the skills of trades people, artists and musicians.[8] In Pisa, the fifteenth-century Dominican prioress, Chiara Gambacorta, initially used her secular connections to solicit the necessary funds for extending her cloister's buildings, but subsequently she appointed artists to decorate the public space of its church.[9] Other Italian nuns similarly sponsored the arts.[10] Patronage therefore represented a medium for pursuing business beyond the immediate economic and political concerns of a cloister. Under the guise of securing their houses' needs, many abbesses were influential in their own right.

Moreover, religious women controlled a resource not purveyed by secular patrons. As mediators between the earthly and heavenly realms they excelled in spiritual patronage, offering devotional guidance and prayers to their clients, or even promoting specific cults and religious practices. The sixteenth-century *beguine*, Maria de Hout, counselled not only her fellow sisters, but also a number of well-educated Carthusian monks of Cologne. In return for her spiritual favours these men patronised her writings, and worked to have them published, thereby increasing her influence.[11] In seventeenth-century Madrid, the *beata*, Mariana de Jesús, provided pious assistance to numerous protégés, including queens, cardinals and civic grandees.[12] Likewise, another *beata*, Madre María de la Santísima Trinidad, courted Seville's elites in her quest to obtain sponsors for her proposed Dominican convent in Aracena, assuming the role of spiritual benefactor and friend in return for their patronage.[13] Clara Hortulana of the Munich Poor Clare cloister has been termed 'a virtual prayerbroker'. She was reputed to have released more than 1,000 souls from purgatory by enlisting nuns in her own and other convents to intercede on their behalf.[14] Spiritual assistance of this kind invested the nuns with an authority beyond that enjoyed by secular women. In the sixteenth century, Ferdinand of Aragon heeded the prophecies of the Castilian seer, María de Santo Domingo, because they bolstered his authority in Castile.[15] Philip III continued his great-grandfather's practice of having recourse to several holy women. In 1612 he consulted a nun believed to survive on the eucharist alone about the expulsion of the Moriscos from his kingdom.[16] Thus, spiritual patronage could lead nuns beyond the usual sites of women's influence onto the very public stage of ecclesiastical and civic politics.

Most early modern religious women participated in the affairs of family, Church and state without leaving the confines of their enclosures. In Italy, the Augustinian visionary, Arcangela Panigarola, denounced clerical corruption and criticised the pope.[17] Similarly, Caterina de' Ricci fostered the cult of the disgraced Dominican reformer Savonarola after he appeared to her in visions. Her convent of San Vincenzo in Prato commemorated the anniversary of his death, sang his devotional music and kept his writings. By flouting the Church authorities' condemnation of Savonarola and promoting his cult, Caterina and her nuns incurred the censure of religious superiors.[18] In the aftermath of the Reformation, religious profession in itself offered a direct challenge to Protestant states. In Augsburg the city council sought to eliminate nuns' rights to control property and resources and to elect convent officials. Both were deemed an affront to the natural order.[19]

Reformers in the Holy Roman Empire were particularly aghast at the concept of nuns' independence because several convents opposed Lutheran efforts to eliminate the religious life for women. Intelligent and eloquent women, like the Poor Clare abbess, Caritas Pirckheimer, articulated a strong defence of monasticism, challenging both the reformers' theological position and the council's authority to interfere in her Nuremburg house's affairs.[20] Therefore nuns were no strangers to conflict with civic authorities if their faith and way of life were under threat. Their freedom from immediate patriarchal supervision enabled them to defend their position actively, and their experience of self-government had equipped them with the requisite skills to do so. Thus, Mary Knatchbull's involvement in royalist conspiracy was by no means at odds with the actions of other religious women across Europe.

Indeed as this chapter will explain, the English nuns mirrored the political activity of their Continental peers in several ways. They tapped into the conduits of informal power to secure their cloisters' survival, but they took it further to establish patronage networks among the exiled English Catholics abroad and their kin in England. For certain nuns these clientage groups offered a platform to wider political influence, both in the English Catholic community and England at large. Despite geographic isolation from their homeland, the cloisters were determined to participate in English religious and political affairs. Underlying their actions was a firm belief that they were the keepers of the monastic tradition for women, and their exile was temporary. They aimed to do all that they could to assist the survival of Catholic belief and practice among their countrymen and women. The approach to achieving this goal varied among orders and houses, and ranged from simply upholding the monastic regimen of prayer, through education and spiritual support, to the overt action of missionary work and political activism on behalf of the Stuarts. Yet patronage underpinned it all, so it will provide the focus of the first section, which examines the networks established by cloisters and their function in monastic governance and influence.

Patronage: maintaining the monastic household

The English nuns' acquisition and maintenance of monastic patrons reflected their social origins. Like secular families, the monastic family sought to advance its interests through alliances with people and institutions most likely to improve its fortunes. In the world, the aristocracy and gentry expanded their estates and prospects by forging lucrative marriages. An ancient and noble lineage counted for much in the competition for sizeable portions and influential connections. Thus, certain cloisters emphasised their impeccable pedigree in the quest to attract novices who were well endowed both financially and socially. In a 1652 publication, the Sepulchrine nuns at Liège highlighted the genealogy of their order, tracing its origins back to James, the apostle. Hinting that the Virgin Mary, Mary Magdalene, and Martha had possibly been Sepulchrines, *A Brief Relation of the Order and Institute of the English Religious Women at Liège* was at pains to establish good family credentials.[21] An account of the Louvain Augustinians' ancestry was written in a similar vein. During the seventeenth century, St Monica's had attracted the daughters of many stalwart recusant families. In an effort to endorse the house's glorious descent, the document listed renowned nuns and benefactors associated with the community.[22] A report on the Ghent Benedictine house sent to Charles Dodd for his history of post-Reformation Catholicism likewise noted members of the cloister 'most illustrious for Birth'.[23]

The play upon social consciousness was even more overt in the 'courting' of women of rank. When in 1692 Lady Lucy (Teresa Joseph) Herbert, daughter of the earl of Powis, decided to enter the religious life, she was fêted as 'a lady of Quality' by the various cloisters she visited.[24] Astute abbesses and prioresses were well aware of the vital patronage she could generate for their community through her family association with the exiled Stuart court at St Germain. Herbert eventually chose the Augustinian house at Bruges, where she rapidly proceeded to the office of prioress. The convent's expansion under her governance confirmed her former suitors' assessments of her patronage capacity. Other aristocratic women fared similarly. Professed in 1634 among the Benedictines at Ghent, in 1667 Mary (Anne) Neville, the daughter of Henry, Baron Abergavenny, was wooed by the superiors of the Pontoise and Dunkirk establishments. Neville chose Pontoise, much to the dissatisfaction of her own cloister, and the disappointment of Abbess Mary Caryll, who had been particularly keen to win her for Dunkirk.[25] A year after her arrival, Neville was elected abbess and held the position for 22 years. The convents' opportunism in securing novices therefore often extended to selection of the houses' principal officers, who would represent its business interests.

The nuns' worldliness in matters of recruitment and promotion even stretched to their choice of benefactors. Most kudos could be garnered from regal associations. Following the Restoration the English monarchs were most commonly approached as patrons, but before 1660 benefactors were cultivated from among the Spanish and French rulers and their consorts. The clothing ceremony of the first eight postulants for the English Benedictine cloister at Brussels was conducted in the presence of the Infanta Isabella, the Archduke Albert and all their court, plus the papal nuncio. Isabella played a prominent part in the ceremony, leading Mary Percy and Dorothy Arundel into the church and providing a banquet for the newly clothed novices and local worthies following the solemnities, declaring herself a 'mother' to the community. Albert bolstered his wife's commitments to the house by promising the nuns whatever assistance he could offer.[26] The consolidation of royal and ecclesiastical support embodied by the ceremony was vital for the new community. Not only did the house gain the promise of patronage from these influential people, it also advertised its credentials to the English Catholic community. The elaborate display of puissant backing aimed to encourage further patronage in the form of money, gifts and postulants.

Despite the convents' preference for princely and aristocratic supporters, they alone did not guarantee security, so the nuns sought further allies, drawn from a circle of family, friends and acquaintances in England and on the Continent. As exiles, it was especially important to attain supporters who had an entrée into local religious and political elites. The English Catholic clergy provided such a link. Unencumbered by the restrictions of clausura, English priests had developed personal patronage systems and their connections proved particularly valuable for newly established convents with few local contacts. When Lady Mary Percy founded the first post-Reformation Benedictine cloister for women she chose Brussels, one of the main centres for expatriate English Catholics. Assisted by the Jesuit, William Holt, who was the former rector of the English College in Rome and agent of Phillip II in Brussels, Percy gained access to Robert Persons in Rome and the archdukes of the Spanish Netherlands. Through Persons the necessary papal briefs were secured, and Holt obtained episcopal sanction and the permission and financial support of Albert and Isabella. He also arranged for the transfer of Joanna Berkeley from the French abbey of St Pierre in Rheims to be abbess, and for two other English nuns of the same community to join the new house.[27] Similarly the founders of the Ghent Benedictine monastery relied upon another Jesuit, John Knatchbull, when they approached the archbishop of Mechelen with a proposal for their cloister. The brother of the first abbess, Lucy Knatchbull, he spoke fluent Spanish and was able to lobby several powerful clergy and lay folk in Flanders to persuade the archbishop, governors and magistrates to permit the English filiation from Brussels, and to garner alms.[28] Once established, these local connections could be called upon for further assistance as needs arose.

However, the quest to secure patrons was only the first element of a complex process. Maintaining networks involved an astute grasp of social protocol, and sagacious religious superiors mobilised those hospitable practices which were least offensive to claustration. The aforementioned custom of lodging wealthy lady pensioners was widespread. The 'Blue Nuns' guests, who included the Duke of Norfolk's daughter, Lady Frances Howard; Barbara Palmer, duchess of Cleveland; and Lady Frances Hamilton (later duchess of Tyrconnel), not only offered their hosts munificent alms, they provided access to other patrons.[29] Mme de Fontenais, the Paris Augustinian convent's great friend, procured other benefactors for the house from among the French nobility and clergy.[30] In the early 1700s, the Augustinians at Bruges regularly accommodated Winefrid Maxwell, countess of Nithsdale, and her entourage. She was Lucy Herbert's sister, and her impeccable Jacobite credentials provided the nuns with a propitious link to the exiled court at St Germain. Moreover, the countess proved a generous supporter, bestowing a succession of gifts upon the convent, including a magnificent marble altar from Rome, valued at 522 pounds.[31] Guesthouse hospitality presented the nuns with an opportunity for regular contact with their lodgers who had firsthand experience of their sanctity and their pressing financial and administrative needs. Accordingly, monastic hosts could count upon patronage and alms from these visitors whose sojourns established bonds of obligation.

Interaction with most patrons, however, was of a more transitory nature. Guests were usually entertained for an hour or so at the grate and in the chapel. Such occasions were conducted according to the customs of polite secular society, but with a monastic flavour. In addition to pious conversation, the nuns served refreshments and sometimes provided musical performances. In 1694, the Catholic earl of Perth and his wife attended *compline* in the Bruges Augustinian nuns' chapel, and were afterwards entertained at the grate 'with a fine collation of milks, fruits, and sweetmeats' by Lucy Herbert, and Catherine and Anne Howard, the daughters of the duke of Norfolk.[32] When the earl and countess visited the English Franciscan cloister in the same town, they were treated to 'an entertainment of musick . . . a hymn and a motette (although it was not an hour of prayer), with the organ, Violes, and violines, and voices'.[33] Most visitors departed with the impression that the convents housed women of good social standing and pious demeanour, and were therefore worthy of immediate assistance and future discourse. In 1660, Anne of Austria visited the Pontoise Benedictine abbey. The French regent was so enchanted by Abbess Christina Forster's command of the French language and her 'very gayning behaviour' that she immediately offered the house anything it needed.[34]

Other patrons rendered assistance without ever enjoying the nuns' social discourse. A cloister providing church services for the public might impress its congregation with the performance of its religious devotions, and thereby attract alms. This was the experience of the Paris Augustinian convent in the 1660s, when it was in dire pecuniary strife. Upon attending evensong Charles Séguier, the French chancellor, was so impressed by the nuns' singing and apparent sanctity that, upon learning that they were in financial trouble, he instantly sent them 1,000 livres. The sum of alms had reached 4,000 livres by the end of the year, and the Séguier family subsequently became staunch supporters of the cloister. By 1664, the confessor of the convent was estimating that patronage from the chancellor and his family totalled more than 10,000 livres.[35] Yet patronage did require some contact, however fleeting, between a benefactor and the nuns. In the eighteenth century, the English Benedictines endeavoured to impress Louis XV by burning 5,000 candles in his honour when he visited Dunkirk. They were competing with several other cloisters for royal favour, and were ultimately unsuccessful. One of the nuns noted somewhat sourly that the neighbouring Poor Clares had received a 600 livres bounty from the king, after cannily sending him a gift.[36] Thus, despite the success of the Paris Augustinians' choir, patronage commonly depended upon direct communication and personalised attention.

The importance of close contact in the maintenance of patronage relationships presented a challenge to the convents whose principal support lay across the Channel in England. Unable to impress these benefactors directly with hospitality, nuns applied letters in the quest to secure and maintain assistance.[37] These epistolary tools usually combined spiritual and secular conventions, mirroring the entertainment lavished upon guests at the chapel and the grate. A religious tone was rarely absent in letters, which invariably assured patrons that they remained constantly in the nuns' prayers. When in November 1660 Abbess Mary Vavasour of the Brussels Benedictines sought the brokerage of the duke of Ormonde, she was quick to reassure him of 'our dayly prayers for your highest present and eternall happinesse'.[38] Similarly, thanking her nephew in 1713 for settling outstanding monies due to the Dunkirk cloister, Abbess Benedicta Fleetwood affirmed that his name had been added to the list of benefactors who enjoyed the nuns' prayers.[39] Yet correspondence also paid attention to social niceties. Abbess Mary Knatchbull of Ghent, who had perfected the practice of strategic letter writing in her incessant pursuit of patrons, tempered her requests for assistance with a warm regard for the health, happiness and salvation of her correspondents. Writing in 1664 to Charles Berkeley, Viscount Fitzharding, keeper of the privy purse, upon whom she depended for the regular payment of a pension provided by the king, she declared:

> As no body can be more obliged to your Lordships Goodness then I am, so I am sure no body hath a tenderer conserne for your happiness, which I dayly make the subject of my best wishes and prayers, and therfore shall proportionably have all wayes my share of comfort in your lordships good fortune which I doubt not is compleated to your harts wish in your Lordships late marryage which I come now to congratulate, with as many tender effects as an obliged hart is capable of produsing. [40]

Through attention to the personal welfare of correspondents and her letters' tone of familiarity, Knatchbull strengthened the bonds of obligation. One acquaintance confided her morning sickness to the nun and joked that she would 'breed girles enough to fill a closter'. Indeed Knatchbull was already god-mother to one of her other daughters.[41] A consummate player like the Ghent abbess understood the importance of establishing a close relationship, bordering on kinship, with her patrons. By offering spiritual favours in return for practical assistance, she drew patrons and clients alike into the Ghent family, binding them with kindred ties.

Yet correspondence was not the only medium for cultivation of long-distance benefactors. Nuns' epistolary expressions of professional and friendly concern could be enhanced by enclosing gifts. Some bestowed devotional objects upon their patrons. From 1685 various convents enjoyed the favour of Queen Mary of Modena. Amidst the many heartfelt wishes in 1688 for her safety in childbirth was a gift from Prioress Mary Wigmore of the Antwerp Carmelites. It was a relic of St Teresa of Avila, comprising 'a peece of her flesh', which the queen was advised to wear during her labour.[42] Other bequests were more typical of secular gift exchange. In the 1690s and 1700s, Abbess Mary Caryll of Dunkirk relied heavily upon the influence of her brother, John, who was secretary to Mary of Modena at St Germain-en-Laye. The abbess and his other relatives at Dunkirk sent a steady stream of gifts to their kinsman, including tobacco and foodstuffs, which he duly acknowledged with gratitude.[43] Often gifts reflected the relationship between patron and client. At the request of her sister with whom she corresponded regularly, Prioress Winefrid Thimelby of the Louvain Augustinians arranged to have her portrait painted and sent to England. The two sisters also exchanged locks of hair.[44] The obligation generated by the exchange of such items and their corresponding rewards more than compensated the inconvenience and expense of purchasing them. When John Caryll was ill, Mary Caryll sent him herbal remedies which she declared she had found to be most effective. She constantly informed him that the nuns prayed for his health and longevity, remarking in 1711, that she believed he owed his life to their many prayers.[45] Although Mary's concern for John was in part that of a devoted sibling, she recognised her cloister's dependency upon his continued support.

The role of John Caryll in the Dunkirk Benedictines' affairs indicates the importance of securing and maintaining reliable patrons. Caryll fulfilled the role of *ex-officio* agent for the Dunkirk community, providing money and financial advice, negotiating vocations and dowries, as well as acting as a broker between the nuns and the Jacobite court. His connections at both St Germain and Versailles proved invaluable for the house's political affairs. He interceded on the nuns' behalf on various occasions, but no intervention generated quite such fulsome gratitude than his action in the Ypres matter. In the aftermath of 1688, the Benedictine community at Ypres was in dire financial straits and, moreover, it lacked sufficient members. In 1699, amidst various proposals to save the cloister, which was patronised by James II and Mary of Modena, the bishop proposed its amalgamation with the Dunkirk abbey. Mary Caryll was aghast, possibly because she did not relish cohabiting with Ypres' abbess, Mary Joseph Butler, with whom she had clashed in 1687 over a Benedictine filiation to Dublin. She immediately enlisted her brother's aid to avert what she and her nuns evidently considered a disaster for their house. His successful intercession to Mary of Modena elicited the cloister's praise. Maura Knightly, writing on behalf of the community, declared that 'after inumerable effects of your Protection and favour, this is esteemed the greatest'. Mary Caryll was similarly effusive, observing 'what would become of us if we had not soe benefitiall a frend as you at Court'.[46] Both letters assured him that his action would be rewarded in heaven. As this incident and others show, John Caryll wielded considerable influence in the Dunkirk convent's affairs by virtue of his position at the exiled court and his consanguinity with the abbess.

The prominence of kinship ties, like those of Mary and John Caryll, within monastic patronage networks proved advantageous to both parties. The close nexus between cloister and kin led to many nuns becoming powerbrokers within their secular families. Not only did Mary Caryll rely upon her brother's access to Mary of Modena and other prominent Jacobite officials to conduct convent business, she also applied to John to secure positions for relatives and friends. Kin who could not afford to dower their daughters petitioned John Caryll through her mediation. Inevitably she tried to settle these nieces within her own cloister.[47] On other occasions she acted as a broker between other monasteries and her brother. In 1706, Mary negotiated possible portions for her two young nieces, Catherine and Barbara Caryll, with Prioress Margaret Mostyn Fettiplace of the English Carmelites at Lierre.[48] Other impecunious relatives used her to plead their case, or to seek preferment at the exiled Court.[49] Winefrid Thimelby of the Louvain Augustinians performed a similar role in the Aston-Thimelby clan. When Walter, Lord Aston provided his widowed aunt, Mary (Mary Bernard) Tateman Aston, with a portion to enter the Liège Sepulchrines, the Augustinian prioress acted as an intermediary. It is not clear whether Winefrid Thimelby negotiated with Prioress Susan (Mary of the Conception) Hawley over dowry details. Nonetheless, an account book noted that the expenses for Mary Tateman before her 1685 profession were paid through the Louvain prioress, suggesting that Thimelby's kin in England relied upon her contacts in their dealings on the Continent.[50]

Royal connections endowed certain nuns with a stature acknowledged by their family and associates, and they became extremely influential. In 1650 Patrick Cary, the Catholic son of the controversial Viscountess Falkland, used his sister at Cambrai to access Sir Edward Hyde. Anne (Clementina) Cary, whose sister Elizabeth had deciphered the encrypted royalist message, was formerly a maid of honour to Henrietta Maria. Patrick, vacillating between a religious vocation and a position among Charles's retinue, declined to make the initial overture to Hyde, instead choosing his sister to press his case. Although Hyde was unable to satisfy her suit, he wrote highly of her virtues, and did all in his power to assist her brother.[51] But it was Mary Knatchbull of Ghent who was considered the accomplished advocate. Family and friends who were eager to advance their prospects petitioned her.[52] She was even approached by out-of-favour royalists in the hope that she could intercede on their behalf. In 1656 the duke of Buckingham sought her advocacy in his endeavour to regain Charles's good will.[53] When in 1658 Colonel Richard Butler, the marquis of Ormonde's brother, found himself in grave debt, the abbess came to his assistance, taking his debts on her credit and beseeching Hyde to approach Ormonde on Butler's behalf.[54] On the eve of the Restoration, clients lobbied Knatchbull seeking positions at the royal court.[55] In Knatchbull the reciprocal nature of patronage is most evident. She achieved her position via a combination of good connections (one of her nuns, Magdalen Digby, was related to the earl of Bristol), her own hard work in establishing mail and client networks, and sheer tenacity. Although ostensibly she forged relationships with powerful figures for the benefit of her impecunious cloister, she could use them to become a patron in her own right.

The abbess of Ghent was not alone in extending favours to those more commonly sought for their benefaction. Letitia (Mary) Tredway, abbess of the Paris Augustinian nuns, showed both the strength nuns wielded as patrons, and the symbiotic nature of patronage when she established a college for English secular priests. Bishop Richard Smith had acted as a useful patron when the Augustinian convent was established in Paris in 1634.[56] A member of Cardinal Richelieu's household, Smith secured the necessary royal approbation for the new cloister. More importantly, with the assistance of the cardinal, the objections of the archbishop of Paris and the *parlement* to the foundation were overturned.[57] After Richelieu's death in 1642, the situation was reversed and the abbess provided Smith with accommodation in a house adjoining the convent. Abbess Tredway later succeeded in achieving the bishop's ambition of founding a community for English secular priests pursuing higher studies at the Sorbonne. In 1667, 12 years after Smith's death, she and Thomas Carre, the confessor of the Augustinian house, established St Gregory's College.[58] The convent provided some land, and Tredway worked tirelessly to secure the political and financial support of English clergy associated with Henrietta Maria in Paris. She later did all she could to enhance the reputation of her clerical foundation, inviting the fathers to preach in the convent church on public occasions when large numbers of English people would be present to hear them.[59] Tredway's patronage of the secular clergy offers one of the clearest examples of nuns' capacity to exert influence over those generally perceived to be in charge of them.[60] Like Mary Knatchbull, the Augustinian abbess was empowered by her formidable web of contacts to extend the munificence usually rendered to her convent to her own not insubstantial clientage.

An analysis of book dedications confirms that these two abbesses were not alone in aiding their clerical assistants in matters of preferment. The

Jesuit translator of Francis Borgia's *Practise of Christian Workes* dedicated his 1620 publication to Abbess Elizabeth (Clare Mary Ann) Tyldesley of the Gravelines Poor Clare cloister. In the preface he noted, 'how far my selfe am growne endebted, for the many benefits I have receaved from your selfe, and your holy Family... and so am forced to excuse my selfe, by paying this interest, until I may be better able to discharge the principall'.[61] Similarly the translator of Vincent Puccini's biography of Florentine Carmelite, Maria Maddalena de' Pazzi, expressed his enormous debt to Abbess Mary Percy of the Brussels Benedictines.[62] Thus, like Mary Knatchbull who in 1660 endeavoured to obtain a benefice in Ghent for her confessor, other superiors patronised the clergy.[63] It is clear that they understood the influence they had attained through their clientage networks, monastic position and, in some instances, social status. Moreover, others recognised their potential power too. Patronage therefore offered religious women an opportunity to participate in affairs beyond the immediate concerns of their cloister. The √ elevated circles in which they moved as patrons and clients, and their identification with the recusant cause in England, encouraged many nuns to engage directly in the civil and religious affairs of their home- √ land. The next section will examine the convents' foray into seventeenth-century English politics. Beginning with a discussion of the political significance of the cloisters, it will then explain the nuns' adaptation of their contemplative apostolate into missionary work, which led some houses into political activism on behalf of the Stuarts.

Politics and the monastic household

As early as 1603, English Catholics recognised the political symbolism of the monastic revival. Commending Abbess Mary Percy for founding the Brussels monastery, Richard Verstegan wrote,

> you [are] the first Abbesse of your holy order revyved in our nation, whose posteritie by the devine providence may come to brighten our country with their shyning sanctitie as your predecessors heretofore have donne: after that Saint Augustyne had brought and taught unto the English people the first knowledge and belief in the true God and his deer sonne and our saviour, Christ Jesus.[64]

This reference England's sixth-century conversion to Christianity from paganism would not have been lost on his readers. More puzzling is the imputation that the Benedictine nuns would mirror their medieval

predecessors and secure the post-Reformation English mission. As cloistered women living in the Low Countries, this was a most unlikely
proposition. Yet Verstegan continued, referring to the abbesses of the
early Church who not only shone as exemplars through written accounts of their 'dying wel', but also by virtue of their holy lives in
which they had learned to die to the world. Thus, the Brussels cloister
was exhorted to provide a saintly model for England's Catholics to
mimic. During the heady early decades of the seventeenth-century
when 'the foundation movement' was blossoming, the new convents
were most certainly perceived by many, both Catholics and Protestants,
as embodiments of the Catholic minority's determination to defy the
Church of England. For the Catholics they stood for the future return of
their homeland to the Roman creed. To Protestants they were reminders
of the papist threat, which forever loomed across the Channel.

The foundation of religious institutions for women was in itself a
politically charged act. Although legislation forbidding English subjects
to join or support seminaries and colleges abroad did not specifically
target convents, there was consternation regarding the flow of women
and young girls across the Channel. Lists of religious houses invariably
included those for women, and English spies mentioned them in dis-
patches.[65] Yet convents did not attract the hysteria directed at the male
houses. This disparity was due in part to perceptions about their role.
Seminaries trained the priests who returned clandestinely to England to
sustain Catholicism and to convert Protestants. Moreover, they were
viewed as breeding grounds for sedition against the English State.
While there was certainly concern about the nuns' capacity for perver-
sion of young children placed in their care, strict enclosure and the
cloisters' geographic isolation from England's shores diminished their
capacity for direct subversive action. Nuns were not expected to appear
in England as missionaries and treasonous activists. Indeed most references to the convents reflected early modern gender assumptions about
women's subservience and incredulity. The nuns were typically portrayed as victims of the clergy, specifically the Jesuits, and credited
with no agency whatsoever. A publication attacking the Bridgettine
convent in Lisbon declared 'it is certain that these silly women thus
muzzled in blindenesse, doe live in very servile obedience to their Superiours'.[66] When Lady Mary Lovel entered the Brussels Benedictine cloister in 1608, the English agent in the town described her as 'the most
passyonate besotted poore woman that ever was with the opinyons of
the Jesuitts'.[67] However, there was no imputation that either the Lisbon
nuns or Lovel would endanger their homeland. Instead they were locked

within their cloisters 'like so many prisoners', completely at the mercy of the avaricious Jesuits.[68]

Yet the convents' minimal threat to national security did not mean they were innocuous. Protestants decried them as hotbeds of superstition and licentiousness, where gullible women were lured to lives of imprisoned futility. At the height of the foundation movement a number of pamphlets attacking the cloisters were published. They all offered similar views about the treacherous Jesuits who ensnared unsuspecting girls for the nunneries, and then denuded them of their fortunes. In 1624 John Gee reported that 'the hungry Jesuits ... dispossesse them of all worldly cares and vanities, and like subtile Alchimists refine them out of their silver and golden drosse into a more sublime estate and condition'.[69] But behind the treatises' derision of 'silly women' and 'lusty priests' lay an obvious fear of the convents' popularity. Gee attributed flourishing recruitment to the nuns who, at the instigation of clerics, 'write over letters ... to the exceeding magnifying of the state wherein they live, that other young Birds of that brood, remaining in England, may be drawn to flie to the same forain nests'.[70] His attempt to downplay their success with lurid tales of a few women who escaped the Jesuit net, failed to disguise his concern that the convents offered Catholic women a haven, beyond the arm of Protestant authorities. For Gee and other polemicists, the religious establishments were perfidious in that they represented Catholic women's capacity to cheat the Protestant state, as well as rivalling its idealised patriarchal household. The anti-Catholic literature ridiculed the religious life as an inversion of marriage in which priests acquired the dowries and sexual favours of women who might otherwise have married upright Protestant citizens. Thus, the convents were a symbol of English Catholic resistance to Protestant social mores. Moreover, the nuns represented a direct challenge to patriarchal authority.

For Catholics the cloisters were no less potent symbols. As I have argued, the establishment of the religious houses and their immense popularity in the early decades of the seventeenth century reflected Catholic optimism for toleration at the very least. They were not essential to the English mission which depended principally upon the sacramental services of the clergy. Yet the convents were most certainly markers of recusant defiance and confidence. Monasticism, which was anathema to Protestant thinking, represented another element of Catholic separatism. Contemplative houses with their prime function of intercessory prayer flew in the face of the Protestant theology of salvation. They further provided the gentry with a refuge for their daughters, where they could avoid the possible danger of a mixed marriage. Moreover, they were tangible reminders of Catholic survival. The Brussels Benedictine foundation in 1598 offered concrete evidence of a healthy religious minority with the resources to diversify its nonconformity. A dedication to Abbess Elizabeth Tyldesley of the Gravelines Poor Clares, one of the most successful communities of the 1610s and 1620s, declared that the religious houses were a source of great comfort to

> our poor countrie... [because] although yee and other virgins of other orders of religion... can not serve God at home in religious houses by reason of the difficulties of the time, yet doe yee in number dayly increase... [and] yee make your houses shine as though they were of yuorie.[71]

Thus, in the face of continued Protestant ascendancy, the cloisters evidenced recusant determination to preserve Catholic institutions, which in the event of a Catholic restoration could easily be transferred to English soil. In 1625, writing of the recently founded Franciscan convent in Brussels, its confessor, Francis Bell, described it as 'newly errected in a forraine contrie, with hope hereafter to transplant the same in to your owne, where Religious discipline is so decayed'.[72] As Bell implied, the cloisters functioned as emblems of optimism, particularly because they were peopled by the 'weaker sex'. Catholic writers were effusive in their praise for the nuns who had forsaken kin and country to maintain the monastic ideal. Sir Tobie Matthew wrote that God 'hath resolved to make mankind see that he knew very well how to compass the highest and hardest things, even by the weakest and most improbable means'.[73] The religious women's unequivocally successful challenge to Protestantism was a positive sign that Catholic faith and practice would prevail in England.

However, in spite of the rousing missionary rhetoric accorded the nuns, they were not expected to assume an overtly political role. They were contemplative and their chief duty was prayer; the clergy was responsible for the work of conversion and political activism. As Abbess Mary Gough noted soon after the Poor Clares moved to Gravelines in 1609:

> we... forsooke our Country, Parents and freindes... to the ende that since we wer not able (in respect of our sex) to doe great matters, yet we might at the least by Penance and Prayer conjoine our selves unto those which labour in Gods vineyard, namely in our afflicted Country of England.[74]

But the cloistered nuns' apostolate was by no means unimportant. Prayer was deemed a potent weapon in the struggle for the faith. Even Mary Ward, who desired a more active missionary role, acknowledged that 'many women outside of England serve God most devoutly in monastic communities, and day and night by their prayers to God and good works, contribute very much towards the conversion of the kingdom'.[75] Contemplation therefore became political when it aimed to achieve the conversion of England. The Rouen Poor Clare convent was founded in 1644 partly on the understanding of its benefactors that it would pray for their homeland's conversion. To that end the nuns recited the Litany of the Saints each night.[76] Their devotions became more explicitly subversive in 1657 when Abbess Mary (Mary Francis) Taylor ordered prayers and penance for the preservation of Dunkirk from Oliver Cromwell's besieging forces.[77] In 1700, the Aire Poor Clares were commissioned to procure 'one Mass every Wednesday for the good and Conversion of England and for the preservation and increase of Gods Holy Church throughout the whole world'.[78] Thus, despite the apparent limitations of the contemplative vocation, prayer presented manifold opportunities for missionary work and political action.

Just as the boundaries of traditional monastic devotion could be stretched into active engagement, the hospitable and charitable activities which were so essential for economic survival also presented occasions for proselytising. Without leaving their enclosure, many women tried their hand at conversion. Monastic schools accepted Protestant lay women, several of whom converted to Catholicism. Between 1672 and 1678, the 'Blue Nuns' successfully persuaded Phoebe Palmer, Anne Browne, Ann Hancock and Elizabeth Davis of their faith's veracity.[79] Other Protestant gentlewomen were drawn towards Catholicism by their contact with nuns whilst living abroad. As a child, Catherine Holland lived briefly in Bruges. When she converted against the wishes of her father, she chose to seek refuge as a nun in the Augustinian cloister she remembered from her childhood.[80] Following the conversion of Sir John and Lady Trevor Warner in 1664, and their joint decision to enter the religious life, they entrusted their little daughters to the Ghent Benedictines for education. The Warners' Protestant relatives were scandalised by their actions, particularly with regard to Catherine and Susan, aged five and one respectively. In 1667 Sir Thomas Hamner, Trevor's father, threatened to gain custody of the girls and raise them as Protestants. Hamner correctly surmised that if left with nuns, they would follow their mother's footsteps. Both took the veil among the

Dunkirk Benedictines.[81] The persuasive power of the cloister over young minds was deemed so great that most assumed, once in a monastic school, a girl was more than halfway to becoming a nun, whether Catholic or not.

For this reason, Protestants were worried about the nuns' proclivity for converting the children sent to their schools. Rising fears concerning the subversive power of education in cloisters led to the calls in 1593 for Catholic children to be schooled by Protestants. This plea was echoed in the 'Commons Petition' of 1621 which also demanded the return of all Catholic offspring being educated abroad. In 1642, Parliament's 'Nineteen Propositions' to the king stated that the children of known recusants should be educated by Protestants.[82] There was no gender bias in these fears, with Protestant divines warning against the perfidy of a convent education. In a sermon of 1623, William Gouge related the case of a young girl who had drowned on her way to one of 'those superstitious places' abroad. Gouge concluded the tale by asking parents whether this story was a sign: 'Judge hereby (O Parents) whether God be well pleased with committing your children to Papists for education'.[83]

On occasions, legislation was invoked against those caught sending youths across the Channel. In 1698, a Middlesex painter, William Seeks, his wife Mary Brittell, and Elizabeth Hollingshead were indicted for sending a nine-year-old girl

> beyond the seas out of the obedience of his Majesty into the Kingdome of ffrance with an intent and on purpose to have the said Child remaine and be trained up in a Nunnery... to be instructed and strengthened in the popish Religion against the forme of the statute.[84]

The case was removed from the Middlesex Sessions Court at Clerkenwell to the court of King's Bench, but ultimately the accused were found not guilty. Although the basis for the verdict is not clear from the documents, it is likely that the courts were persuaded that Weeks was sending the girl to her father who lived in Paris. Nonetheless, concern about the seditious nature of a convent education was apparent in a King's Bench record which declared that sending a child abroad to a cloister was 'in contempt of the king and his laws'.[85] Indeed, in 1700, the English government reaffirmed the Elizabethan and Jacobean anti-Catholic legislation in 'An Act for the Further Preventing the Growth of Popery' which rewarded informants who reported the dispatch of children overseas for the purpose of a Catholic education.[86]

Monastic schools represented one opportunity to proselytise, but many nuns also took advantage of social intercourse at the grate to catechise Protestants. In the late seventeenth and early eighteenth centuries, young men passing through Flanders on their 'Grand Tour' often included English monasteries in their list of sights to visit. They attended public services in convent chapels, and then talked at the grate with a few nuns. Some were even treated to special musical performances. In 1671, when John Walker visited the Franciscan house in Bruges, the abbess introduced him to several women. Later they sang for the visitors. Walker described the experience in glowing terms: 'We heard a most harmonious consort of viols and violins with the organ. Then a ravishing voice of a nun singing in Italian a treble part alone; the rest now and then keeping the chorus'.[87] The nuns could not expect such visitors to act as patrons, so the trouble to which they went in this case and in similar instances suggests they had other motives.

When in 1687 Thomas Penson visited the Carmelite convent in Antwerp he talked about religion with one of the older nuns. His account of their discussion made clear her missionary intent. When he confided that he had spoken to several Catholics about religion during his trip, and that he intended to pursue the subject further upon his return to England, she was obviously heartened. Almost as if to tempt him with what delights Catholicism held, she brought a novice to the grate. Penson was completely overcome:

> There soon appeared (as an angel of light) a delicate, proper, young, beautiful lady, all in white garments and barefaced, whose graceful presence was delightful to behold and yet struck an awful reverence, considering she was devout and religious. And having paid my respects and fed my greedy eye a short moment on this lovely creature, I thus spoke: 'Madam, may heaven bless and enable you in your undertakings, which to us that are abroad in the world seem so hard and difficult. For we account it no less than being buried alive to be immured within the confines of these walls.' To which she answered: 'Sir, the world is much mistaken in their harsh censures of these religious houses, not considering the felicities we here enjoy in the service of God...I would not change conditions with any princess or noble lady in the world'.[88]

Penson was clearly impressed by these nuns, as well as being dazzled by the youth and beauty of the novice. Upon his departure, they assured him that they would pray for him, a fact he faithfully recorded.

The incident suggests that the nuns hoped to secure conversions to Catholicism by such meetings at the grate. In his travel memoirs of 1718, Lord Egmont commented that nuns were more inclined to discuss religious controversy than the monks and priests he had encountered.[89] Indeed, at Ghent in the 1640s, Abbess Mary Roper became renowned for converting Protestant visitors by conversing with them at the grate.[90]

Some nuns were able to conduct their missionary endeavours beyond the enclosure. Despite clausura, under certain circumstances women could leave the cloister. Apart from the obvious occasions necessitated by wars, natural disasters, and the need to establish new houses, with a permit from the bishop nuns could break cloister to retrieve dowries or collect other monies owing them. The precarious financial position of many convents enabled the religious women to take advantage of this provision and return to England to conduct convent business.[91] The 'Blue Nuns' spent inordinate amounts of time in England in this way. Anne Timperley went to England on three occasions during her 20 years as abbess.[92] Other communities stationed nuns in London to conduct business. Following the Restoration, Abbess Mary Knatchbull of Ghent was eager to receive Charles II's promised financial reward for her assistance during the Interregnum. After letters, messengers and personal visits to the king had failed to elicit more than 1,000 pounds of her promised 3,000 pound bounty, in 1663 she located Anne Neville and Paula Knatchbull in London to collect the money in the form of an annual pension. The two nuns remained in England until 1667 when it became obvious that they would no longer receive the funds.[93]

In England the nuns stayed with kin and they solicited alms, scholars and postulants for their cloisters. Anne Neville's account of her time in England hints that she and her companions lived openly as nuns within their family circle. This was not the strategy employed by Mary Ward's Institute, which included missionary work in its charter of practical charity. Although greatly criticised for their worldliness because they lived and dressed as secular gentlewomen, Ward's sisters were effective in gaining converts to the faith. The narrative of the Institute's Sister Dorothea demonstrates the ease with which women could proselytise under the guise of teaching children and practising herbal medicine. Disguised as the kinswoman of the Suffolk gentlewoman with whom she lived, Sister Dorothea was able to convert several people. In the account of her endeavours, she claimed that 'I never gain one alone, but more'.[94] Ultimately, Ward's sisters were censured for working in this way. The undisguised presence in England of contemplative nuns was unwelcome and attracted similar criticism. In the 1660s both Charles II and Catherine of Braganza complained to Philip Howard, the queen's almoner, of the scandal which could ensue from 'nuns gadding about . . . in these parts'.[95] There is no evidence that they were engaged in missionary work. However, Mary Knatchbull's inclination for converting her correspondents, suggests that she would not have been averse to subtle proselytising on their part.

The nuns made their missionary intentions most explicit in efforts to establish convents and schools in England and Ireland. From the 1620s, various communities sent small groups of women across the Channel to return monasticism to their native land. Encouraged by the apparent success of Mary Ward's Institute and the marriage of Charles I to Henrietta Maria, the Poor Clares of Gravelines sent a filiation to Dublin in 1625. This community collapsed in 1649 upon Cromwell's entry into Ireland.[96] In 1639, the poverty-stricken Franciscan nuns of Nieuport sent three sisters to England 'for the setting up of a Seminary in our native Soyle of England, of Yong Gentlewomen'. In spite of the Civil War, the nuns remained in their homeland until 1650, when they were finally forced to abandon their cloister and return to the Continent.[97] In the 1640s Katherine Manners, formerly the duchess of Buckingham, who had subsequently married the earl of Antrim, obtained permission to sponsor a Benedictine filiation to Ireland, and asked for three or four nuns from the Ghent monastery to undertake the work.[98] The fate of these early attempts became entangled with the political upheavals of the 1640s and 1650s. Possibly some of the failed settlements spawned nuns who continued educative and missionary work on their own. However, they apparently lost contact with their mother-houses abroad, so it is difficult to trace the impact they had in England.[99]

The restoration of the monarchy in 1660 encouraged the expansionist ambitions of many cloisters. Between the 1660s and 1680s there was a revival of religious foundations in England. In the light of the Ghent Benedictines' close relationship with the royalists, it was assumed that Abbess Knatchbull would be among the first to return. There had been talk in 1659 of her obtaining St James' Park with a view to settling there.[100] Instead, in August 1662, she established a new house in Dunkirk, which was English territory (until its sale to Louis XIV in October of that year).[101] Other orders were less circumspect and sent women directly to England. Mary Ward's revised Institute opened schools in Hammersmith in 1669 and Yorkshire in 1677.[102] However, most convents were underwhelmed by Charles's desultory efforts to aid English Catholics. Instead they pinned their hopes on their co-religionist, James II's, assistance. In 1686, James assured Mary Knatchbull that he would make good his brother's broken promises, declaring his intention 'to have your cloyster, our Darling monastery, the first in my kingdom'.[103] However, even he balked at installing nuns on English soil. Ultimately, he invited the Benedictines of Ypres to relocate to Ireland in what he termed 'Our chief and first Royal Monastery of Gratia Dei'. Abbess Mary Joseph Butler and her companions set out for Dublin in 1687. The hopes raised by Abbess Butler's presentation to the queen at Whitehall, dressed in her religious habit, were dashed by the events of November 1688. While James sought refuge in Ireland, the nuns were confident of his restoration, but the Battle of the Boyne in 1690 saw them flee back to Ypres.[104] The 'Blue Nuns' fared no better. They chose April 1688 to send Frances (Clare) Crane to England in the company of a French lady 'who designed to sett up a scoole for us in England'. They were forced to abandon the scheme. In September, Jane (Francis) Sanders set out to establish a house in Ireland, but the Glorious Revolution ensured that she proceeded no further than England before the plan had to be abandoned.[105] Despite the failure of most attempts to recolonise their homeland, the filiations highlight the convents' determination to accelerate by whatever means possible the return and toleration of their religion in England.

Obviously the nuns' geographical dislocation, combined with the limitations of clausura, hampered their active participation in affairs of state. However, the exile at various junctures of both Charles II and James II, enabled the cloisters to demonstrate their loyalty to the Stuart monarchy. Most houses offered hospitality to the royal family during the 1640s and 1650s. In Paris, the Augustinians regularly offered Henrietta Maria and her sons 'dutiful and respectful entertainments', and upon visits to the Benedictine cloister founded by her former favourite, Anne Cary, Henrietta 'showed herself a constant friend'.[106] Charles II reputedly lodged with the Benedictines upon visits to Ghent in 1658 and 1659, and other leading royalists, like Sir Edward Hyde, also enjoyed monastic visits.[107] However, the nuns' allegiance to the Stuarts amounted to far more than hospitality. Like their families in England, they were staunch royalists during the Civil War. Anne Neville expressed well the sentiments of all the cloisters when she referred to the execution of Charles I as 'that horrible sacrilegious murther'.[108] In its aftermath, they offered whatever assistance possible to his son. In 1650 the prince visited Benedictine abbess, Mary Roper, at Ghent, commending his concerns to the convent's prayers. The nuns evidently impressed Charles, and he likewise touched their sensibilities. The prince apparently told the bishop of Ghent 'that if ever God restorde him to his kingdome this Comunity shold ever find the effects of his favour'. The sight of him in mourning for his father moved the nuns 'to pray hartily for his Conversion, and the good success of his bleeding affairs'.[109] In 1651 the failure of divine mediation at the Battle of Worcester was at least mitigated by Charles's miraculous escape. Upon his return to the Continent, he received several cloisters' allegiance. The Bruges Augustinians regularly entertained him during his residence in their town. In 1656 they gave 1,000 florins to further his cause.[110] Other cloisters doubled their prayers for the restoration of the monarchy. In 1660 Abbess Mary Vavasour of the Brussels Benedictines claimed that her nuns had prayed night and day for Charles.[111]

The staunchly royalist abbess of Ghent offered the prince's supporters even greater assistance. In addition to manifold prayers and regular hospitality, she conducted their mail, arranged loans, gathered information, conveyed the contents of deciphered letters, and provided her own advice about the situation in England. Like the Bruges Augustinians, Knatchbull financed the royalists. Despite Charles's inability to meet repayments, she organised credit for him, using the monastery as security.[112] From 1657 she put her mail network at the royalists' disposal, and by 1658 she was receiving, sorting and dispatching the correspondence of the main plotters to Hyde, as well as to the marquis of Ormonde and Sir Edward Nicholas, Charles's secretary. The Ghent postal service was exceptionally reliable, and despite some incidences of interception, Hyde endorsed the abbess's conveyance, writing in March 1660 that it 'brings many other letters very exactly to mee'.[113] Mary Knatchbull was also in receipt of newsletters and information about the situation in England from her various contacts, and she channelled these to Hyde.[114] By 1659 her letters to the chancellor increasingly offered not simply news, but her interpretation of events and the best course of action. In the aftermath of Sir George Booth's failed uprising, she was gloomy, noting 'a scourge hangs over the nation and a greater cannot be inflicted then a conquest by strangers and yett it now growes more then evident, his Majesty is not to attemp to enter with out an Army'.[115] Knatchbull's willingness to offer political advice reflected her confident status as a royalist conspirator. It was also a precursor to the nuns' political stance after 1688.

James II had befriended the recusant exiles during the Interregnum. His conversion to Catholicism exalted the nuns' regard for him, and in the 1680s they eagerly anticipated his accession to the throne. As duke of York, he and his first wife, Anne Hyde, were generous benefactors to several houses.[116] Upon his second marriage, Mary of Modena became an important intermediary with the king, and a patron of the nuns in her own right. The indefatigable abbess of Ghent recognised Mary as a willing advocate and showered her with spiritual patronage. In 1687, the convent sent her 'a poore New Yeares Guift with two thousand communions, Masses, paires of Beads and acts of penance', and received a gracious acknowledgement from Whitehall.[117] In 1686, the queen praised the Dunkirk Benedictines for their loyalty and devotion, and promised to assist them.[118] The nuns understood the importance of a Catholic heir, and many prayers were directed to that end. In 1688, news of the safe delivery of a prince of Wales elicited a jubilant congratulatory letter from Mary Knatchbull, who reported the convent's thanksgiving *Te Deum* for 'this saving Guift to the 3 Nations' and expressed hopes for the 'speedy addition of a Duke of York'.[119] Five months later, William of Orange quashed the nuns' expectation of Catholic consolidation under James and his heir.

In the aftermath of the Glorious Revolution the cloisters became ardent Jacobites, refusing to acknowledge William and Mary and their successors as legitimate monarchs. The annals of the Paris Augustinians articulated the disappointment felt by many convents, when they pledged their loyalty to

> Holy King James II . . . [who] was by the perfidious, undutiful and unnatural baseness of his son-in-law and nephew, the Prince of Orange, dethroned and driven out of the kingdom; that detestable Prince joining with the treacherous defection of the Protestant subjects of England, and a malevolent party which were the dregs of the Cromwells Vipers blood. [120]

The convent often entertained with great pomp and ceremony the deposed king, his queen and their children, and through its confessor, Edward Lutton, maintained regular contact with the exiled court at St Germain.[121] At Ghent the nuns resumed their prayers for the reinstatement of the Catholic monarch. In 1694, Mary of Modena thanked them for their divine petitions on her behalf.[122] The death of James in 1701 gave rise to widespread mourning. The Bruges Augustinians 'performed a solemn service, with scutcheons and hearse', and thereafter prayed for 'James III'. In 1708 they entertained the pretender within their enclosure.[123] Abbess Anne Tyldesley of the Paris Augustinians obtained a relic of the deposed king's arm, which the nuns venerated in their chapel, and they lavished spiritual support on his son.[124] Several nuns had

Jacobite relatives. Mary Caryll of Dunkirk, whose brother was in the exiled queen's service, regularly alluded to her nuns' prayers for a Catholic restoration.[125] Prioress Lucy (Teresa Joseph) Herbert at Bruges was in regular contact with her sister, the Jacobite countess of Nithsdale, who had masterminded and executed the daring escape of her condemned husband after the 1715 rebellion.[126] Other establishments pursued Mary Knatchbull's 1650s approach and placed their resources at the Stuarts' disposal. The Pontoise Benedictines' support for the uprisings of 1715 and 1745 was widely acknowledged.[127] At the Dominican convent in Brussels, Mary Rose Howard performed the same conspiratorial tasks for James Stuart that the Ghent abbess had undertaken for Charles II. She was an intermediary between the pretender and Jacobites in England, transporting news and mail.[128] Ultimately the nuns' confidence in a similar outcome to that of 1660 proved unfounded, but their determination to overthrow the Hanoverians cemented their dissatisfaction with the English crown, and marked the shift in their allegiance which had been firmly behind the monarchy from 1642 to 1688.

The intrigues into which nuns entered for the Stuart cause did not escape the attention of English authorities. At times of heightened tension, the convents might be considered seriously. In the hysteria of the Popish Plot, a letter to a member of the House of Commons detailed all monasteries for English women, along with the seminaries and colleges for priests. The purpose of the list was 'to inform the People of England of the Measures taken by the Popish Party for the Re-establishing of Popery in these Nations'.[129] Yet, as I have argued, the conspiratorial endeavours of religious women were commonly deemed more an amusement than a threat. In 1717 the spy, Le Brun, reported the espionage activities of the Gravelines Poor Clare abbess, Catherine (Catherine Dominic) Bagnall to the duke of Malborough. He wrote dismissively, 'you can judge what secretaries nuns are, but more particularly my Lady Abbess, who can keep nothing longer than she can find occasion to tell it'.[130] However, gender assumptions which denied women any capacity for political cunning, coupled with Protestant stereotypes of the 'silly nun', might well have enhanced the convents' ability to engage in English affairs of state. The authorities' refusal to take seriously their actions on behalf of the Stuarts permitted nuns like Mary Knatchbull and Mary Rose Howard to conduct the rebels' business. While by no means central to the success and failure of their respective ventures, the monastic plotters could offer secure passage for sensitive information by virtue of their perceived political incapacity, and accordingly they became valuable allies to the Stuarts.

These forays by the nuns into English politics were by no means incompatible with their understanding of their religious duty. The conversion of England lay at the heart of their political actions. Following the marriage of Charles I to Henrietta Maria, the nuns remained optimistic about the future for Catholicism in their homeland. Although they perceived the Civil War and Commonwealth as a disaster, they endeavoured to benefit from the ensuing contact with the future Charles II, his advisers, and his brother, James. The regular royal intercourse of the 1650s inspired confidence in the princes' return to the Roman faith, and prayers for the conversion of England became synonymous with petitions for Charles's and James's salvation. Hence the religious communities greeted the news of Charles II's supposed deathbed conversion with delighted satisfaction. The 'Blue Nuns' congratulated themselves because since 1667 they had offered special weekly religious devotions 'for the conversion of our King and country'.[131] Mary Knatchbull was even encouraged to extend her missionary efforts to other royalist friends. In 1686 she urged the duke of Ormonde to follow the late king's example (and that of other Court converts) and embrace Catholicism, warning him 'not to delay the execution, since perhaps what was granted them in the Article of death may not be alowed you, if you differ till then'.[132] Although her advice fell on deaf ears in this instance, she might well have been instrumental in the duke of York's conversion. James was apparently swayed by 'the nun's advice in a monastery in Flanders . . . to pray every day that if he was not in the right way God would bring him into it'. Her counsel rang in his ears until he adopted the Roman faith.[133] Ironically, the royal conversion mitigated against the very end that Knatchbull and her monastic compatriots aimed to achieve.

In conclusion, it can be said that although they were often on the periphery of events in England, the nuns participated actively in their homeland's religious and political upheavals. Ironically, it was by virtue of their own experience of isolation that they proved invaluable allies to the Stuarts and other exiles. The uncertain financial situation of most cloisters, and their reliance upon supporters across the Channel, forced abbesses to develop communication and patronage networks, which could then be placed at the disposal of others. Thus, the very weakness of the cloisters' constant insolvency empowered them to propel their influence well beyond their enclosure walls. The conventions and tools of patronage underpinned this activity. As with their understanding of female governance and appropriate work, the nuns employed their social skills to advance their economic and political agendas. However, as I have suggested, the religious women did not see any conflict of interest between their actions and their religious vows. Founded to preserve the monastic tradition for women and to pray for the conversion of England, the nuns defined the boundaries of their apostolate far wider than the Council of Trent's definition of contemplation. As the next chapter will reveal, the spirituality of the English cloisters, like all other aspects of their daily lives, was infused with an active sense of mission.

5
Active in Contemplation: Spiritual Choices and Practices

If a soul would give herself wholly to thee and to be instructed by
thee, good Lord, how is she persecuted? She is esteemed worse
then a Turk or Infidel; and this by those who would fain be
esteemed holy; O me what kind of spiritual guides are now a
days, who do tyrannise our souls, worse by far than heretofore
did the heathens over the christians; nay, they are so far transported, that they will not stick to say, that having recourse to thee
by prayer, is idleness and a mere vanity; and because their brutish
senses cannot comprehend the wonderful grace that thou bestow-
est upon Ideots in prayer, they will not beleive [*sic*] that it is true
and good . . . It seems to me that they think it impossible for thee to
bestow the grace of contemplation upon an ignorant woman,
because they cannot or do not enjoy it by their curiosity of wit
and learning; they forget, it seems, that thou art omnipotent, and
can yield more knowledge to a simple Ideot in one hours
prayer, (being interiorly pure and converted to thee) than they
with all their plodding can obtain in twenty years yea all their life
time; O my God what an age is this, when we are more afraid to
serve and love thee truly and perfectly than some are to offend
thee.

(Barbara Constable, 'The Complaints of Sinners', 1649)[1]

Barbara Constable of the Cambrai Benedictine abbey penned this invec-
tive during a period of spiritual controversy in her community. The
teachings of its spiritual director, Augustine Baker, had been questioned
and she, like most of the convent, feared that their devotional life was
under threat. Although vindicated in this instance, the spiritual method
developed by Baker and the Cambrai nuns continued to attract criticism

and the convent was forced to defend its reputation on subsequent occasions. At issue was the degree of freedom Baker encouraged in individuals to choose the pious regime most suited to their capacity for meditation. In the Catholic Church of the seventeenth century, such autonomy was considered dangerous. Spirituality was to be carefully prescribed and regulated by a competent confessor well versed in the supervision of religious women. Other English convents conformed to this ecclesiastical preference; many allying themselves with the popular Society of Jesus, which dominated the early modern missionary and spiritual landscape. Yet the closer moderation of the Jesuits did not necessarily make for trouble-free monastic piety. During the course of the century, several cloisters were rent with dissension over spiritual practices and alliances. At the same time, numerous religious women negotiated personal devotional paths, which enabled them to give meaning to their cloistered existence. For some, mysticism opened themselves and their sisters to the spiritual and temporal fruits of divine favour. Most, however, carved out a daily existence of formal prayer and good works in their quest to achieve salvation. This chapter will explore the spiritual avenues pursued by the English nuns, which on the whole located them firmly within the traditions of the Continental Church. They prayed for England, but did so within the framework of reformed devotion.

R. Po-chia Hsia recently highlighted the contrasting gender dynamic of Catholic spirituality in post-Tridentine Europe, writing that women's 'heroic struggle took place not at the pulpit and in the market square preaching sermons, nor in the torture chamber and execution grounds undergoing martyrdom, but in the enclosed confines of the convents and in the boundless imagination of the mind'.[2] The imposition of strict enclosure on all houses of religious women in 1563 had aimed to prevent nuns from pursuing an active missionary apostolate but, as the previous chapter suggested, many women were not deterred by their convent's walls. As with their temporal labours and willingness to engage in politics, they negotiated the terms of contemplation within their convents. Yet of all the restrictions placed upon nuns, those relating to spirituality were the most fraught. In the confessional age, the Catholic Church was at pains to regulate the pious behaviour of the faithful, especially those behind grilles and walls. The witchcraft hysteria and a series of high profile cases of demonic possession highlighted the dangers posed by supernatural intercourse. In convents, the claustration-imposed separation from secular discourse and an intensive monastic regimen of prayer and meditation provided fertile ground for mysticism. By the seventeenth century most nuns also had access to vernacular biographies of the late medieval mystics and the early modern best-selling life of Teresa of Avila, presenting them with handbooks for sanctity. While the Church could not prevent those of a mystical inclination from communicating directly with the divine, it did all in its power to regulate them. The spiritual director took on the mantle of supernatural moderator, prescribing suitable devotions for his penitents and filtering their spiritual experiences to ensure their orthodoxy and divine origin.

The religious women of early modern Europe variously responded to the Tridentine restriction of their spiritual expression. Many prominent female reformers challenged the traditional contemplative vocation. Angela Merici, Jeanne de Chantal, Louise de Marillac and Mary Ward were among several founders who rejected the apostolate of prayer in favour of a more active piety, attuned to the religious and social needs of the day. Ultimately such a vision for female monastic spirituality, which conflicted with the Church's desire to segregate the holy from the profane, necessitated compromise, and the innovators were required to submit to ecclesiastical demands and modify their ambitions. Yet amidst their struggles a precedent was established for the social apostolate, which was to become the lodestar for Enlightenment spirituality.[3] However, not all reformers interpreted the missionary imperative so literally. At the other end of the spectrum, Teresa of Avila's reform of the Carmelites encapsulated the Tridentine preference for incarceration. Rejecting worldly intercourse for her nuns, Teresa advocated a life of strict asceticism and prayer behind convent walls. This espousal of contemplation did not mean the discalced Carmelites opted out of the Church's christianisation programme. Teresa argued that her nuns would participate in the missionary field, actively supporting the catechising labour of male religious through their prayers.[4] Moreover, like Teresa herself, many sisters transcended the cloister's confines through mystical engagement with the supernatural world which, in turn, brought public fame. Thus, the reformed Carmelites embodied a dynamic contemplative spirituality, whose acceptance and interpretation of clausura contrasted sharply with the apostolic orders' pleas for freedom from enclosure to pursue a religiosity centred upon social activism.

The spiritual experience of most seventeenth-century nuns fell between the extremes of mystical contemplation and active charity. Commonly coerced into claustration against their wills, religious women realigned their devotional life within the circumference of the enclosure. Often this necessitated inventive negotiation of the rigid strictures placed upon them. The Pütrich convent in Munich represents an excellent example of how this might occur. The Franciscan house was reformed in the 1620s putting an end to the nuns' ability to perform commemorative prayers for the dead outside their cloister, and their engagement in the commercial textile trade. With their economic foundation and spiritual traditions thus jeopardised, the nuns adopted a creative solution to counter their potentially devastating invisibility. They arranged the purchase of an entire skeleton of St Dorothea which they dressed sumptuously for public veneration in their Church. Thus, they tapped into reformed Catholicism's fervour for saints, prayers for the dead and public devotion, while preserving claustration, their textile skills and access to alms.[5] Other nuns were similarly adept at securing their spiritual preferences within the framework of Tridentine law. Women who longed for a missionary apostolate followed Teresa's dictum that prayer equated preaching. During mystical trances, the Spanish Conceptionist, María of Agreda, was transported to New Mexico where she preached conversion to the Indians.[6] Those desirous of martyrdom became their own persecutors, at the least depriving themselves of sleep, food and any vestige of comfort, and at the most inflicting pain and wounds upon their tortured flesh in living embodiments of the *Imitatio Christi*. Rose of Lima, a Dominican tertiary, conducted her early spiritual training attired in a hair shirt, waist chain and crown of thorns, which she supplemented with daily flagellation.[7] Likewise, the Florentine mystic Maria Maddalena de' Pazzi practised extreme asceticism to the point that she was rewarded by the receipt of the stigmata.[8] Early modern nuns' piety thus encompassed an innovative mix of late medieval devotion with the ideals and directives of the post-Reformation Church.

This fusion was abundantly obvious in the traditional monastic communities where contemplation formed the backbone of both collective and individual spirituality. As Teresa's reform of the Carmelites showed, it was possible to lead a cloistered existence centred upon prayer and yet still pursue the missionary impetus of the post-Tridentine Church. Women who had either accepted claustration willingly or by default sought to redefine the contemplative life within the parameters of Catholic reform. Through their regular prayers, religious ecstasies, promotion of specific devotions, and determination not to be rendered invisible by their convents' walls, cloistered nuns across Europe actively promoted their faith and Church as the best vehicle for salvation. Therefore the religious fervour which swept through Catholic countries in the late sixteenth and early seventeenth centuries was not the fruit of the missionary orders' labour alone. The renewed enthusiasm for the religious life among women, evident in the proliferation of new orders and houses, bears witness to the convents' influence both locally and in the wider Church. Counter-Reformation spirituality's dynamism was encapsulated in the Jesuit ideal of 'contemplative in action'. Coined to explain the Society's practical realignment of daily canonical prayer into an active pastoral ministry, a reworking of the term to 'active in contemplation' illustrates the traditional monastic communities' understanding and lived experience of reformed Catholicism. Just as the Jesuits grounded their missionary work in the Spiritual Exercises, a similarly exertive regime of mental prayer; so could enclosed nuns direct their contemplative labour into the crusade for endangered souls in Europe and beyond. Moreover, 'active in contemplation' necessitated a rereading of rules and statutes for many women. In the same vein of pragmatism which translated prayer into income generation and patronage into politics, the boundaries of contemplation were expanded to incorporate not simply the devotional but also the daily operations of the monastic household.

However, the religious women's efforts to reinterpret their prayerful apostolate in the light of the new activist spirituality did not always meet with the approval of those appointed to regulate their religiosity. In many instances their endeavours were understood differently by their clerical superiors who were determined to extinguish any belief or practice which might be construed as heretical. The confessor-spiritual director who monitored collective and individual piety was most often intent upon channelling the faithful into officially-sanctioned religious observances. For many monastic communities this supervision resulted in the imposition of the most popular spirituality of the seventeenth century, that of the Society of Jesus. Liberating and abundantly successful for some, other nuns found the Spiritual Exercises and the men who administered them, an impediment to a fulfilling spiritual life. The discord between ecclesiastical control and the freedom to choose the most suitable devotional path reverberated though many of the exiled English convents.

Finding the right path: spiritual direction

No discussion of the English convents' spirituality is possible without reference to the Society of Jesus, which constituted either the devotional orthodoxy or the 'other' against which alternative approaches were measured. The role of the Jesuits in religious training hinged upon a contradiction between their immense popularity as directors, and their constitution's injunction that 'they ought not to take a curacy of souls and still less ought they to take charge of religious women or any other women whatever to be their confessors regularly or to direct them'.[9] Their renown as religious guides can be attributed to the widespread success of Ignatius Loyola's Spiritual Exercises, which comprised a systematic approach to prayer, based upon the principle of 'affective piety'. This meditation technique employed the imagination and emotions so that the penitent could identify with the joy or suffering of the contemplated event, usually taken from the life of Christ. Although originally prescribed for potential missionaries, the Exercises' simplicity and flexibility enabled their adaptation to a wider audience. They could be adjusted for individual preferences, and were deemed ideal for religious cloisters where spiritual capabilities were diverse. Moreover, all spiritual experiences were filtered through the Jesuit director who judged their orthodoxy. Thus, the Society was well equipped to supervise monastic religiosity, but it was limited by the constitutional embargo. Ultimately the nature of the Jesuits' christianising mission across Europe provided a convenient loophole. Although Loyola had envisaged clerical troops free from the ties of regular chaplaincy, the spiritual guidance of the laity was central to reforming Catholic belief and practice. The Society's priests invariably directed individual piety among the laity, and their success inspired former penitents to demand their participation in monastic piety. The ensuing compromise permitted the fathers to infiltrate convents as both ordinary and extraordinary confessors and directors. However, this solution which solved the anathema of Jesuit convents, created pockets of Ignatian spirituality within cloisters under the auspices of rival orders. This disjunction was at the crux of much dissension over the Society's involvement in monastic devotion.

Whatever the ultimate pitfalls of Jesuit supervision, it proved a popular choice in the newly established English convents. The gentlewomen who initiated the monastic foundations allied themselves with specific clerical friends, with whom they determined a devotional programme which was both in sympathy with their rule and appropriate to their needs. They did so at a time when the faithful were encouraged to choose their own confessor-spiritual director. In his devotional guide, Jean Surin echoed the advice of François de Sales and Teresa of Avila when he insisted that such aides 'must be chosen in good faith and by an entirely free choice and not by force'.[10] Therefore the spiritual persuasion of a community was the choice of its founders, rather than an imposition by the hierarchy, and within cloisters individual preferences might be satisfied by access to advisers beyond the established chaplain. St Teresa had set an enviable precedent in this respect, having at least nineteen confessors.[11] Given the participation of Jesuit clergy in the erection of several exiled English convents, their continued involvement with the nuns in a devotional capacity was not surprising. Indeed for many women it provided continuity with their worldly piety which had been managed by Jesuit confessors. Thus, the Society's prominence in nuns' spiritual direction was in part a consequence of their success on the English mission. Mary Ward presents a case in point. Ward grew up in houses served by Jesuits, and she found solace in the piety they recommended. The devotional influences of her childhood and adolescence were to govern Ward's adult life. Upon the foundation of her English Poor Clare house at St Omer, Ward and the other postulants undertook the Spiritual Exercises. Ward was so concerned that the women gain a good grounding in matters of the spirit that she procured an English Jesuit to conduct the Exercises and to act subsequently as the nuns' confessor.[12]

Mary Ward's commitment to the ideals and spirit of the Society of Jesus led her to believe that she was called to undertake 'contemplative in action' in its fullest apostolic sense. Other nuns adapted Jesuit spirituality to the contemplative life. Elizabeth (Lucy) Knatchbull of the Brussels Benedictines undertook the Spiritual Exercises as a postulant at a time when she doubted her religious vocation. As a consequence, she not only resigned herself to the will of God, but she also began to experience the visions which characterised her subsequent devotional life. Although the resolve to persevere with her troubled vocation soon faltered, Knatchbull remained convinced that the Society's direction was essential to her spiritual progress. In 1609, when it was mooted that Abbess Joanna Berkeley might withdraw the house from Jesuit influence, Lucy Knatchbull joined others who left the Brussels cloister to found a new convent which would be subject to the Society's jurisdiction. This venture failed and the troubled postulant was eventually clothed and professed in her original monastery. Gradually, with the assistance of the Exercises and other forms of Jesuit prayer, Knatchbull's mystical experiences returned and she achieved spiritual satisfaction as well as a reputation for sanctity. However, dissension within the Brussels community over the issue of Jesuit influence continued and, in 1624, Knatchbull was one of the four founders of the Ghent filiation which was to ally itself firmly to the techniques of Loyola.[13]

Other women went to similar lengths to secure the Society's direction. Lady Mary Roper Lovel loomed large in the annals of several early

English cloisters. In 1608, Lovel had joined the Brussels Benedictines, but in the following year she headed the ill-fated attempt to found a separate house under Jesuit guidance which Lucy Knatchbull had joined. Lovel had disagreed with the founder, Mary Percy, and Abbess Berkeley over their move to exclude the Society.[14] Unlike Knatchbull, she did not return to the Benedictines. She investigated the likelihood of founding a Carmelite cloister in Liège, and a Bernardine house at Bruges, but it was not until 1619 that she finally achieved her goal of a Teresian convent in Antwerp.[15] Yet her firm adherence to Ignatian spirituality led to further dissension. Lovel had endowed Antwerp on the provision that the nuns would enjoy the privilege of choosing their confessors. She did so because she knew that the Belgian Carmelite fathers who had overall jurisdiction of her foundation would oppose Jesuit direction. When Anne (Anne of the Ascension) Worsely, the first prioress of the new community, appointed a Jesuit spiritual director, the Belgian superiors commenced a campaign which was to beset the convent with problems for its first five years until the pope intervened and placed the nuns under the jurisdiction of the local bishop, making Jesuit direction possible.[16]

Although there were several women like Lucy Knatchbull and Mary Lovel who found Ignatian spirituality the best path to communicating with the divine, others were not so convinced. During the 1620s and 1630s several English convents were divided over the issue of Jesuit direction. The Brussels Benedictines represented the most serious case. However, as we have seen in Chapter 2, the Poor Clares at Gravelines were struck by similar strife, occasioned by those nuns who supported the Society's methods refusing to submit to Franciscan direction.[17] Decades later similar conflicts flared in other houses. In 1675 rumours were abroad of 'strange and monsterous miscarrages' among the 'Blue Nuns' in Paris.[18] Tensions had arisen between Henry Browne, the established confessor, and the Jesuit provincial, John Warner, which pitted Abbess Elizabeth Anne Timperley against two of her flock, Agnes Lathom, a lay sister, and Mary Gabriel Huddlestone, a young choir nun. The two sisters supported Warner in his putative bid to replace Browne. Lathom in particular acted out of her attachment to the Jesuits of whom she reputedly declared 'Religion could not stand with out'.[19] The dispute was eventually resolved in the abbess's favour. However, a 1680 postscript to the quarrel in which Abbess Timperley herself ousted Browne made it abundantly clear that tensions remained in the cloister. Her nuns opposed the decision and she was forced to resign the following year.[20] Likewise in 1697 the Pontoise Benedictine cloister was divided over access to extraordinary confessors, with the Jesuits again at the centre of the controversy. In this instance Abbess Elizabeth D'abridgecourt was determined that her nuns should patronise the Society to the irritation of the secular chaplain, Lawrence Breers, and his supporters.[21] Dissension regarding the Society's role in the cloister had evidently been brewing for several years. A book of Pontoise's customs defended the celebration of Ignatius Loyola's feast day, wryly noting that 'new comers out of the world may not perhaps so rightly relish such devotions till they have binn more accustomed to the practis'.[22] Thus, despite their popularity with individual nuns, the Jesuits sparked widespread controversy among the exiled cloisters.

Scholars have attributed the disunity to various factors. While many concede that spirituality was at its core, its devotional origins have been subsumed within broader issues of politics and power. Most common has been the assumption that the nuns were simply re-enacting the clerical tensions which split the English Catholic community in the late sixteenth century. Peter Guilday's thoroughly researched account of the Brussels Benedictine fracas acknowledged that spirituality was at issue, but characterised the unrest as another instance in which 'the dissensions which separated Seculars and Regulars were re-echoed'. He interpreted the Gravelines unrest as an indirect consequence of the 'faction-spirit' infecting Brussels.[23] Likewise Placid Spearritt, who suspected that differing perceptions of spirituality were at the root of the Brussels dilemma, ultimately concluded that the nuns were caught in the political struggles of the clergy.[24] David Lunn explained the furore as 'a sidelight on the conflict between Bishop Richard Smith and the Regulars, then raging'.[25] The Brussels Benedictine affair, which is the best documented, has received the most scholarly attention, and the complex nature of that dispute has resulted in the war between Abbess Mary Percy and the rebel nuns being interpreted principally as a struggle over authority. In her dissertation, Colleen Seguin discussed it as an episode of familial dysfunction during which the 'unruly children' challenged their 'mother's' right to impose her will upon them. Seguin cast the 'Blue Nuns' splintering in 1675 in the same light.[26] Guilday had earlier recognised the centrality of power in the Gravelines Poor Clare furore which amounted to a struggle between the nuns and the friars over jurisdiction.[27] In all instances the nuns' opposition to their abbess's choice of confessor most certainly compromised her due allegiance. However, significantly, the bone of contention in each instance was competing spiritualities. Indeed, the question regarding the suitability of Ignatian devotion for women professed in Benedictine, Franciscan and other monastic traditions is the key to understanding the bitter acrimony which rent several communities. The Brussels dispute offers a case in point.

Writing about the mêlée David Lunn observed that the rebellious nuns seemed to have been fighting for Teresa of Avila's principle of free access to confessors.[28] This view is borne out by the rebels' copious correspondence. Within a decade of its foundation questions had arisen concerning the Jesuits' participation in the house's spiritual governance, spawning the departure of Mary Lovel in 1609, and the Ghent founders in 1624. In these early episodes the dissenting nuns confidently articulated their right to the Society's guidance. In 1623 Potentiana Deacon explained that since its beginning the convent had benefited from Jesuit assistance with spiritual matters and that most of the nuns owed their vocation to the Society.[29] When the dispute resurfaced in 1629 numerous distressed nuns petitioned the archbishop on the same grounds, citing their inability to receive religious comfort from Anthony Champney, the convent's new anti-Jesuit secular chaplain. Joyce (Flavia) Langdale sought a licence to confess to her chosen director, or at least to discuss with him matters weighing on her mind, claiming that he was best able to assist her because he more than anyone understood the state of her conscience.[30] Others, like Benedicta Hawkins, begged leave to transfer to another monastery where 'I may serve god in peace as I have allwaies done for in my contience I cannot live insecurite of my soul, in this goverment, without the assistance of the Societe to ayed me in my present difficultes'.[31] Unhappy with the manner of Champney's appointment as ordinary confessor, the rebels accused the abbess of contravening the house's statutes which, they insisted, required the consent of the convent's Chapter.[32] Frustrated in their efforts to secure Champney's dismissal, and thereby access to a more suitable confessor, certain nuns took matters into their own hands, and the breakdown of order described in Chapter 2 ensued. Therefore what began as a spiritual issue degenerated into a severe political, economic and religious crisis, which contrary to their intentions, caused the Society's supporters unimaginable anguish. Anne Healey, a lay sister who sympathised with the pro-Jesuit faction, claimed that the situation was 'grevously dangerous to many a soule: and I fear my own exceeding much, though my whole studdy be its preservation'. She described her inner turmoil, writing 'I live as in a prison, oppressed with discontent: wher formerly as in a paradice I abounded with delight'.[33] Thus, the sensitive issue of access to suitable confessors was not simply a question of clerical sympathies, nor of monastic obedience, for the likes of Langdale,

Hawkins and Healey, it was central to their religious vocation and their salvation.

Abbess Mary Percy would not have disagreed that the situation imperilled her nuns' immortal souls. However, she identified the very right for which the rebels were fighting as the spiritual malaise afflicting the cloister. At the outset Abbess Percy blamed the fracas on the freedom of choice and variety of spiritual direction permitted during the convent's early years.[34] The first abbess, Joanna Berkeley, had allowed nuns the option of a Jesuit confessor if they did not want the services of the house's appointed secular chaplain. There is ample evidence to confirm that many nuns took advantage of this option. When the Cambrai Benedictine convent was founded in 1623, Brussels sent three nuns to govern the fledgling community and train the founders in the monastic life, all of whom were all staunch believers in Jesuit prayer.[35] Indeed, in 1612, Mary Percy and Anthony Hoskins SJ had co-translated a prayer manual written by an Italian mystic and her Jesuit director, showing that at this point the future abbess was not opposed to Ignatian religiosity.[36] In 1619 the English translation of the Florentine ecstatic, Maria Maddalena de' Pazzi, was dedicated to her. The preface noted that Percy had read the Italian original and 'planted, not only in your owne Religious hart, but in the harts also of your own excellent Religious, a most tender, and deere remembrance of her rare vertue'.[37] Other members of the community gravitated towards different spiritual methodologies. The 1609 mystical treatise of an English Capuchin friar, William Fitch (alias Benet Canfield), was dedicated to his cousin, Winefrid (Agatha) Wiseman at Brussels.[38] Canfield's, *The Rule of Perfection*, combined Franciscan spirituality with elements of late medieval English mysticism.[39] Thus, in its early years, the Brussels Benedictine cloister embraced an eclectic mix of spiritual trends. Certain senior nuns considered this variety divisive. Agnes Lenthall, later abbess herself, explained the problem to Archbishop Jacob Boonen:

> We finde by experience that the speret and derections of the fathers of the Societie of Jesus is quite diferent from the simplicities of our holye Rule, and that ther directions and examples hath wrought such effects that ther is little since left of the Rule of S Benedict amoungst us esspeciallye in those that hath most frequented them, and allso now standeth most for them.[40]

Lenthall, a staunch ally of Mary Percy's campaign to introduce spiritual conformity, implied that she had never benefited from Ignatian techniques. However, Percy had patronised the Society in previous years, in 1618 even writing to the Jesuit provincial praising its spiritual support.[41] Why did she withdraw allegiance from her former religious guides? The answer may be found in the evolution of Ignatian piety in the early seventeenth century. Its supposed flexibility had been the reason for its tremendous appeal and widespread application by reforming Catholics. The main difficulty with the Jesuit school lay in differing interpretations of how the faithful should meditate. Loyola's original schema offered a methodical procedure for praying which allowed for a broad range of experiences, from simple meditation on the scriptures to mystical contemplation. Subsequent Jesuits modified the founder's regimen in accordance with their personal preferences, and in response to specific clerical fears about spiritual independence. Proponents of the later school believed that visions, revelations and raptures were dangerous because they took the mystic beyond the controlling influence of the Church. They accordingly adopted a cautious approach to the spiritual life which focused more on good works, attendance at the sacraments, frequent confession, and set meditations, and discouraged any contemplative activity which might encourage mysticism. One of the best proponents of this school was Alfonso Rodríguez whose *Practice of Perfection and Christian Virtues* reduced Loyola's spirituality to conventional practicality.[42] Rodríguez's compilation comprised 40 years of spiritual advice to novices and encompassed three volumes, each of which was divided into smaller treatises dedicated to specific virtues and how best to attain them. It appeared in English translation not as a complete work, but variously as the individual treatises, or compilations of them.[43] The Benedictines at Paris held a manuscript digest of it, titled the 'Treatise of Temptions', and the dedications in two published abridgements, to Abbess Lucy Knatchbull of Ghent and to Prioress Anne Worsely of the Antwerp Carmelites, suggest that English translations of Rodríguez's book were being recommended to nuns.[44] In monasteries, where the primary goal was the contemplative rather than the active life, reductive treatises like those of Rodríguez which were 'less concerned to arouse enthusiasm and inflame the imagination than to lead to action' alienated some nuns for whom mysticism was the ultimate spiritual experience.[45] Helen (Gertrude) More, the Cambrai Benedictine mystic, argued that Jesuit spirituality was predicated upon an active principle which did not sit well with cloistered nuns. She believed the limitations of sensible devotion frustrated cloistered women who, lacking 'sufficient action to imploy themselves in', yearned for a 'more spiritual prayer of the will'.[46] Obviously not all women felt constrained by the evolution of a more rigid Jesuit regime. Lucy Knatchbull, to whom Rodríguez's work was dedicated, meditated upon set texts and events but she used them as a springboard to mystical union.[47] However, it is significant that Mary Percy came to reject the methodology she had previously supported. The abbess's translation of the *Breve Compendio* placed her firmly within the school of broader Ignatian spirituality which encompassed mystical activity. Evidence that some within her house were adherents of the reductionist school of Rodríguez and his ilk can be found in a copy of his book which was sent to the Cambrai Benedictines.[48] Significantly, this occurred in the 1620s, when the abbess was beginning her campaign against the Society.

Mary Percy's rejection of the Society can perhaps best be understood as a reaction against the narrowed focus of particular Jesuits which conflicted with her broader spiritual sympathies. There is evidence that she favoured placing the convent under the control of the English Benedictine congregation, thereby grounding it firmly within her order's spiritual tradition.[49] Yet this was not how she chose to present the conflict. Her version of the affair suggests that the anti-Jesuit camp blurred the dispute's focus so the question of spiritual direction was obscured by broader issues of authority and power. The abbess's correspondence reveals how she characterised the affair as a matter of monastic obedience, rather than as a question of spiritual guidance. In a defence of her stance reputedly read to the entire convent in November 1629, Percy acknowledged that certain nuns had 'Masters and Directors' beyond the official chaplain, but asserted her right as their 'Mother' to deny access to these priests.[50] In letters to ecclesiastical authorities in Rome, Mary Percy argued that the dissident nuns were contravening not only their vow of obedience to her as their abbess, but also the dictates of Trent which had placed the monastery under the jurisdiction of the archbishop of Mechelen.[51] Archbishop Jacob Boonen supported Abbess Percy. In the opposite camp, the dissenting nuns acquired the vital support of the papal nuncio in Brussels. Thus, the issue evolved into a question of monastic government and obedience which had to be dealt with by the ecclesiastical authorities, and was largely taken out of the nuns' hands. Beyond the convent walls, the rhetoric of both sides inevitably reflected the Jesuit/secular debate and entered the purely political realm, all but obscuring its spiritual origin. Brussels served as a warning to other cloisters of the politically charged nature of monastic spirituality.

Other houses took heed and rejected the Society outright. Letitia (Mary) Tredway was adamant the Jesuits would have nothing to do with her cloister when she founded the Augustinian convent in Paris in 1634. She admired the secular clergy to the extent that her co-founder, Thomas Carre (*vere* Miles Pinckney), a priest from the English College at Douai, later noted that 'she conceives her holie father hath made her' an honorary member.[52] From the outset Tredway was determined to tolerate no extraordinary confessors beyond the secular clergy, 'apprehending it much to the comon peace and quiete of the Monasterie, since she sees so much discord and scandall by the Jesuits medling with English monasteries in these parts'.[53] Upon Carre's retirement as confessor in 1666, Tredway sought a suitable replacement who would 'conserve one hart, and one soule among us, which is the spirit of our Rule and all religion'.[54] Therefore for her the spiritual formation of her nuns was the province of the secular clergy alone. Similarly, in 1623, in the light of emerging chaos at Brussels, the Cambrai Benedictine cloister was established under the auspices of the English Benedictine congregation. A string of Benedictine confessors, who were more attuned to missionary work than spiritual direction of a convent, proved wanting and the novices struggled to establish personal prayer regimes. Gertrude More recalled that in this time of confusion 'I was as great a stranger to Almighty God as I was in England when I scarce thought...whether there were a God, or no'.[55] The three nuns sent from Brussels to assist the new establishment had been schooled in Jesuit spirituality, and they attempted to train the Cambrai novices in the way of prayer they found profitable. Significantly, before the nine founders had been in the habit six months, they begged the president of the English Benedictines to send them someone qualified in their own order's spirituality.[56] The monk sent to Cambrai to assist the young novices was Augustine Baker.

Baker's nine years at Cambrai established a particular form of spirituality there, which endured beyond his departure in 1633, and his death in 1641. Dissatisfied with the rigidly methodical meditation they had hitherto encountered, the nuns were attracted by Baker's non-interventionist approach. Rather than impose a universal contemplative regimen, he encouraged individuals to pursue the devotional path which best suited their ability and temperament. To assist spiritual self-discovery, Baker translated the writings of the great late-medieval mystics, and he supplemented these texts with devotional treatises and prayer manuals, composed in response to problems experienced by the nuns. Thus, his religiosity comprised a combination of established contemplative methods and the nuns' modification of them.[57] Moreover, he was fiercely critical of contemporary Ignatian piety, which he derided as 'the

ABC in a spiritual life'.[58] He was especially scathing about heavy-handed spiritual direction in contemplative cloisters, writing:

> the director... should advise according to the character of each soul, remembering that his office is not to teach his own way of prayer, nor any definite way, but to instruct his penitents how to discover their way for themselves by observing what is profitable and what harmful. In a word, he should know that he is God's instrument, and must lead souls in God's way, and not in his own.[59]

Baker's warning about interventionist confessors struck a resonance with the religious women, who later wrote contemptuously about their encounters with such men. Gertrude More sarcastically denounced the efforts of priests from whom she had sought guidance prior to accepting Baker, confirming his accusation that many simply trained inexperienced nuns in their own prayer techniques. In her experience the bewildered soul was confused further by the conflicting advice tendered by each priest consulted in the quest to find spiritual satisfaction.[60] Barbara Constable concurred, complaining that

> in former ages... there was but one way to tru sanctity; but now there are a thousand ways, and every man will affirm his way to be the best and only way; and how should a simple Ideot know, for they do so pelt her so with their learning... that I see not how they can be resisted.[61]

Convinced by the veracity of Baker's opinion and buoyed by its successful application in their own lives, many in the community attained divine union through prayer. In the 1670s Abbess Catherine (Christina) Brent explained the theology to her sisters, advising:

> the knowledge you can learne from men or bookes, (though that be also to be sought in due measure) is weake unconstant and easily passes with out much effect; but that of god brings strength, the former is superficiall and shines in our eyes; the later peirces into the bottome of our soules, and with out such recource to god and help from him the way of vertue can never truly be walked.[62]

Thus, as Brent made clear, the Cambrai community espoused a spirituality in which the soul was led by God alone, thus rejecting the discourse, set meditations, and close supervision that characterised Ignatian piety.

The religious women who benefited from Baker's method proclaimed its efficacy both within and beyond the confines of their enclosure. 'Bakerism' was disseminated principally through the copying and circulation of his treatises among the nuns at Cambrai and Paris and in the wider Benedictine congregation. It even spread beyond adherents to Benedict's rule when in the mid-1630s copies of Baker's books were sent to the English Carmelites at Antwerp.[63] Several nuns also imparted Baker's methodology directly to others. Upon his departure in 1633, Baker endorsed Abbess Catherine Gascoigne as a capable instructor of his ideology, insisting that she and her sisters were 'sufficiently entered and founded in their spirituall course... to undertake the office of teaching the younger [nuns]'.[64] His confidence in their capacity for spiritual tutelage was shared by the archbishop of Cambrai who in 1642 commissioned Abbess Gascoigne, Bridget More and Anne (Clementina) Cary to reform the local French Benedictine monastery of St Lazare. In the process of restoring regular discipline there, Gascoigne taught the precepts of 'Bakerism' and provided the convent with its principal texts.[65] Her success elicited the admiration of the archbishop and other local worthies who 'affirmed they had never met a person of greater light and experience than she had in the conduct of souls'.[66] Yet transmission of 'Bakerism' did not rely solely upon the monk's ideas and writings. Many Cambrai sisters wrote pious works of their own which aimed to explicate the religiosity. Spiritual diaries and compilations of devotional material were composed in the light of evolving personal and communal needs, and circulated among the Cambrai and Paris communities.[67] Barbara Constable, who was responsible for many copies of Baker's writings, even wrote an advice book for confessors and spiritual directors.[68] In 1658, the nuns' spirituality reached a wider audience with the publication of Gertrude More's devotional writings, titled *The Spiritual Exercises*. The role of the cloister in propagating what it termed 'Fr Baker's Way', coupled with the nuns' own development of the ideology, led to its increasing identification with the Cambrai convent.[69] However, the nuns themselves attributed the method and their successful appropriation of it entirely to its progenitor. Baker was revered as the founder of the spirituality and it has even been suggested that the nuns were working towards the canonisation of their former spiritual director, for they referred to him as 'the Venerable Father Augustine Baker' as if the canonisation process was under way.[70] Inevitably, as Cambrai's spiritual reputation flourished, questions were raised about Baker's orthodoxy.

The novelty of Baker's approach lay not in its content, or even the principle of individual self-direction, but in proposing it to nuns in the reforming Catholic Church. At a time when greater scrutiny of private religiosity was deemed paramount, Baker effectively encouraged the religious women to become their own spiritual directors. Some fellow Benedictines feared that the monk went too far in his insistence upon the sensitive issue of spiritual autonomy. In 1633 matters came to a head when Cambrai's official Benedictine chaplain, Francis Hull, accused Baker of preaching anti-authoritarian doctrines, and the charge brought Baker before the General Chapter of the English Benedictine congregation. Both Gertrude More and Abbess Catherine Gascoigne wrote eloquent defences, in which they articulated the deep and abiding spiritual content they had drawn from his guidance, and an exhaustive audit of the monk's writings by several learned scholars exonerated him entirely.[71] However, the male branch of the order became concerned that Cambrai might degenerate into another Brussels and withdrew both Baker and Hull from the convent. Baker resided at St Gregory's College in Douai, until he was sent on the English mission in 1638, where he died three years later. The concern of those who were sceptical about his orthodoxy in 1633 was no doubt inflamed later that year by the death from small pox of the saintly Gertrude More. The night before she died, More was asked if she would like to speak with a priest, but she reportedly declined saying 'give [Baker] thanks a thousand times, who had brought her to such a pass that she could confidently go out of this life without speaking to any man'.[72]

No one questioned Gertrude More's orthodoxy, but doubts about Baker's doctrine simmered below the surface to erupt over 20 years later in a bitter dispute. In 1655, Claude White, the president of the English Benedictine congregation demanded Abbess Catherine Gascoigne relinquish the original Baker treatises, so that their 'poysonous, pernicious and diabolicall doctrine' could be expunged.[73] Gascoigne's refusal to submit to his command unleashed a torrent of threats in which White denounced the nuns' determination to resist him and declared their abbess was 'in a damnable way running to perdition'.[74] When his terrifying speeches to the assembled convent had failed to sway the nuns' resolve, the president resorted to blackmail, announcing that he would not approve the profession of three novices 'before he had satisfaction in what he desired'.[75] Ultimately the abbess triumphed and preserved Baker's writings intact, but not before she had considered taking the momentous step of removing her convent from the jurisdiction of the English Benedictines and placing it under the archbishop of Cambrai.[76] The dispute between Gascoigne and White undoubtedly centred upon spirituality but it revealed how, like at Brussels, religiosity was inextricably bound with political and economic issues. The Cambrai convent paid financially for the furore with a sharp slump in recruitment during the next decade. Moreover, in arguments reminiscent of Mary Percy's correspondence to the rebels, White couched the struggle over the manuscripts in terms of monastic obedience, telling the nuns that their opposition to his wishes amounted to 'absolut disobedience'.[77] It was implicit in his condemnation of Baker's teaching that although heretical in themselves, the writings were doubly subversive in that they encouraged nuns to assert their independence in other areas of monastic life too.

Spirituality in the English convents therefore encompassed the wider issues of monastic jurisdiction and authority, as well as personal interaction with the divine. The Jesuit injunction against administration of women's cloisters placed many English communities in an impossible position regarding spiritual direction. Ignatian spirituality dominated Catholic Europe, but there was often a conflict of interest between a convent's official chaplain, and Jesuits overseeing specific nuns' pious programmes. The problem of spiritual direction, however, was not limited to conflict between Jesuits and the secular clergy. As events in the Cambrai house showed, disputes over devotional methodology could still arise among those of the same order. Yet Gertrude More was correct in her plea for contemplative women's freedom to access the divine. She warned 'living in Religion (as I can speake by experience) if one be not in a right course between God and our soul: Ones nature growes much worse; then ever it would have been if they had lived in the wor[l]d'.[78] Although fighting for a different devotional path, the Brussels rebels would have concurred, as anxious letters concerning their salvation attest. In the contest for close supervision of nuns' religiosity, their supervisors and indeed some women themselves, ranked political and economic issues ahead of the spiritual. The politicisation of spirituality visited great anguish upon many individuals and their communities, but amidst the struggle most nuns were able to carve out a meaningful prayer life. Certain women succeeded in overcoming the obstacles to the ultimate form of divine union which was at the root of so much of the dissension. The seventeenth-century English mystics will feature in the next section.

Mysticism and authority

The English nuns were particularly well placed to engage in mysticism. Early modern understandings of female physiology, combined with the common belief that women were the more devout sex, rendered all women potential mystics. Enclosed nuns were deemed particular candidates for divine union because clausura theoretically removed them from the distractions of the world to concentrate upon matters of spirit. The cloister also provided a fertile environment for the practices of self-abnegation and physical punishment which gave expression to supernatural discourse. In addition, the explosion of printing in the late sixteenth century made available an ever-increasing corpus of devout literature which detailed the mystical process and the lives of those who had successfully pursued it. The books provided aspiring holy women with ready-made blueprints from which they could fashion their personal sanctity at a time when alternative pieties were limited. Given that nuns were physically restrained within their enclosures, mysticism offered a gateway to supernatural and worldly action. As Ulrike Strasser has noted, it 'allowed cloistered women to move beyond convent walls and to counter exclusion from public life by entering into another world altogether'.[79] Women renowned for intense spiritual relationships often had their biographies and spiritual writings published, thus becoming exemplars; and many mystics achieved secular power in the form of election to high conventual office. Indeed, as Caroline Bynum has argued, intense piety did not necessitate rejection of the world; medieval women's mysticism was 'historical and incarnational', reflecting their experience as women.[80] Links between the spiritual and temporal spheres were similarly prominent in the religiosity of seventeenth-century English nuns. Although they tried hard to reject secular associations and habits by embracing the rituals of bodily and mental discipline, worldly images defined their visions and devotional writings. Mysticism therefore represented a contemplative activism in which a strongly secular discourse mediated the mystic's relationship with the divine.

In early modern Europe, Protestants and Catholics alike believed that women were more devout than men. The Elizabethan divine Richard Hooker observed that as the weaker sex women were naturally 'propense and inclinable to holiness'.[81] Augustine Baker attributed this phenomenon to female physiology:

> Women in their verie nature are more religious then men. This is verified not onlie . . . in the Catholick church where you see farre more women then men to frequent the sacraments but allso in false religions . . . And though we cannot enter into all the reasons of nature, yet we maie conjecture . . . that women being of a colder complexion are more fearefull and have lesse confidence in them-

selves which urgeth them uppon occasions of feare . . . to recurre unto God for help as by the verie instinct of nature . . . And thus in the verie course of nature have they some advantage over men; for the divine grace finding a better disposition in nature commonlie worketh her effect the more effecaciously.[82]

Seventeenth-century medical discourses remained indebted to the texts of the ancient physicians which in the middle ages had been interpreted through the prism of Christian theology. As a consequence, the female body was commonly understood to be inferior to the male anatomy. Hence Baker's explanation interpreted women's greater religiosity in terms of Galenic theory, in which the more problematic cold and moist humours dominated female biology causing numerous physical, intellectual and moral defects. Yet, although widespread belief in women's corporal and mental incapacity restricted their official participation in public affairs and justified their seclusion as wives, mothers and enclosed nuns; as Baker implied, it also had more positive implications for their spiritual status. Phyllis Mack has suggested that women's supposed weak intellectual capacity made them more suitable receptors for divine energy. Men who filled their minds with earthly concerns and prided themselves on the strength of their reason were less able to conduct heavenly messages.[83] The visionary, mystic or prophet was likened to an empty vessel into which God poured his message. This symbolism was concordant with the Christian doctrine that the weak and humble would be exalted over the powerful and proud. The Flemish mystic, Antonia Bourignon, questioned God's proposal to use her as a messenger, citing her gender as a reason why people would not take her seriously. In response, a heavenly voice told her, 'I will serve my self of vilest matter to confound the pride of Men. I will give thee all that thou shalt need; be faithful to me.'[84] Thus, women's innate passivity and inferiority were understood as qualifications for mystical experience.

Early modern people might have attributed the greater religiosity of women to nature, however it can better be understood as a cultural and social construction. The 'good woman' of sermons and conduct books exhibited qualities and behaviour commensurate with Christian virtue. Of course both men and women were expected to be devout, but the latter generally had more opportunity to practice piety. Confined to domesticity, women were encouraged to occupy their time profitably, and religion provided appropriate employment via personal prayer and charitable action.[85] If ideology, opportunity and location were prerequisites for godliness, then the convent offered the ideal devotional

environment. Augustine Baker's biography of the saintly young Margaret Gascoigne, who died at Cambrai in 1637, described the cloister as
God's gift. He wrote

> And for the enabling of souls the better to observe the Divine Inspir-
> ations, so necessary for salvation, hath the Holy Ghost invented and
> instituted the Holy State of Religion, especially Contemplative
> Orders (as ours is) in which is provided much Extern Solitude with
> all other helps and commodities conducing to the said purpose of
> being the better to observe the Divine Inspirations.[86]

Within the sheltered confines of the convent, the ordered monastic
routine aimed to transform its inmates into models of religious virtue
through 'mortification', a programme of strict behavioural regulation.
Beginning in the noviciate the attributes of humility, modesty, charity
and obedience were instilled into the nun through its disciplining
rituals of self-denial.[87] Such qualities reflected common early modern
prescriptions for ideal womanly comportment, but within the cloister
they acquired a spiritual imperative. Intensive periods of prayer, fasting,
chastisement of the flesh, and public humiliation enabled the nun to
'die to the world' so that she could access the divine unhindered by
bodily and worldly concerns. Phyllis Mack described a similar process
enacted by Quakers as the attempt 'to dissolve the habits, passions,
gestures, and little secret sins that made them who they were; to expose
themselves as creatures without status, without intelligence, without
gender; to become blank'.[88] Margaret Gascoigne expressed it in comparable terms, declaring that to give herself entirely to God's 'will and
worshipp':

> I would see nothing,
> Heare nothing,
> Feele nothing,
> Know nothing,
> Understand nothing,
> Be moved at nothing,
> Have nothing,
> But thee and thy will.[89]

In his account of the extraordinary mystical experiences of Lucy
Knatchbull of Ghent, Tobie Matthew attributed the abbess's 'Supernatural Favours' to the way in which she made 'a total Sacrifice of

herself . . . with all her affections and appetites, to the greater glory of our Blessed Lord'.[90] Gertrude More saw 'mortification' as a total surrender of the self to God's will, writing a 'soul can never be pure, and free for the ascending to the praise of God, til it be very humble, which the more a soul endeavoureth to be . . . the freer accesse doth she find to God, and the lesse impediments between him and her soul.'[91] Thus, determined adherence to its discipline within the cloister facilitated a nun's chance of achieving religious ecstasy.

In reality, divine union was notoriously difficult to attain, and only a small coterie of nuns ever accomplished it. Tobie Matthew noted that charismatic experiences were not open to 'all God's Court' but only to a chosen few, like the ecstatic, Lucy Knatchbull.[92] Augustine Baker referred to Gertrude More's 'propensity' for the higher forms of contemplation.[93] The clerical biographers clearly attributed mystical success to divine favour rather than to any human ability, suggesting that supernatural causation overrode nature and nurture in this ultimate spiritual achievement. The nuns also believed that the hand of God guided their charismatic sisters' sacred intercourse, but they remained convinced that successful adherence to mortification was a prerequisite. Hence even the mystical elect emphasised their struggle for abstraction and thus union. Clare Vaughan, whose eminence in prayer was acknowledged by the Pontoise Benedictines upon her death in 1687, steeled herself to spurn all disruptive thoughts and activities, remarking in her spiritual diary, 'in the first place now that my mind is a litle recollected from the distractions of the world, I must endea[v]our to keepe it soe, by beeing blind deaf and dumb, endeavouring to know nothing but christ crucified'.[94] Gertrude More despaired of success, begging 'O my God, when shall I find and possess Thee in the bottom of my soul? When shall the eyes of my body be so closed from beholding all vanity that the eyes of my soul may be cleared by Thee, to the discernment of truth?'[95] Vaughan's determination for self-control and More's anguish at the failure to conquer her will belie the notion that divine union was God's gift to an inert vessel, pointing instead to the need for intensive personal endeavour. Mysticism therefore must be considered an active rather than a passive spiritual mode.[96] ✓

Indeed, far from a natural attribute, charismatic religiosity was socially constructed, and in the early seventeenth century, it was an intrinsic feature of female convent culture, advanced by ready access to devotional literature, including the highly prescriptive lives of holy men and women.[97] The hagiographies presented models for sanctity, detailed painstakingly from the exemplars' portentous birth, precocious piety, virtuous, mystical and often punishing adult religiosity, to their final suffering, death and posthumous intercession. In some instances the textual account was fortified by illustrations of the more momentous events in the saint's life.[98] Accordingly, despite the post-Tridentine Church's endeavours to downplay the more sensational features of late medieval sanctity, typified by the physical manifestations of Christocentric raptures and visions, accounts of ecstatic women remained popular, fuelled by the more contemporary examples of Teresa of Avila and Maria Maddalena de' Pazzi.[99] By the 1620s and 1630s the lives of the late medieval and sixteenth-century mystics were available in English translation, and the convents' familiarity with them is implicit in their prefaces.[100] Francis Bell, confessor to the Franciscans at Brussels, presented an account of the visionary, Joan of the Cross, to Margaret and Elizabeth Radcliffe, the convent's temporary abbess and vicaress, noting 'I finde myselfe bound to promote you in the way of Pietie'.[101] The translated life of Maria Maddalena de' Pazzi was dedicated to Abbess Mary Percy of Brussels, who had reputedly extolled her nuns to emulate the Florentine Carmelite.[102] Likewise the English version of Teresa of Avila's autobiography encouraged its religious readers to embody their founder's virtue in deed and prayer.[103] Evidence that the nuns imbibed the books' contents can be found in their writings. Barbara Constable of Cambrai quoted Maria Maddalena de' Pazzi in her advice manual for confessors.[104]

However, the impact such material made upon the faithful is difficult to gauge. Some nuns had evidently been swayed by youthful familiarity with the hagiographies. The Benedictine, Catherine (Justina) Gascoigne, who was professed at Cambrai in 1640, later becoming prioress of the house's Paris filiation, reputedly read the saints' lives during her childhood and they inspired her passion for mortification and charity.[105] Other women more obviously self-fashioned their spirituality in accordance with the texts. At the age of 16 the Carmelite mystic, Catharine (Mary Xaveria of the Angels) Burton, encountered the writings of Teresa of Avila and read the life of Catherine of Siena. In her autobiography, she recalled imitating the saints' self-denial and devotional rituals before entering the Antwerp convent in 1693.[106] Given Burton's subsequent extraordinary mystical career, replete with trances, visions, levitations, and eucharistic miracles, it is clear that this literature styled her religiosity. Indeed it is possible that she chose to fashion a saintly identity modelled upon Teresa and Catherine, both in her life and in her written account of it. Evidence of so-called 'false saints', who faked mystical union and its bodily imprints, testify to the influence such books exercised over their readers' imaginations and ambitions.[107] However, the English cloisters apparently did not engineer a Benedetta Carlini or a Cecilia Ferrazzi, and no one questioned Burton's veracity.

Indeed, it was commonplace to construct quasi-sanctity in obituary and chronicle accounts of deceased women. A copy of the Gravelines Poor Clares' annals, made for the 1644 filiation to Rouen, ended with various accounts of 'severall holy Religious...conspicuous for sanctity'.[108] The obituary notices of the Ghent Benedictines offer several examples of this literary imperative to interpret individual spirituality within a saintly framework. Margaret (Alexia) Grey was remembered for her 'intence prayer and application to Spirituall things', but her life had not always been so devout. In true Augustinian style she had led a youthful life of vanity 'earnestly pursuing her pleasures in all kind of Recreation, Balls, maskes and the Like', until she had an arresting dream of her own final judgement which partially reformed her gay abandon. It took another divine jolt, this time while she was dancing, to propel her into the cloister whereupon she immediately 'run'd on a full race towards perfection'. The full measure of her success was revealed upon her untimely death from consumption in 1640, when a priest who happened to see her body laid out in the cloister's choir, declared that her soul had bypassed purgatory and gone straight to heaven.[109] Obituary narratives like Grey's served to authenticate a cloister's spirituality by detailing the singular holiness of its members and evidence of divine certification. However, they also perpetuated an internal hagiographic tradition by promoting women with whom the nuns had lived as exemplars to be emulated. Some went so far as to write actual biographies. In her memoir of Margaret Clement, Elizabeth Shirley made clear its instructive imperative, writing 'because the lives of the belssed Sainsts is principally to stire us up to the Imitation of their heroicall vertue: Let us make that profitt, that we follow them in spirituall devotions and mortification, but allso in some corporall exercises'.[110] Shirley unashamedly promoted Clement as a proto-saint, whose devotional regime could serve as a pattern for others.

Inevitably the publicity surrounding charismatic religious women, like Alexia Grey and Margaret Clement, allowed them to transcend monastic anonymity. While the death notices and chronicles might have been composed for the instruction of the convent, the exploits of exceptionally devout sisters often reached a wider circulation. Sir Tobie Matthew prepared Lucy Knatchbull's life for publication in 1651 'for the edification of the Catholics of our Country'.[111] The 1630 obituary of the worthy Benedictine lay sister, Jane (Cecily) Price concluded abruptly with the explanation 'The latter part of this holy Religious woman's life was unluckily lost by some seculars who for their edification Desir'd the reading of it.'[112] Part of the missing material resurfaced in Tobie Matthew's biography of Lucy Knatchbull and reveals that the lay sister attained great heights through prayer, including a vision of Christ on the cross.[113] Price's fragmented obituary suggests that there was a lay audience for mystical literature, and the saintly nuns' lives, whether self-fashioned or constructed by their sisters, provided a devotional avenue between the cloister and the world. Claustration ensured that this spiritual connection was a mediated rather than a direct link. Unlike the priests, religious women were unable to train the faithful in Catholic piety, but as exemplars they could indirectly promote early modern religiosity outside their enclosures. Gertrude More's writings were published in 1658, making available her exemplary prayer to a wider audience.[114] Serenus Cressy, the Benedictine who compiled Augustine Baker's writings for print, noted that, in addition to inspiring and teaching her religious sisters,

> Many others, of divers Conditions, have not only Received much Edification, but Great Profit, by the sight of the said writings, in being drawn and Encouraged by them to Give themselves very seriously to prayer; as her Example and Counsell, when Living, did work the like Effects in Many.[115]

Certain women advanced beyond the status of mere pious models to become living saints with direct intercessory powers. Convent guests commonly demanded discourse with these powerbrokers at the grate. The company of the celebrated Lady Trevor (Clare of Jesus) Warner, whose conversion and religious vocation led her husband and sister-in-law into monasticism too, was much desired by visitors to the Liège Sepulchrines. Rumours of her holiness no doubt intensified when she relocated to the more austere Poor Clares at Gravelines, after a eucharistic vision convinced her to join a stricter order.[116] In Paris various people revered the Benedictine prioress, Justina Gascoigne. One devout woman made an annual New Year's day pilgrimage to the convent to obtain Gascoigne's blessing, and she commissioned the prioress's 'picture to be drawne, which she keepes still, as a Relique'.[117] Thus, the demand for physical contact persevered even after the holy women's deaths. In 1679, upon the death at Lierre of the Carmelite prioress, Margaret (Margaret of Jesus) Mostyn, lay mourners at her funeral requested pieces of her habit and other possessions as relics.[118] The 1745 death of the pious Dunkirk Benedictine, Mary Agnes Poulton, likewise inspired appeals for items associated with her.[119] More spectacularly, the discovery in 1716 of the uncorrupted body of the Antwerp Carmelite Margaret (Mary Margaret of the Angels) Wake, who had died in 1678, initiated a veritable stampede into the monastery by visitors who wanted to venerate the 'saint' and seek her intercession. When the sheer volume of devotees forced Prioress Mary (Mary Francis of Teresa) Birkbeck to bar entry into the enclosure, the crowds reportedly complained, 'God has not given this saint for the monastery alone but for all the people.'[120] Thus, the perceived potency of such holy women could not be contained within the cloister alone. Their reputation as mediators between God and the faithful spread into the lay community, encouraging as much veneration as emulation.

The English mystical nuns' transmutation of clausura did not however compromise their contemplative apostolate because they conducted their action within the parameters of monastic piety. Clerics sent Margaret Clement of St Monica's the spiritually destitute, hoping that her saintly demeanour and mediation would assist them. Many subsequently affirmed the efficacy of her prayers, declaring that 'next unto god they did ascribe unto her the whole cause of ther salvation'.[121] The prioress's assistance combined spiritual guidance and support with regular religious practices. Elizabeth Shirley recorded Clement's 'devout prayers, her watchings, her tears, her continual exhortations, [and] her long suffering with unspeakable patience'.[122] Intercession, like mortification, thus necessitated exertion and suffering, not unlike Christ's agony for humankind's salvation. Indeed, many common features of monastic devotion characterised the labour of other mediators. Cecily Price preserved a sister's wavering religious vocation by appealing to the Virgin Mary. A third party testified to witnessing Price carrying the doubtful novice's soul in the form of a dove to each Marian shrine in the convent, thereupon the woman changed her mind and proceeded to take her vows. Price spoke of the incident as a dream, commenting, 'God knows...how often I was likely to have lost it in a great Mist; but still I procured with care to keep it safe from all danger.'[123] Price's saving 'dream' reflected ceremonies performed by the nuns in devotion to the Virgin. Ghent's Helen (Aloysia) Beaumont, who died only four years after her 1631 profession, regularly visited 'every Image of our blessed lady' in the convent, and offered 'some pious salutation prayr and petition'.[124] Moreover, it combined elements of regular piety with charismatic religious experience. Other nuns operated entirely within the mystical framework. Catharine Burton comforted a disturbed nun who questioned her salvation. Upon receiving communion, Burton acquired the scrupulous sister's anguish, and transferred her own consolation to the woman. The surrogacy was temporary, lasting only ten days, but it was sufficient to sustain the anxious nun during future bouts of desolation.[125] Intercessors like Margaret Clement, Cecily Price and Catharine Burton therefore drew upon the sacred resources intrinsic to their orders' spiritual traditions to arbitrate between heaven and earth. Yet in so doing they transformed contemplation into a missionary apostolate, soothing troubled souls, securing vocations and sometimes even converting Protestants, all from within their enclosures.

The active nature of mysticism had other worldly ramifications too. Religious authority was thought to translate well into temporal governance, and several saintly nuns were elected to lead their religious communities, often at a very young age. Margaret Clement was only 30 when chosen prioress. Catharine Burton's confessor scoffed when she predicted her election two months later, saying a woman in her early 30s was too young and inexperienced.[126] Various apparitions of Christ and his cross forewarned the Lierre Teresian, Margaret Mostyn, of her impending superiority. Reluctant to assume the mantle of government after a unanimous vote, Mostyn reminded the bishop that she was not yet 30, but he declared the hand of God was evident in her election and confirmed her appointment.[127] The willingness of both nuns and bishops to ignore the Tridentine requirement that prioresses should be 40, but at the very least 30, emphasises the perceived connection between spiritual and secular leadership. The principle that saintly superiors would guide their communities to religious perfection clearly persuaded the Pontoise Benedictines to elect unanimously the reclusive Elizabeth D'abridgecourt as their abbess in 1689, declaring that her mystical successes qualified her as 'the Candlestick to Enlighten this Community'.[128] They had already reaped the benefits of such a choice in Abbess Anne Neville, who reputedly had possessed 'soe familier a conversation and strict union with allmighty god, that what she spoke in publicke of edification to her community, she generally drew from the intertainements she had with him interiourly'.[129] However, there were more practical reasons for choosing a saintly superior. One so close to God would secure heavenly assistance in her task, and this might prove crucial for houses in economic difficulties. After Margaret Mostyn's rise to power, the Lierre Carmelites attributed their improved fortunes to God's providence, secured in part by their admirable prioress. Mostyn was adamant that all needs would be supplied, telling those who questioned her confidence 'my Infant Spouse has promised me He will take care of our concerns Himself'. Various accounts of miraculous recovery from financial embarrassment and her seemingly abundant charity to the poor and displaced when there was scarcely enough to sustain the community were duly attributed to her special understanding with God.[130] Catharine Burton, who apparently never failed to obtain whatever she asked of God, similarly sustained the Carmelites at Antwerp.[131] Likewise, the Paris Benedictines were virtually destitute upon the election of Prioress Justina Gascoigne in 1665, and they attributed their economic survival and the convent's expansion during her 25 year rule to divine patronage.[132] The religious superior's temporal authority was thus grounded in her spiritual power. Not all mystics advanced to this principal office in the monastery, but none could escape the authority their spiritual success conferred on them.

Paradoxically, therefore, religious women who accomplished supernatural union through claustration and mortification invariably garnered the public scrutiny they had striven so hard to shun. As exemplars, intercessors and monastic superiors they realised a power at odds with the weak and humble vessel requisite for divine communion. For this reason, the spiritually eminent commonly resisted efforts to prise them from self-imposed ascetic obscurity. Elizabeth (Colette Clare) Thwaites, professed at Gravelines in 1615, was respected within and beyond her community for 'her peace and constant union with God' which were reflected 'in her exterior'. In the 1654 abbatial election, Thwaites and Luysia (Luysia Clare) Taylor received an equal number of votes. Thwaites was apparently so horrified at the prospect of authority that she 'went round the quire...saying deare Sisters I renounce, I renounce'. They acquiesced and elected Taylor, but the reluctant administrator was subsequently made vicaress, a position she held for 24 years.[133] Likewise the saintly Mary Wright, professed an Augustinian at Bruges in 1657, refused to accept any offices for over 30 years because she feared that temporal concerns would endanger her profound relationship with God. Wright also assiduously avoided any form of contact with the outside world, and when she was elected prioress in 1693, the cloister's lay friends expressed amazement because they knew nothing of her. Upon her death in 1709, it was said that 'she was not humble, but – humility'; a comment borne out by the discovery that to preserve her anonymity she had burned all records of her spiritual life.[134] However successfully Mary Wright shunned publicity, many others in her position could not escape the adulation which, theoretically, was an obstacle to their supernatural intercourse. The innate tension in the mystic's life therefore centred upon striking the right balance between the mortification necessary to achieve direct union, and the fame and power emanating from such an achievement. If only the well-mortified soul could interact with the divine, then nuns who were lauded as mystics constantly needed to remind themselves of their human frailty, and they had to intensify the practices necessary to instil its principles in their weak bodies. Thus, mortification became self-perpetuating. This ambivalence might explain why at the very moment when a nun entered a mystical state and was most empowered by the regime of denial she had pursued, she couched her experiences in highly metaphorical language which was replete with images of feminine passivity, humility and emotion.

In the English nuns' encounters with the divine, the soul was ostensibly female in its reception of the male God. The women commonly described their connection with Christ using metaphors of secular love. Lucy Knatchbull spoke of her spiritual relationship as a love affair. When she was experiencing visions and trances at Brussels, prior to the Ghent filiation, she described herself as 'one deeply stricken in Love'.[135] Gertrude More characterised her association with God in terms of a lover seeking her beloved. She asked him to forgive her shortcomings and to teach her the requisite perfection for divine union, begging

> be mercifull to my desolate hart, and stirre it up to perfect *love* of *thee*, that I may simply seek *thee*, and sigh after *thee* my beloved... Lett me long to embrace *thee* with the armes of my soul, and think it litle to endure any misery in body, or soul, to be at last admitted into the boosom of my *Love, fairest, and choicest of thousands*... O when shall my soul, having transcended it self, and all created things, be firmly united to *thee*, the *beloved* of my hart.[136]

This gendered relationship between the believer and God was most explicit in its characterisation of the nun as the 'bride of Christ'.[137] As Christ's spouses, many nuns extended the metaphor into every aspect of their existence, couching their relationship with the Lord in conjugal terms. Several Paris Benedictine obituaries likened the bond between a nun and God to that of the 'spowse in the Canticles'.[138] The priest, Peter Lupus, was even more explicit, reassuring Margaret Clement that at death Christ would call 'come my spouse to thy marriage come to the nuptiall beed; that I may kisse thee'.[139] Tobie Matthew likewise declared divine intercourse was granted 'to such only, as be admitted to be of his own bed Chamber, as true Spouses are, and ought to be'.[140] Some nuns' visions encompassed this sexually explicit construction. Margaret

Mostyn related how 'our Lord Himself would suddenly appear and show Himself to her in the Holy Sacrament, which excited in her the most fervorous desires of Communion, with which our Lord sometimes favoured her'. On other occasions he 'seemed to pierce her heart with a most curious dart like unto a little spear, which filled her heart and breast with the most vehement pain, of which afterwards she remained very sensible'.[141] Certain nuns extended the sexual metaphor to encompass a more permanent contract. In one vision, Catharine Burton saw herself marrying Christ:

> I seemed to be admitted to the spiritual marriage with my heavenly Spouse, which He Himself did declare, when, in His Sacred Humanity, He came to make His abode and habitation with me, as in His own palace, giving me to understand by clear and distinct words, that now these spiritual nuptials were completed He would make me partaker of his heavenly treasures and riches, giving part of them, even now, in my own hands, to dispose of them to my relations and friends.[142]

Burton understood that her mystical marriage would bestow upon her in spiritual terms all the rights and privileges gained by a secular wife through her husband's social position. The account makes an explicit analogy between the dignity bestowed upon both the earthly bride of inferior social status and her relatives through her marriage to a secular prince, and the benefits Burton's family and friends were to achieve through the nun's nuptials with Christ.[143] Thus, as women, nuns were able to appropriate metaphors which conformed with their gender to explain their experience of the divine. Furthermore, these images were drawn from the social reality of women's options in early modern society.

The expression of the English nuns' spirituality generally conformed to that of their medieval predecessors. Caroline Bynum argued that women's spiritual orientation towards the humanity of Christ, which led them to employ images of physicality, was continuous with their own ordinary experience of social inferiority. While for men characterisation of religious experience often entailed a reversal of both social position and gender (because the divine was accessed through empty vessels and the divine was often male), women operated within the realm of common female experience.[144] Certainly, in order to live a life of strict asceticism, nuns renounced the world, the privileges of their birth into gentry and aristocratic families, and the comfort of intimate human contact with parents, husbands and children. How-ever, they spoke of their association with Christ in images commensur-ate with their female gender; they perceived the divine as father, lover and bridegroom. Where the early modern English nuns differed from their medieval sisters was in their representations of Christ. He was always a male figure for them: the infant Jesus in the arms of the Virgin, their bridegroom, the suffering Christ on the cross. While he comforted them and allowed them to witness the signs of his incarnation and Passion, neither Christ nor God possessed maternal attributes. Jesus was rarely 'mother' in the writings of seventeenth-century English nuns.[145] Instead there was a clear emphasis upon the Virgin Mary as maternal comforter. While relationships with Christ and God the father were constantly depicted by the nuns in terms of interaction between women and their male relatives, the Virgin, and to a certain extent the female saints, fulfilled a distinctly feminine function. In visions Mary was most often seen with her infant son, or, if alone, she would remind the nun concerned of her monastic vows and obligations to Christ. Thus, the Virgin Mary became the nun's mother because of the religious woman's status as spouse of Christ.

This strictly gendered relationship between the mystic and those in heaven was most clearly delineated in the visions of Margaret Mostyn. Her devotion to the Virgin began when she was about six years of age. The young Margaret spent hours adorning a picture of Mary holding the infant Jesus with her bracelets and other ornaments. This image, coupled with saying her beads and other prayers to the mother of God, reassured her that she was under the Virgin's protection.[146] At the age of 11 or 12 she had her first vision of Christ in the eucharist and longed to receive him. Upon making her first communion these visions continued.[147] From this early age she desired only to be a nun but initial family opposition to the vocation, and then her own reluc-tance to enter the religious state, frustrated the plan until she was in her late teens. Significantly, it was the Virgin who assisted her by appearing with St Teresa to reassure the troubled girl that they would guide and protect her in the cloister.[148] Mostyn believed that Mary and Christ were present at her clothing, and when prior to her profession in 1645 she was having doubts about the monastic life, Christ again appeared to her and assured her that he would not forsake her.[149] Throughout the remainder of her life, Mostyn's visions of the Virgin and Christ con-tinued. Sometimes Mary would hand her the infant Jesus to hold; on other occasions she would be visited by the adult Christ displaying all the marks of his Passion, or as a member of the trinity.[150]

Margaret Mostyn's interaction with the divine reflected early modern notions of what constituted appropriate masculine and feminine behaviour. For her the authoritative male figure was God the father. During a vision in which the trinity entered her heart, she understood that she 'possessed in her soul her Father, Spouse and Comforter'.[151] Yet it was the alternating conceptions of Christ as either an infant or her spouse which revealed her sense of her own position. Mostyn either held Christ in her arms, or she was joined with him in her soul. While the adult Jesus appeared to her frequently, she seemed to be more comfortable with his embodiment as an infant. On one occasion when the Virgin called her to see the risen Christ on his heavenly throne, introducing him as Margaret's spouse, the nun drew back. Mary turned to her son and said, 'See she is more afraid of you now than when she enjoys you a Child in my arms.'[152] By the very nature of Christ's incarnation in her visions, it is obvious that the prioress felt most comfortable when she could adopt a maternal position in her interaction with him. While she had several visions in which Christ entered her heart, suggesting consummation of their relationship as spouse and bridegroom, Mostyn preferred to identify with the role of the Virgin who constantly appeared as a mediator between Margaret and her son, whether he was child or adult. Mary's role was clearly defined when she declared her position to Margaret: 'those who trust in me, and acknowledge me for their Mother, shall find by experience that I will carry them through this world in my arms'.[153]

As prioress it was Margaret Mostyn's duty to be 'mother' to her nuns. The power of female superiors was commonly couched in maternal imagery, so in her relationship with the infant Christ Mostyn was performing a familiar role. Yet, as I have suggested, monastic 'mothers' were authoritarian figures.[154] Thus, in choosing maternal imagery, Mostyn was assuming a powerful identity. Margaret's control was abundantly evident in several visions where she adopted an intermediary role. She prayed for nuns who were afflicted with devils, and acted as mediator between souls in purgatory and their relatives in the cloister.[155] The Carmelite mystic was by no means alone among the women who became abbesses in appropriating maternal imagery which had been applied to the 'mother-God' in medieval spiritual literature. Religious superiors were commonly likened to mother hens caring for their chickens, a popular image for Christ who compared himself with the hen who gathers her chicks under her wings for protection in Matthew 23:37.[156] Yet, the meaning of this simile went much further than mere scriptural allusion. In his analysis of the visions of sixteenth-century

Spanish mystic, Mother Juana de la Cruz, Ronald Surtz argues that the nun adopted the mother hen image in order to identify with the sufferings of Christ.[157] Margaret Mostyn's visions were replete with images which suggest that she performed a protective and redemptive role. Once she had been made subprioress, she had a series of visions of Christ with his cross. These culminated in a trance during which she felt Christ imprint his sufferings upon her heart.[158] The Carmelite's charismatic experiences therefore suggest that she constructed for herself a complex identity. She related to the male trinity as a daughter, spouse and mother, while seeming more comfortable with the Virgin Mary whom she considered her 'Mother and Sister'.[159] However, although she often assumed a passive position, she also appropriated a powerful maternal persona in her dealings with the infant Christ. Such postures of authority were commensurate with her experiences as a woman. As nun and prioress, Mostyn was well aware of women's potential to rule others, and to make representations on their behalf to patriarchal authorities.

Mysticism therefore empowered several English nuns to assume supernatural and earthly jurisdictions not open to all. Those who perfected mortification were liberated from the cloister into a divine discourse, which left them spiritually exhilarated and desperate to repeat the experience. Yet divine union encompassed more than the individual and God. The charismatic nun became a channel for heavenly favours to members of her community and lay folk outside the enclosure. She accordingly received publicity and authority seemingly at odds with the self-abnegation she had undergone to attain her elevated spiritual status, and incompatible with her gender. It was this disparity between the female monastic ideal of enclosed contemplation and the very public identity of the mystic which coloured the debate and conflict about the English convents' spirituality. As Alfonso Rodríguez and the opponents of Augustine Baker had implied, women's unmediated access to the divine enabled them to challenge their apostolate and appropriate, both vicariously and in reality, the activist piety enjoyed by the male religious orders. However, as in all other spheres of convent life, cloistered spirituality functioned more or less within the limits imposed by Trent and the nuns' clerical superiors. Hence the mystics couched their action within an acceptably humble and feminine discourse, and they submitted to the sometimes heavy-handed oversight of their spiritual directors. In a sense their charismatic experiences and reputation counted on acquiescence; those who neglected the discipline of mortification would be denied the favours of their divine spouse. Yet there was another dimension to the practice of regular piety which gave impetus to assiduous adherence to it. For the majority of women in the cloister the rituals of mortification constituted the central plank of their spirituality. Unlike the 'Marys' who excelled in prayer and abstraction, the 'Marthas'' piety encompassed the rituals and routines which punctuated their day from *matins* to *compline*. Although not so exalted as mysticism, this piety was considered an equally valid path to salvation. Moreover, by seeking God through work and other mechanical activities, the nuns' religiosity was not entirely at odds with the Jesuits' 'contemplative in action'. The next section will examine its operation in the English cloisters.

The pursuit of piety

In a comforting address to her religious community at Cambrai, the Benedictine abbess, Christina Brent, acknowledged that not everyone would attain heaven through mystical rapture. Instead God directed individuals along whichever path best suited their temperament and circumstances.[160] For reluctant nuns, the over-scrupulous, those who found meditative prayer impossible, and the officers and lay sisters distracted by household business, an acceptance of spiritual diversity and the reassurance that they might be saved via different channels was vital. Such women turned to piety, 'a regime of godliness, devotion or religious discipline', as an alternative route to heaven.[161] The pious nun injected religious meaning into every moment of her day, no matter where she was or what she was doing. Her formal monastic obligations and prayer might provide the opportunity for devotion, but she might equally dedicate her domestic chores and recreational periods to it. Constructing one's self and one's daily routine in accordance with holy principles was not unique to religious women, nor indeed to Catholics alone, but the importance of 'mortification' in a nun's religious formation, suggests that piety underpinned monastic spirituality. Moreover, in a Church increasingly orientating towards ministry, the active principle implicit in piety had a particular resonance for contemplatives. The individual and collective exertion necessary for reforming characters and performing good works presented them with an effective paradigm for action. While certain women embarked on missionary and political ventures from within their enclosures, most nuns practised 'active in contemplation' within the compass of their daily religious and temporal obligations.

Monastic rules and statutes prescribed the mechanisms of piety, articulating the virtues, rituals and structure of individual and collective behaviour. The 'Blue Nuns' were recommended to heed their constitutions 'as most serviceable to their advancement in their way of Perfection'.[162] Likewise, Thomas Carre recommended his translation of the Augustinian rule to the Paris nuns, as 'the Rule and Measure of your actions'.[163] The cloisters' prescriptive handbooks outlined the desirable religious qualities of humility, modesty, charity and obedience, how they might best be attained, and the way they were manifested in the pious sister. The Benedictine statutes commenced with a chapter titled 'piety', which focused specifically upon religious devotion, defined as prayer, meditation, confession, communion and mortification, before detailing the essential virtues and ordering of monastic life.[164] Other constitutions concentrated more intently upon the daily routine of prayer, work and recreation, prescribing the obligations and desirable comportment of everyone from the abbess to the novices.[165] Implicit in these instructions was the principle that all activities must be undertaken in a religious spirit, thus piety breached purely devotional boundaries to infiltrate every aspect of monastic existence. In other words, just as the Bruges Franciscans were required to arrive in the choir early 'to prepare their heartes to God, and offer up their intentions unto him', so too did they have to 'eate with all modestie and silence attending to the reading' in the refectory.[166] The prescriptive literature therefore promoted the sister who followed her rule diligently and led an exemplary life as the epitome of monastic piety.

The extent to which religious women subscribed to such blueprints for godliness is evident in their writings. Spiritual advice, letters, chronicles and obituaries all provide some clue as to how far the nuns internalised it. Chastising her nuns in the weekly convent chapter, Abbess Christina Brent of Cambrai reminded them that 'according to the rules of religious mortification, the whole lives of religious persons, should be lives of mortification, silence humilitie charity and the practise of all vertues as you may sufficiently see in our holy rule'.[167] Individuals took such advice to heart. In her spiritual diary, Barbara Constable wrote despairingly of ever succeeding in a pious life:

> O when shall I by true and perfect mortification, overcome my evil inclinations and passions? When shall I go about conversion of manners seriously as I have promised. It is now almost ten years... since I promised the conversion of my manners, and obedience according to the rule, but I cannot perceive as yet that I have done any considerable thing towards it; when therefore, O my God, shall I begin? Surely it is high time.[168]

Alexia Grey of Ghent was so convinced that the Benedictine rule would guide her and her sisters to perfection that she published an English translation in 1632. In her preface to Abbess Eugenia Poulton, she pointed to the innumerable saints, church leaders, and 'purest Virgines, fruites, which this holy rule, as a most comfortable sunne, hath produced, fostered, and brought up to inlighten and illustratt, both with word, writinges and examples, of singular sanctitye'.[169] However, the clearest indication that the rule and statutes shaped collective and individual piety comes from obituary notices. Every convent was required to keep a book of the dead to record the passing of all members. Although the death notices varied in length and detail depending upon religious order and house, compiler (usually the abbess), and rank of the deceased woman, they invariably documented the main tenor of her piety. At Ghent, Abbess Mary Roper, who died in 1650, was praised for her 'Prudence, Modesty, Zeal, Gravity, recollection silence, Devotion and Charity to all, especially to the poor'. In 1657, Cornelia Corham, a former sacristine, cellarer, and procuratrix was remembered for 'Devotion to our blessed Lady, Abstinence, modesty, meekness, frugall poverty and a neat cleanlyness'. The lay sister, Catherine (Teresa) Matlock, was commended in 1650 for her 'Generall charity, a Religious simplicity and obedience to others, having the Rule in perfection'.[170] Although formulaic and constructed in accordance with a house's statutes and devotional orientation, the obituaries record an individual's successful (and sometimes failed) application of the sacred in prayer and in daily life. They also reveal that communities accepted action, like contemplation, as intrinsic to their religious identity.

The prescriptive literature and death notices show that first and foremost true piety constituted fervent application to all religious observances. In the Brussels Benedictine statutes each nun was enjoined to spend daily an hour in 'mentall prayer' beyond the obligations of the divine office and sacred reading. Significantly, those who lacked an aptitude for meditation were exhorted to spend this time 'eather in vocall prayer or in sume other devout imployment'.[171] However, the statutes affirmed that piety entailed not simply the act, but also the spirit in which it was performed. The Third Order Franciscans were exhorted to undertake their choir obligations solemnly, and those found wanting were to be punished, for disruptive attitudes and behaviour 'doe ill become Religious persons'. Accordingly, all choir nuns had to arrive early 'to prepare their heartes to God, and offer up their intentions unto him'.[172] The Benedictine constitutions advised nuns that the divine office should be conducted with 'due modisty and desent composition of ther carrage... they must pronounce each word with moderat leasure, distinctly, and truly with so loude voyce that they may be heard and understoode by those that ar out of the Quire'.[173] Such decrees were evidently necessary. In 1620, during a visitation, Archbishop Mathias Hovius of Mechelen reminded the Brussels Benedictines about attendance at religious services and appropriate silence.[174] Similarly in the 1670s, Abbess Christina Brent of Cambrai reprimanded her nuns for laxity in formal religious observances. She complained that some came late to the divine office, others laughed and whispered during services, and the overall standard of answering at high mass was so poor that lay worshipers in the church had noted the apparent lack of dedication.[175] These common breaches in collective piety guaranteed accolades to individuals who applied themselves zealously at the formal ceremonies. Catherine Sheldon who died at Cambrai in 1650 was singled out for her 'great love for regular observances, particularly the office of the quire' which she ardently attended.[176] Likewise, in 1654 at Nieuport, the Franciscan, Frances (Frances Clare) Massey, was praised for her constant devotion and contribution to the divine office.[177] Moreover, communal laxity was not universal. When the earl of Perth passed through Bruges in 1694 he was impressed by the Augustinian nuns' performance at *compline*.[178] In the 1650s Charles Séguier, the French chancellor, patronised the Paris Augustinians not only for their music, but also the dignified manner in which they conducted their services.[179]

The pious regulation of conduct extended beyond religious duties into secular activities. The Augustinian rule advised 'nor are you to receave foode with your mouth onely, but also the word of God by your eares'.[180] Thus, the everyday actions of dressing, eating, working, and recreating became sacred rituals. A Franciscan ceremonial manual detailed the morning rite of dressing. Washing symbolised the cleansing of sin. While tying the cord around her waist, a nun recited, 'Garde me o lord with the girdle of fortitude that manfully I may persevere in thy service.' The scapular was invoked as a reminder of Christ's passion. Finally the veil and cloak represented her complete separation from the world to become a committed spouse of Christ. Upon drawing the cloak around her shoulders she intoned, 'Our Lord cover me with the cloake of puritye and chastitye that no lover but Jesus I may admitt.'[181] Partaking of daily bodily sustenance also took on a holy aura. In the refectory dining commenced and ended with prayer, and while eating a public devotional reading piously focused the diners' attention and guarded against idle chatter. Even the menu and frequency of meals varied according to the liturgical calendar of feasts and fasts.[182] The conduct of monastic work was similarly sacralised. In the workroom nuns were encouraged to stitch in silence, and their labours were accompanied by prayers. The 'Blue Nuns' commenced with a *Veni Creator*, listened to a 'pious Lecture' for the next 15 minutes, and mutely applied their needles until concluding with a *Te Deum*.[183] The Paris Augustinians were advised 'while their hands are busied about their worke, let their minds be exercised in good and holy thoughtes'. To assist they were to murmur 'fervent aspirations' and prayers.[184] Labourers in the kitchens and laundry were similarly encouraged to accompany their chores with divine invocations. While washing the dishes, the Franciscans had to recite a *Miserere* and a *de Profundis*, and at the conclusion they kneeled bare-headed together to beg forgiveness of each other's faults.[185] Even recreation was imbued with spiritual meaning. The Franciscans were permitted to chat by the fire, but they had to 'charitably and Religiously give way to one another' to share the warmth. The Ghent Benedictines were bidden to speak moderately, but only about spiritually edifying matters.[186]

Obituaries and chronicles suggest that individual and communal piety were crafted in accordance with these official expectations. At St Monica's, the Augustinians fasted one day per week, and their consumption of meat reflected the liturgical calendar.[187] In addition to this collective observance, certain nuns further limited their diet as part of their personal godliness. Margaret (Winefrid) Blundell, who was professed in 1615, was over strict with herself, scrupling that she ate too much. The sisters assumed that her small appetite matched her petite stature, but upon her death in 1647 they conceded her 'vertue' had instead shaped her skinny frame and poor health.[188] At Louvain's daughter-house at Bruges, Xaveria Stanley likewise mortified her body through an inadequate diet. She reputedly ate only scraps of food, pretending they nourished her sufficiently.[189] Other women meticulously regulated their conduct. At Ghent, Mary Trevelyan, who died in 1634, firmly adhered to rules regarding restricted access to the dormitory during periods of silence and formal prayer. Although her business was often in rooms beyond the sleeping quarters, she always chose the longer route through the kitchen.[190] To guard against idle chatter while attending her temporal affairs, Abbess Mary Roper murmured a *de Profundis* for the souls of the faithful departed as she passed through the monastic buildings.[191] The widow, Dorothy (Bridget) Dorvolie Gildrige, who was professed in 1640 at the age of 60, took to heart the guidelines for the workroom. She memorised part of her morning meditation and recited it during the afternoon work session. Although blind she refused to sit idle, instead learning to knit, and occupied her free hours in that 'humble work in Doing charitys' for her sisters.[192] Such women concurred with Abbess Christina Brent who recommended that her Cambrai sisters offer 'themselves readely simply and entirely to him in the performance of each dutie how small soever'.[193] Others went further, transforming their work into a form of religious observance which incited others to reverence. Ghent's Elizabeth Bradbury disliked her duties at the grate which involved interaction with the outside world, but her quiet and efficient manner so impressed the lay people with whom she dealt that they deemed her a saint. Likewise, as sacristine 'she order'd all things with Exquisite nateness . . . and [made] such pritty and curious works for the sepulcher in tenebre times accommodating the Alter and all pertaining to the church, so clean, Desent and handsome, that it moved to Devotion.'[194] Through the meticulous performance of her household offices Elizabeth Bradbury attained credit similar to that enjoyed by the mystics.

Nowhere was the identification of work with godliness so crucial as it was for those women who had entered monasticism with physical, rather than spiritual, labour as their vocation. Lay sisters were reminded that 'they are taken into Religion to assist the Quire-Sisters by their work', and the toil of housework reduced their opportunity for prayer.[195] Ascribing religious meaning to their duties therefore constituted a vital aspect of many sisters' devotion. Scholastica Higginson of the Pontoise Benedictine cloister was applauded upon her death in 1730 for 'having a marvelous art att mingling Martha and Mary together' in her daily duties.[196] Likewise, Gravelines Poor Clare, Helen Bernard Lasley, was remembered in 1703 for 'her diligent employing each moment . . . in the service of holy Religion, perseverantly joining prayer with Labour, and never making a reply to what was required of her'.[197] The spiritual dimension of housework was particularly vital for lay sisters like Dorothy Skrimshaw, who was professed at Ghent in 1642. Addicted to prayer, Skrimshaw had assumed that in the convent she would do little else, and she was distressed to discover the true nature of her vocation. However, the reluctant lay sister persevered, whenever possible stealing time from work to spend in the chapel. This unsatisfactory state of affairs continued for three years until a divine revelation persuaded Skrimshaw that 'it was an errour not to find God and his holy will in everything ordain'd by superiours'. She accordingly transformed herself into a 'True saint Labouring in the hardest works Continually, never desiring or admitting rest'. Sadly, Skrimshaw died not long after this reformation, however she was remembered as an edifying example of monastic obedience.[198] Moreover, it was no coincidence that the Ghent lay sister was enlightened during a Jesuit-led retreat. Ignatius Loyola had insisted that one should 'find God in all things' not just prayer, and the Society specialised in a 'spirituality of service'.[199] Although their ministry differed from the strict Jesuit meaning of 'contemplative in action', Ignatian piety presented traditional monasticism with a viable alternative for lay sisters, and others distracted by temporal offices.

Identification of the holy in secular affairs was vital too for choir nuns who were unable to fulfil the requirements of their vocation either physically or spiritually. Women who through illness or advanced years could not attend formal devotions contributed in other ways. Louvain's sickly Frances Burrows possessed a weak voice and was not able to contribute adequately to the choir. She compensated for her shortcomings in this area by doing 'willingly what she could in the service of the convents, as looking to the workmen or such like employments'.[200] Choir nuns who found it difficult to meditate, and those suffering periods of spiritual desolation, also required some other means by which to achieve spiritual fulfilment. Margaret Tremayne of the Louvain Augustinians, who died in 1624, was much beloved by her sisters for her excellence in temporal duties. Tremayne had channelled her energies into 'exterior things' because throughout her 26 years of profession she had never been able to attain 'the gift of prayer'.[201] Another Augustinian, Mary Clopton, who likewise lacked 'so great a gift in prayer' sought comfort in her office as sacristine. Prior to her death in 1653 she reputedly derived great solace from working for God in the very place where his presence was most certain.[202] Piety further compensated those who doubted their salvation. Although encouraged to pray to combat their scruples, many also turned to more tangible acts of devotion to overcome their fears. Catherine Sheldon, who died at Cambrai in 1650, mitigated her 'many interior conflicts and temptations' by embracing the Benedictine rule's prescribed religious virtues and dedicating herself to regular observances.[203] Even women who had attained divine union experienced spiritual desolation. Clare Vaughan of Pontoise suffered endless scruples about her commitment to God, and despaired of ever adhering perfectly to the rule. She resorted to such an intense pious regime that she was made novice mistress in the belief that her example would incite others to imitate her.[204] Thus, Vaughan's godly routine to combat periods of spiritual drought advantaged the convent almost as much as her charismatic experiences.

The communal benefits of piety ensured that it, like mysticism, propelled successful practitioners into the limelight. Nowhere was this more apparent than in women whose talents enhanced a cloister's spiritual and economic circumstances. Worldly skills which should otherwise have been stifled by the rigours of 'mortification' were applauded if they served the convent well. Mary Southcott, who died at Ghent in 1641 was renowned for her sharp wit, grasp of Latin, writing technique, good speaking and singing voice, and musical ability.[205] Likewise, Mary Coyney possessed the best and strongest singing voice at St Monica's, where the choir reputedly suffered upon her death in 1672.[206] Directing one's talents towards the common good thus constituted an important element of piety. The musically inclined were particularly well placed to foster collective devotion, and even to attract external credit, as the renowned example of the Paris Augustinian choir made clear. Certain adroit musicians garnered widespread acclaim. At Bruges, the Franciscan, Anne (Cecilia Mark) Smith, not only assisted the choir, she also drew lay people to attend religious services. Smith had been accepted by the convent in 1664 for her 'most delicat Voice, and Excellent skill to teach' and she served its musical needs for the next 50 years.[207] Accompanied by other gifted musicians, like the sisters Anne (Seraphia of St Winefrid) and Frances (Frances Henrietta Stephen) Garnons, who between them played the organ, violin, viol de gamba and sea trumpet, Smith enhanced the Franciscans' reputation by singing at divine services and special performances for visitors. In 1671, an English tourist, John Walker was treated to a recital by the Franciscan choir. He described Anne Smith's voice as 'ravishing', while Frances Garnons played the sea trumpet 'to admiration'.[208] When the earl of Perth visited the convent in 1694, he was entertained with a hymn and motet, commenting that Anne Smith 'sung the best of any woman I have heard in these Countries'.[209] Upon her death in 1715, Smith was said to have 'render'd by her voice so greate honour to God and service to this holy Community that the like hath never preceded her'.[210] Music as a form of religious expression and prayer enabled nuns like Mary Southcott, Mary Coyney, Anne Smith and the Garnons sisters to be active in contemplation. Like their sisters who transformed personal comportment, daily rituals and physical labour into acts of devotion, they manipulated the terms of their vocation to encompass something of the spirit of early modern activist spirituality.

The dynamism implicit in piety, like that in mysticism, shows clearly that, despite enclosure, the English nuns were not constricted by their contemplative vocation. Instead they pursued the full gamut of reformed Catholicism's spiritual options from within its parameters. The obituaries and other literature articulate the tremendous diversity in aims, ability and achievement among cloisters and individuals. Women of an otherworldly bent were encouraged in their charismatic religiosity, while those who yearned for a more practical calling could find meaning within their household offices and daily activities. Although mystical activity attracted greater prestige, the assiduous pursuit of piety could confer sanctity too. Moreover, both spiritual paths fostered not simply personal and communal devotion, they also contributed to the English mission. As exemplars and intercessors, the mystics became spiritual conduits between their cloister and the lay communities beyond its walls. Paragons of piety similarly advertised their convent's holiness, and focused secular attention on religious women's proximity to the divine. The laity therefore sought contact with the nuns; either indirectly via their devotional literature and attendance at their religious services; or directly at the grate and in the boarding facilities and schools. This intercourse facilitated the transmission of the cloisters' religiosity locally and into England. As well as sustaining lay piety, it promoted the benefits of Catholicism to Protestants and to the less committed adherents of Rome. Although the barrier of clausura ensured that in most instances the nuns' spiritual direction and proselytising was vicarious, the nuns nonetheless understood, like Teresa of Avila, that theirs was an active apostolate; their missionary work simply took another form to that of the clergy and orders like Mary Ward's Institute.

The English nuns' willingness to choose and fight for particular spiritual schools reflects their perception that contemplation took many guises. Already limited by strict enclosure, those who defied their superiors to uphold the methodology they found efficacious were fighting for their freedom to interpret their contemplative vocation. At the height of the Brussels mêlée the rebels sought permission to establish another Benedictine cloister where they would be able to follow their understanding of their rule and constitutions, which they believed had been corrupted under Abbess Percy.[211] Abbess Catherine Gascoigne of Cambrai, who unswervingly maintained her allegiance to the methods of Augustine Baker, spoke for all early modern contemplatives who understood the complexity of their vocation and the importance of a spirituality which facilitated it, in her submission to the Benedictine General Chapter of 1633. She wrote:

My prayer I know not how to expresse, but it seemes to me to be a longing and vehement desire of the soule thirsting after the presence of God, seeking and intending only and wholy his will and pleasure with as much purity of intention as my imperfection will permitt... This way of tending and aspiring toward God by Love and affection, doth in no sorte hinder a soule from the due performance of her other duties, obligations and externall obediences, much lesse doth it cause her to neglect misprise or disesteeme of her superiors their ordinations and actions (as hath bene feared) for it doth teach and cause her to observe and performe the more cheerfully readily and with more purity of intention, regarding God and his will in the doing of them rather then the workes that she doth. And a soule that is caried in this maner with a great and affectuous inclination towads God carefully observing the divine call and motions, and abstracting herselfe from impertinences and all things which doe not belong to her to doe or undergoe, she will be able to make use of all things in their due time to her advancement in spirit, for nothing is required of us in o[u]r state of Life but that if we know how to make right use of it, it will further us in our way, and especially the divine office and service of the Quier, as being an exercise more immediately belonging to the praise and worshipe of God, so doe I most commonly finde it a great helpe and incitement therto, except when the body is too much weared or otherwise indisposed. And this exercise of love seemes to me to be the best meanes and way to purchase all vertues.[212]

Conclusion

The spiritual, political and economic vitality of the post-Reformation English cloisters belies their historical anonymity. As active players in the quest to maintain English Catholicism, and determined participants in promoting (and modifying) Church reform of the religious life and post-Tridentine devotion, the nuns' endeavours were acknowledged by their contemporaries; but they have failed to resonate subsequently in the scholarship on the English and Catholic reformations. This absence reflects the preoccupations of early modern scholars, who for a long time prioritised the political implementation and consequences of the reforms. Debates have since centred upon the processes and successes of confessionalisation in the towns and villages of England and Europe. The English historiography has focused upon the extent to which the Protestantisation of the populace was impeded by Catholic conservatism, and on the role of the Continentally-trained missionary priests in shaping the contours of English Catholic belief and practice. The experiences and contributions of the nuns, who did not physically partake in the missionary effort because they were locked up in convents across the Channel, have been absent from these scholarly deliberations. In Europe, the early modern explosion of female monasticism was more difficult to ignore, and ecclesiastical and social historians have discussed its economic, social and religious dimensions. More recently, scholars interested in gender have advanced our understanding of the convent's civic and cultural significance. Although the full extent of spiritual interaction between the highly regulated monastic enclosure and the confessionalised society beyond its walls and grilles demands further consideration, an ever-increasing interest in contemplative nuns promises fruitful analyses of the religious women's influence over institutional and lay piety in the future.

To date the most stimulating studies of the early modern convent have been grounded in the cloister's relationship with its surrounding local community. This orientation highlights the anomalous situation of the English houses, which were in a liminal position – geographically separate from the families and English Catholic population they served, and culturally distinct from the neighbourhoods in which they were situated. The nuns' isolation from both communities not only accounts for their historical marginalisation, it also raises interesting questions about the convents' function in the overall scheme of English Catholic nonconformity. The institutions clearly operated in totally different circumstances to European religious establishments which were intimately linked to their sustaining community both physically via kinship connections and their buildings' presence in its midst, and psychologically through shared religious, dynastic and civic ideologies. As I have argued, the English nuns identified closely with their co-religionists in England, and they were supported financially by them, but this relationship was truncated by distance. Thus, although the exiled houses performed many of the economic, social and symbolic roles undertaken by their Continental counterparts, they could never fulfil them to the same extent as cloisters residing in the midst of their familial and civic supporters and beneficiaries. Like other English Catholics, who were not unified under a single leader, and therefore tended to be fragmented geographically and socially throughout England, the convents were seemingly dislocated pockets of resistance to the Protestant Church and state. But this does not mean that the cloisters performed no role for the Catholic minority, beyond comprising convenient economic and social institutions where their daughters might live securely and honourably. Rather, the nuns' schooling and boarding facilities ensured open channels of exchange with their homeland, with kin moving backwards and forwards between the convents and England. Moreover, the recusants expressed their nonconformity and their piety through the professions and prayers of their daughters in the expatriate religious establishments, which offered tangible evidence that Catholicism was surviving, even thriving, in the face of an enduring Protestant ascendancy. Hence the convents helped to unify the disparate elements which comprised the English Catholic community. They did so socially through family use of parlours, schools and guest houses, politically through their relatives' collective disobedience in patronising these facilities and the cloisters themselves, and spiritually via an unwavering belief in the efficacy of the nuns' devotions on their kin's and country's behalf.

The nuns' isolation from the community with which they identified nationally and spiritually also stamped a particular character upon the expatriate religious institutions. Separation from their homeland invariably moulded them into tight-knit groups which fostered the traditions of their own and their friends 'persecution' at the hands of the Protestant authorities. The convents' registers, annals, letters, obituaries, and spiritual obligations recorded and revered the stories of personal and family suffering for immediate consumption and for future generations. Thus, the identity of individuals and cloisters was bound closely with their degree of proximity to the English martyrs and others who had sacrificed much for the preservation of their faith. If any one thing united the religious communities, it was this sense of confessional adversity and the agony of exile from kin and co-religionists. This common heritage of affliction, coupled with a web of kinship connections among different houses, drew the potential monastic competitors together into a loose congregation of mutually supportive independent institutions, which was reflected in exchanges of stories, alms and prayers. For example, when the Gravelines Poor Clare convent was badly damaged by the 1654 arsenal explosion, the nuns' vivid account of their terror and misfortune was circulated among houses.[1] Similarly when part of the Paris Augustinian nuns' choir and church collapsed in the eighteenth century, Prioress Lucy Herbert of the Bruges cloister directed alms towards its reconstruction.[2] Of course, the shared traditions did not always secure such sisterly support, as the squabble among several Benedictine cloisters regarding the future of the Ypres house showed.[3] Nor did it ensure internal cohesion. As other scholars have noted, many of the internal disputes over governance and spiritual matters were grounded (in part) in the rivalries which fragmented English Catholics. While, as I have argued, the furore at Brussels and its counterparts elsewhere were far more complex than simply a re-enactment of English clerical tensions, they might not have become so contentious had the cloisters not identified closely with the troubles and aspirations of their co-religionists across the Channel. Likewise, the disputes' escalation beyond the enclosure would have been less likely, had the nuns' families not had such vested spiritual and political interests in their daughters' convents. Thus, the English cloisters replicated the symbiotic relationship that existed between Continental houses and their locales, but they did so from a considerable distance signified both by miles and a distinctive *mentalité* shaped by the experiences of religious dissent.

Yet, despite their primary affiliation with England, it was impossible for the English convents to remain entirely disconnected from their local environs. They did not recruit many indigenous women and thereby maintained an aloofness which might well have been mitigated by kinship ties between their inmates and the local populace. However, the cloisters' tenuous economic circumstances, the need to do business with local tradespeople and merchants, the importance of patrons who had influence with regional religious and civic authorities, and the physical presence in towns of their buildings and church services, inevitably garnered relationships with their neighbours. The dependence of some houses upon local charity at certain junctures, and the bountiful munificence of benefactors, like the Paris Augustinians' Mme Fontenais, revealed the importance and benefits of establishing indigenous connections. However, while the benefits for the nuns were obvious, the townspeople's willingness to assist the foreigners raises some interesting questions about the early modern convent's function for the wider civic community. Without the bonds and obligations of kinship, the English cloisters did not constitute the same kind of moral, social and civic resource that locally founded and populated convents did, so why did the citizenry support them? There was clearly a degree of compassion for well-born women exiled from their heretical homeland, and the nuns played upon this sympathy whenever they required financial assistance. However, it is evident that the English houses were incorporated into existing networks of local lay piety. In the absence of kinship ties, the alms, pious bequests, and attendance at the nuns' services point to a continuing respect for contemplative women's prayers, despite the missionary imperatives and sacramental orientation of post-Tridentine piety. Moreover, it is possible that for the local populace the expatriate convents provided tangible evidence of the horrific consequences of Protestantism which had rendered the nuns religious exiles, and their example accordingly bolstered individual and communal resolve to uphold the veracity of Rome's teaching. Indeed, perceptions of how they had suffered for their faith, may well have invested them with a spiritual kudos not shared by locally-born nuns and their religious houses. Thus, although they maintained their distance, the nuns were very much a part of the local landscape and confessional *mentalité*.

A final question remains regarding the convents' wider significance for our understanding of the early modern Church and society. What can the English nuns possibly reveal of women's experience in the seventeenth century, particularly the situation of English women? Like many others of their gender and social status, the religious women successfully combined the dual pursuits of salvation and household management. They did so in the face of religious, economic and political upheaval, relying upon their faith in divine intervention, coupled with their own resourcefulness and ability to negotiate with local ecclesiastical and lay bodies, to stave off ultimate failure. Although their religious profession, exile, and independence from immediate patriarchal supervision set them apart from most of their female compatriots (and indeed other European women), they nonetheless governed themselves and their domestic affairs using the skills and strategies wielded by lay women in gentry and aristocratic households. They lacked husbands and children, but still conceptualised and ordered their convents in familial terms, as well as forming close and supportive relationships with God, one another, kin and friends. Like Continental nuns, they joined their convents for diverse voluntary and involuntary economic, social and religious reasons. For the most part, they made the best of their incarceration behind convent walls, negotiating the terms of their existence with clerical and lay bodies outside and, in the process, achieving spiritual and political stature in the wider community. In many respects therefore the convents can be considered as microcosms of the post-Tridentine Church and elite society. Thus, far from the historically marginal institutions and women they have hitherto been, the English contemplative cloisters and nuns attest to the importance of the convent as a key to understanding the early modern family, Church and state. The nuns' distinctive separation from the usual spheres of the domestic household and royal court bring into sharp relief the myriad ways women organised their domestic and spiritual lives, and moved beyond 'traditional' female roles to engage in secular and religious politics. Accordingly, the post-Reformation English nuns need to be integrated more fully into the histories of early modern women, religion, politics and society in both England and Europe.

Notes

Introduction

1 J. Mush, *An Abstracte of the Life and Martirdome of Mistres Margaret Clitherow* (Mechelen, 1619), sig. A2–A2v.

2 *Troubles of Our Catholic Forefathers Related by Themselves*, ed. J. Morris (London, 1877), vol. 3, p. 432; *The Chronicle of the English Augustinian Canonesses Regular of the Lateran, at St Monica's in Louvain (now at St Augustine's Priory, Newton Abbot, Devon) 1548–1644*, ed. A. Hamilton, hereafter *Chronicle of St Monica's* (London, 1904), vol. 1, pp. 33–4.

3 *Chronicle of St Monica's*, vol. 1, pp. 16–17, 33, 46–55, 80–4, 175–9, 189–90, 205–6; vol. 2, pp. 164–8.

4 H. Peters, *Mary Ward: A World In Contemplation*, trans. H. Butterfield (Leominster, 1994); J. Cameron, *A Dangerous Innovator: Mary Ward 1585–1645* (Sydney, 2000); M. Wright, *Mary Ward's Institute: The Struggle for Identity* (Sydney, 1997); P. Guilday, *The English Catholic Refugees on the Continent 1558–1795* (London, 1914), pp. 163–214; *St Mary's Convent, Micklegate Bar, York (1686–1887)*, ed. H. J. Coleridge (London, 1887).

5 Their publications on the history and archives of convents and individuals are too numerous to list, but the principal journals include: *Recusant History; Downside Review; Ampleforth Journal; Essex Recusant; London Recusant; Northern Catholic History; Staffordshire Catholic History; Catholic Archives*. See also the CRS records and monographs series. The two standard studies of the convents abroad are Guilday, *Catholic Refugees*; and B. Whelan, *Historic English Convents of Today: The Story of the English Cloisters in France and Flanders in Penal Times* (London, 1936).

6 M. J. Havran, *The Catholics of Caroline England* (Stanford, Ca., 1962); P. McGrath, *Papists and Puritans Under Elizabeth I* (London, 1967); J. Bossy, *The English Catholic Community, 1570–1850* (London, 1975); A Pritchard, *Catholic Loyalism in Elizabethan England* (London, 1979); C. Haigh, 'From Monopoly to Minority: Catholicism in Early Modern England', *Transactions of the Royal Historical Society*, 31 (1982), pp. 129–47; M. L. Carrafiello, 'English Catholicism and the Jesuit Mission of 1580–1581', *HJ*, 37 (1994), pp. 761–74. For an overview of the debates, see A. Dures, *English Catholicism 1558–1642* (London, 1983); and M. A. Mullett, *Catholics in Britain and Ireland, 1558–1829* (Basingstoke, 1998), pp. 2–26.

7 D. Mathew, *Catholicism in England 1535–1935: Portrait of a Minority: Its Culture and Tradition* (London, 1936); J. Bossy, 'The Character of Elizabethan Catholicism', in *Crisis in Europe, 1560–1660*, ed. T. Aston (London, 1965), pp. 223–46; C. Haigh, *Reformation and Resistance in Tudor Lancashire* (Cambridge, 1975); J. C. H. Aveling, *The Handle and the Axe: The Catholic Recusants in England from Reformation to Emancipation* (London, 1976); Bossy, *Catholic Community*; C. Haigh, 'The Continuity of Catholicism in the English Reformation', *P&P*, 93 (1981), pp. 37–69; Dures, *English Catholicism*. For a good overview of the

historiography, see A. R. Muldoon, 'Recusants, Church-Papists, and "Comfortable" Missionaries: Assessing the Post-Reformation English Catholic Community', *CHR*, 86 (2000), pp. 242–57.

8 C. Hibbard, 'Early Stuart Catholicism: Revisions and Re-revisions', *Journal of Modern History*, 52 (1980), pp. 1–34; C. Hibbard, *Charles I and the Popish Plot* (Chapel Hill, NC, 1983); A. Walsham, *Church Papists: Catholicism, Conformity and Confessional Polemic in Early Modern England* (Woodbridge, 1993), pp. 73–99.

9 Mullett, *Catholics in Britain*, pp. 82–3.

10 E. Power, *Medieval English Nunneries, c.1275–1525* (Cambridge, 1922); S. K. Elkins, *Holy Women of Twelfth Century England* (Chapel Hill, NC, 1988); S. Thompson, *Women Religious: The Founding of English Nunneries after the Norman Conquest* (Oxford, 1991); R. Gilchrist, *Gender and Material Culture: the Archaeology of Religious Women* (London, 1994); M. Oliva, *The Convent and the Community in Late Medieval England: Female Monasteries in the Diocese of Norwich, 1350–1540* (Woodbridge, 1998); K. Cooke, 'The English Nuns and the Dissolution', in *The Cloister and the World: Essays in Medieval History in Honour of Barbara Harvey*, ed. J. Blair and B. Golding (Oxford, 1996), pp. 287–301.

11 M. Norman, 'Dame Gertrude More and the English Mystical Tradition', *RH*, 13 (1976), pp. 196–211; R. Warnicke, *Women of the English Renaissance and Reformation* (Westport, Conn., 1983), pp. 173–7; S. Bowerbank, 'Gertrude More and the Mystical Perspective', *Studia Mystica*, 9 (1986), pp. 34–46; I. Grundy, 'Women's History? Writings by English Nuns', in *Women, Writing, History 1640–1740*, ed. I. Grundy and S. Wiseman (London, 1992), pp. 126–38; P. Crawford, *Women and Religion in England 1500–1720* (London, 1993), pp. 63–4, 83–5; J. K. McNamara, *Sisters in Arms: Catholic Nuns through Two Millennia* (Cambridge, Mass., 1996), pp. 448–9, 462, 491, 496–7; H. Wolfe, 'Reading Bells and Loose Papers: Reading and Writing Practices of the English Benedictine Nuns of Cambrai and Paris', in *Early Modern Women's Manuscript Writings*, ed. V. Burke and J. Gibson (Aldershot, 2002).

12 D. L. Latz, *'Glow-Worm Light': Writings of Seventeenth-Century Recusant Women from Original Manuscripts* (Salzburg, 1989); *The Tragedy of Mariam The Fair Queen of Jewry with The Lady Falkland: Her Life by One of her Daughters*, ed. B. Weller and M. W. Ferguson (Berkeley, Ca., 1994); *Women's Worlds in Seventeenth-Century England: A Sourcebook*, ed. P. Crawford and L. Gowing (London, 2000), pp. 51–3, 54–7; *The Early Modern Englishwoman: A Facsimile Library of Essential Works*, ed. B. S. Travitsky and P. Cullen, vol. 13, *Recusant Translators: Elizabeth Cary and Alexia Grey* (Aldershot, 2000); *Elizabeth Cary, Lady Falkland: Life and Letters*, ed. H. Wolfe, RTM vol. 4, MRTS vol. 230 (Cambridge and Tempe, AZ, 2001).

13 K. Norberg, 'The Counter Reformation and Women: Religious and Lay', in *Catholicism in Early Modern History: A Guide to Research*, ed. J. W. O'Malley (St Louis, 1988), p. 134.

14 G. Zarri, 'Ursula and Catherine: The Marriage of Virgins in the Sixteenth Century', in *Creative Women in Medieval and Early Modern Italy: A Religious and Artistic Renaissance*, ed. E. A. Matter and J. Coakley (Philadelphia, 1994), pp. 237–78; G. Zarri, 'Living Saints: A Typology of Female Sanctity in the Early Sixteenth Century', in *Women and Religion in Medieval and Renaissance*

Italy, ed. D. Bornstein and R. Rusconi (Chicago, 1996), pp. 219–303; G. Zarri, 'Gender, Religious Institutions and Social Discipline: The Reform of the Regulars', in *Gender and Society in Renaissance Italy*, ed. J. C. Brown and R. C. Davis (London, 1998), pp. 193–212; *Women and Faith: Catholic Religious Life in Italy from Late Antiquity to the Present*, ed. L. Scaraffia and G. Zarri (Cambridge, Mass., 1999). For a review of this literature, see S. Evangelisti, 'Wives, Widows, and Brides of Christ: Marriage and the Convent in the Historiography of Early Modern Italy', *HJ*, 43 (2000), pp. 233–47.

15   R. Burr Litchfield, 'Demographic Characteristics of Florentine Patrician Families, Sixteenth to Nineteenth Centuries', *Journal of Economic History*, 29 (1969), pp. 191–205; R. C. Trexler, 'Le célibat à la fin du Moyen Age: les religieuses de Florence', *Annales ESC*, 27 (1972), pp. 1329–50 (trans. 'Celibacy in the Renaissance: The Nuns of Florence', in *Dependence in Context in Renaissance Florence* (Binghamton, NY, 1994), pp. 343–72); V. Cox, 'The Single Self: Feminist Thought and the Marriage Market in Early Modern Venice', *RQ*, 48 (1995), pp. 513–81; E. A. Lehfeldt, 'Convents as Litigants: Dowry and Inheritance Disputes in Early Modern Spain', *Journal of Social History*, 33 (2000), pp. 645–64.

16   K. J. P. Lowe, 'Patronage and Territoriality in Early Sixteenth-Century Florence', *Renaissance Studies*, 7 (1993), pp. 258–71; H. Hills, 'Iconography and Ideology: Aristocracy, Immaculacy and Virginity in Seventeenth-Century Palermo, *Oxford Art Journal*, 17 (1994), pp. 16–31; J. G. Sperling, *Convents and the Body Politic in Late Renaissance Venice* (Chicago, 1999); C. Blaisdell, 'Religion, Gender, and Class: Nuns and Authority in Early Modern France', in *Changing Identities in Early Modern France*, ed. M. Wolfe (Durham, NC, 1997), pp. 147–68; S. Broomhall, ' "In My Opinion": Charlotte de Minut and Female Political Discussion in Sixteenth-Century France', *SCJ*, 31 (2000), pp. 25–45; J. Bilinkoff, 'A Spanish Prophetess and Her Patrons: The Case of María de Santo Domingo', *SCJ*, 23 (1992), pp. 21–34.

17   *The Crannied Wall: Women, Religion, and the Arts in Early Modern Europe*, ed. C. A. Monson (Ann Arbor, Mich., 1992); *Creative Women*; M. Winkelmes, 'Taking Part: Benedictine Nuns as Patrons of Art and Architecture', in *Picturing Women in Renaissance and Baroque Italy*, ed. G. A. Johnson and S. F. Matthews Grieco (Cambridge, 1997), pp. 91–110; L. Lierheimer, 'Redefining Convent Space: Ideals of Female Community among Seventeenth-Century Ursuline Nuns', *Proceedings of the Annual Meeting of the Western Society for French History*, 24 (1997), pp. 211–20; M. N. Taggard, 'Picturing Intimacy in a Spanish Golden Age Convent', *Oxford Art Journal*, 23 (2000), pp. 99–111; P. Ranft, *A Woman's Way: The Forgotten History of Women Spiritual Directors* (New York, 2000); A. Weber, 'Spiritual Administration: Gender and Discernment in the Carmelite Reform', *SCJ*, 31 (2000), pp. 123–46.

18   C. Monson, *Disembodied Voices: Music and Culture in an Early Modern Italian Convent* (Berkeley, Ca., 1995); J. M. Wood, 'Breaking the Silence: The Poor Clares and the Visual Arts in Fifteenth-Century Italy', *RQ*, 48 (1995), pp. 262–86; U. Strasser, 'Bones of Contention: Cloistered Nuns, Decorated Relics, and the Contest over Women's Place in the Public Sphere of Counter-Reformation Munich', *Archive for Reformation History*, 90 (1999), pp. 255–88.

19   *Till God Will: Mary Ward Through her Writings*, ed. M. Emmanuel Orchard (London, 1985), p. 58.

1 Female Monasticism Revived: Foundations and Vocations

1 'Abbess Neville's Annals of Five Communities of English Benedictine Nuns in Flanders, 1598–1687', ed. M. J. Rumsey, hereafter 'Abbess Neville's Annals', in *Miscellanea V* (London, CRS 6, 1909), p. 2.

2 Upon investiture, most women were given a religious name to replace their baptismal name. This signified their relinquishment of the world and new spiritual life within the cloister. I will identify individuals by both names upon first reference, and thereafter use the name by which they are commonly known. As some religious names were long and unwieldy, I will refer to lesser-known women by their baptismal name. Hence, at first mention the woman professed a canoness of the Holy Sepulchre at Liège on 18 Aug. 1649, would be Elizabeth (Flavia of St Joseph) Daniel and, subsequently, Elizabeth Daniel.

3 'Abbess Neville's Annals', pp. 2–3, 5, 7; *Chronicle of the First Monastery Founded at Brussels for English Benedictine Nuns AD 1597* (Bergholt, 1898), pp. 24–42; DL, Hazlemere MSS 1887 and 1888; PRO, SP Flanders 77/6, fol. 73; P. Arblaster, 'The Infanta and the English Benedictine Nuns: Mary Percy's Memories in 1634', *RH*, 23 (1997), p. 522.

4 M. E. Perry, *Gender and Disorder in Early Modern Seville* (Princeton, NJ, 1990), pp. 76, 78.

5 E. A. Lehfeldt, 'Convents as Litigants: Dowry and Inheritance Disputes in Early Modern Spain', *Journal of Social History*, 33 (2000), p. 645.

6 P. Ranft, *Women and the Religious Life in Premodern Europe* (New York, 1996), p. 111.

7 S. Evangelisti, 'Wives, Widows, and Brides of Christ: Marriage and the Convent in the Historiography of Early Modern Italy', *HJ*, 43 (2000), p. 241.

8 H. Hills, 'Cities and Virgins: Female Aristocratic Convents in Early Modern Naples and Palermo', *Oxford Art Journal*, 22 (1999), pp. 38–41.

9 E. Rapley, *The Dévotes: Women and Church in Seventeenth-Century France*, (Montreal and Kingston, 1990), pp. 19–20.

10 Ranft, *Religious Life*, p. 106.

11 C. Harline, 'Actives and Contemplatives: The Female Religious of the Low Countries Before and After Trent', *CHR*, 81 (1995), pp. 556–9.

12 Rapley, *The Dévotes*, p. 20; E. Rapley, 'Women and Religious Vocation in Seventeenth-Century France', *French Historical Studies*, 18 (1994), pp. 626–30; J. G. Sperling, *Convents and the Body Politic in Late Renaissance Venice* (Chicago, 1999), p. 28.

13 Perry, *Gender and Disorder*, p. 78. See also J. K. McNamara, *Sisters in Arms: Catholic Nuns through Two Millennia* (Cambridge, Mass., 1996), pp. 527–9, 546–7.

14 R. C. Trexler, 'Celibacy in the Renaissance: The Nuns of Florence', in *Dependence in Context in Renaissance Florence* (Binghamton, NY, 1994), pp. 354–5; J. C. Brown, 'Monache a Firenze all'inizio dell'età Moderna', *Quaderni Storici*, 85 (1994), pp. 120–2; Evangelisti, 'Wives, Widows', pp. 241–2.

15 Sperling, *Convents and the Body Politic*, pp. 26–8.

16 Ibid., pp. 23–4, 71; S. Chojnacki, 'Daughters and Oligarchs: Gender and the Early Renaissance State', in *Gender and Society in Renaissance Italy*, ed. J. C. Brown and R. C. Davis (London, 1998), pp. 71–5; Harline, 'Actives and Contemplatives', pp. 564–7. See also Hills, 'Cities and Virgins', pp. 44–6.

17 Lehfeldt, 'Convents as Litigants', p. 657.
18 B. B. Diefendorf, 'Give Us Back Our Children: Patriarchal Authority and Parental Consent to Religious Vocations in Early Counter-Reformation France', *Journal of Modern History*, 68 (1996), p. 274. See also Rapley, 'Religious Vocation', pp. 624–5.
19 Rapley, *The Dévotes*, p. 19.
20 For an overview of this debate, see A. R. Muldoon, 'Recusants, Church-Papists, and "Comfortable" Missionaries: Assessing the Post-Reformation English Catholic Community', *CHR*, 86 (2000), pp. 242–57.
21 M. A. Mullett, *Catholics in Britain and Ireland, 1558–1829* (Basingstoke, 1998), pp. 2–9, 19–21 summarises this point.
22 J. Bossy, *The English Catholic Community, 1570–1850* (London, 1975), pp. 150–9; A. Walsham, *Church Papists: Catholicism, Conformity and Confessional Polemic in Early Modern England* (Woodbridge, 1993), pp. 78–81; M. Rowlands, 'Recusant Women 1560–1640', in *Women in English Society 1500–1800*, ed. M. Prior (London, 1985), pp. 149–80; R. Warnicke, *Women of the English Renaissance and Reformation* (Westport, Conn., 1983), pp. 164–85; C. Seguin, '"Addicted unto Piety": Catholic Women in England, 1590–1690' (PhD dissertation, Duke University, 1997), pp. 1–17; J. D. Hanlon, 'These Be But Women', in *From the Renaissance to the Counter-Reformation* (New York, 1965), pp. 371–400; A. F. Marotti, 'Alienating Catholics in Early Modern England: Recusant Women, Jesuits and Ideological Fantasies', in *Catholicism and Anti-Catholicism in Early Modern English Texts*, ed. A. Marotti (Basingstoke, 1999), pp. 1–34.
23 Mullett, *Catholics in Britain*, pp. 16–19, 21–2; M. Questier, 'The Politics of Religious Conformity and the Accession of James I', *Historical Research*, 71 (1998), pp. 14–30; A. Dures, *English Catholicism 1558–1642* (London, 1983), pp. 41–2.
24 Dures, *English Catholicism*, pp. 40–2.
25 The cloisters in the sample include the Brussels, Cambrai, Pontoise and Ghent Benedictines, the Gravelines Poor Clares, the Louvain and Bruges Augustinians, the Third Order Franciscans, the Liège Sepulchrines, and the 'Blue Nuns' of Paris. My data includes women who joined foreign houses and transferred to English convents, but the recruitment statistics exclude those professed prior to the 1590s. They also exclude the Ghent Benedictines for whom the registers are incomplete.
26 *The Chronicle of the English Augustinian Canonesses Regular of the Lateran, at St Monica's in Louvain (now at St Augustine's Priory, Newton Abbot, Devon) 1548–1644*, ed. A. Hamilton, hereafter *Chronicle of St Monica's* (London, 1904), vol. 1, pp. 1–3, 24–5.
27 P. Guilday, *The English Catholic Refugees on the Continent 1558–1795* (London, 1914), pp. 56–61; J. R. Fletcher, *The Story of the English Bridgettines of Syon Abbey* (South Brent, 1933), pp. 37–111.
28 Guilday, *Catholic Refugees*, pp. 413–15.
29 M. W. Sturman, 'Gravelines and the English Poor Clares', *London Recusant*, 7 (1977), p. 2.
30 *Chronicle of St Monica's*, vol. 1, pp. 26–8; W. Peryn, *Spirituall Exercises and Goostly Meditations* (Caen, 1598), p. 2.
31 'Registers of the English Poor Clares at Gravelines, including those who Founded Filiations at Aire, Dunkirk and Rouen, 1608–1837', hereafter 'Poor

Clare Registers', in *Miscellanea 9* (London, CRS 14, 1914), pp. 25–6, 32–4;
M. C. E. Chambers, *The Life of Mary Ward (1585–1645)*, ed. H. J. Coleridge
(London, 1882), vol. 1, pp. 171–2; H. Peters, *Mary Ward: A World In Contem-
plation*, trans. H. Butterfield (Leominster, 1994), pp. 89–92.

32 Guilday, *Catholic Refugees*, p. 362.
33 Ibid., pp. 302–3.
34 *Chronicle of St Monica's*, vol. 1, pp. 68–9, 77–8, 110–11, 119–20.
35 Ibid., vol. 2, pp. 67–8. The foundation was thwarted by Lovel's death.
36 *In a Great Tradition: Tribute to Dame Laurentia McLaughlan Abbess of Stanbrook
    by the Benedictines of Stanbrook* (London, 1956), p. 7.
37 Chambers, *Life of Mary Ward*, vol. 1, pp. 128, 159; Peters, *Mary Ward*, pp. 75,
    80.
38 *Chronicle of St Monica's*, vol. 1, pp. 34–5, 64.
39 Ibid., vol. 1, p. 63.
40 Ibid:, vol. 1, pp. 203–13; C. S. Durrant, *A Link between Flemish Mystics and
    English Martyrs* (London, 1925), p. 254.
41 'The Register Book of Professions...of the English Benedictine Nuns at
    Brussels and Winchester, now at East Bergholt, 1598–1856', ed. J. S. Hansom,
    hereafter 'Brussels Benedictine Registers', in *Miscellanea 9* (London, CRS 14,
    1914), pp. 175–84; 'Poor Clare Registers', pp. 32–54; Priory, St Monica's MS J8,
    fols. [1]–3, List of All the Religious Professed from Elizabeth Woodford...to
    1897; *Chronicle of St Monica's*, vol. 1, p. 58.
42 Priory, St Monica's MS J8, fols. 3–5; *Chronicle of St Monica's*, vol. 2, p. 68.
43 'Brussels Benedictine Registers', pp. 184–6; 'Poor Clare Registers', pp. 54–65.
44 T. Matthew, *The Life of Lucy Knatchbull*, ed. D. Knowles (London, 1931),
    pp. 83–95; Darlington, MS Aire Register, [fol. 3]. The Poor Clares also sent a
    group of nuns to Dublin in *c*.1625. See Chapters 2 and 5 for the dissension
    behind the filiations.
45 'Records of the English Benedictine Nuns at Cambrai (now Stanbrook),
    1620–1793', ed. J. Gillow, hereafter 'Cambrai Records', in *Miscellanea VIII*
    (London, CRS 13, 1913), pp. 1, 76–8; 'Brussels Benedictine Registers', pp. 176,
    179–80, 184.
46 When a widow entered a cloister she was referred to by either her father's or
    her husband's surname. To avoid confusion both her family and her married
    name (when both are known) will be used.
47 The Brussels cloister was administratively subject to the archbishop of
    Mechelen, and largely under Jesuit spiritual supervision.
48 Guilday, *Catholic Refugees*, offers a good survey of these foundations.
49 I have only included English contemplative foundations which survived into
    the eighteenth century in this table. It does not include filiations to England
    and Ireland, nor houses of Mary Ward's Institute. The Ypres Benedictines
    (exclusively Irish after 1684) are included because they were originally Eng-
    lish and the house figured prominently in the other convents' affairs.
50 Rapley, *The Dévotes*, pp. 48–60.
51 Sperling, *Convents and the Body Politic*, p. 249.
52 Mullett, *Catholics in Britain*, pp. 25–6; Dures, *English Catholicism*, pp. 70–4.
53 Arundel, Franciscan MS Annals, fols. 25–26, 31, 35–43, Annals of the Religious
    of the 3rd Order of St Francis of the Province of England from the Year 1621 to
    (1893); *Franciscana· The English Franciscan Nuns, 1619–1821 and the Friars*

Minor of the Same Province 1618–1761, ed. R. Trappes-Lomax (London, CRS 24, 1922), pp. v–vi, 22, 35; *The Diary of the 'Blue Nuns' or Order of the Immaculate Conception of Our Lady, at Paris, 1658–1810*, ed. J. Gillow and R. Trappes-Lomax, hereafter *Diary of the 'Blue Nuns'* (London, CRS 8, 1910), pp. 7–13; S. M. F., *Hidden Wheat: The Story of an Enclosed Franciscan Community 1621–1971* (Glasgow, 1971), pp. 8–10, 19–22, 28–34.

54   'Abbess Neville's Annals', pp. 42–6.

55   Guilday, *Catholic Refugees*, pp. 415–16.

56   C. Walker, 'Prayer, Patronage and Political Conspiracy: English Nuns and the Restoration', *HJ*, 43 (2000), pp. 16–18.

57   These foundations are discussed in Chapter 4.

58   This pattern is remarkably similar to the picture of women entering French teaching congregations for the same period, see Rapley, *The Dévotes*, pp. 197–201. Rapley's subsequent book appeared too late for comparison, see E. Rapley, *A Social History of the Cloister: Daily Life in the Teaching Monasteries of the Old Regime* (Montreal and Kingston, 2001).

59   The absence of Gravelines and Brussels from the data has resulted in a significant decrease in the professions of choir nuns for the 1620s.

60   *A Brief Relation of the Order and Institute of the English Religious Women at Liège* (Liège, 1652), pp. 52, 54.

61   Lille, 20 H 1, fol. 85, Constitutions of English Benedictines at Cambrai, 1631.

62   Priory, St Monica's MS Qu2, fols. 88–9, Instructions for a Religious Superior.

63   The Franciscans professed 37 choir nuns in the 1620s, 12 during the 1630s, and 20 between 1641 and 1650. In the same period (1621–1650) only 8 lay sisters were professed. *Franciscana*, pp. 123–41, 151–4.

64   Arundel, Franciscan MS Annals, fol. 44.

65   Priory, St Monica's MS J8, fols. [1–2]; *Chronicle of St Monica's*, vol. 1, pp. 35–6.

66   Durrant, *Flemish Mystics*, pp. 241–3, 263; Priory, Bruges List, pp. 163–5.

67   The Gravelines' registers do not distinguish lay sisters from choir nuns until the 1650s, so some of these women were most likely lay sisters.

68   Darlington, MS Gravelines Chronicles, fols. 145–63.

69   Buckfast, Pontoise MS 'An Account of the Blowing-up and Destruction of the Town of Gravelines', fol. 1.

70   'Poor Clare Registers', pp. 54–114.

71   'Brussels Benedictine Registers', pp. 184–92; 'Poor Clare Registers', pp. 83–121; Priory, St Monica's MS J8, fols. [7–9]; 'Registers of the English Benedictine Nuns of Pontoise, now at Teignmouth, Devonshire, 1680–1713', hereafter 'Pontoise Registers', in *Miscellanea X* (London, CRS 17, 1915), pp. 267–326.

72   AAW, A XXXIV, fols. 327, 329–31, 333–5, 337, 339, 343, 345–7, 349–60; *Diary of the 'Blue Nuns'*, pp. xxii–xxiii, 25, 29–31.

73   'Cambrai Records', pp. 39–59; *Obit Book of the English Benedictines from 1600–1912*, ed. H. N. Birt (Edinburgh, 1913), pp. 213–23.

74   Bodl., Rawlinson MS A.36, fols. 45, 49–50, 89–90, Catherine Gascoigne to Augustine Conyers 3 March 1655, Gascoigne to Anselm Crowder 3 March 1655, Crowder to Gascoigne 26 Jan. 1655; J. McCann, 'Some Benedictine Letters in the Bodleian', *Downside Review*, 30 (1931), p. 467; 'Cambrai Records', pp. 48–50; *Great Tradition*, pp. 18–19.

75 A. F. Allison, 'The English Augustinian Convent of Our Lady of Syon at Paris: Its Foundation and Struggle for Survival during the First Eighty Years, 1634–1713', *RH*, 21 (1993), pp. 464–5, 468, 471–2.

76 Durrant, *Flemish Mystics*, pp. 241–2.

77 'Obituary Notices of the Nuns of the English Benedictine Abbey of Ghent in Flanders, 1627–1811', hereafter 'Ghent Obituary Notices', in *Miscellanea XI* (London, CRS 19, 1917), pp. 16–18; Matthew, *Life of Lucy Knatchbull*, p. 185.

78 *Chronicle of St Monica's*, vol. 2, pp. 155–61.

79 *Franciscana*, pp. 178–80.

80 *Chronicle of St Monica's*, vol. 2, pp. 161–2.

81 A. M. C. Forster, 'The Chronicles of the English Poor Clares of Rouen – I', *RH*, 18 (1986), pp. 68–95.

82 Allison, 'English Augustinian Convent', p. 459.

83 *Chronicle of St Monica's*, vol. 1, pp. 194–6.

84 Ibid., vol. 1, p. 246.

85 P. R. P. Knell, 'The Southcott Family in Essex, 1575–1642', *Essex Recusant*, 14 (1972), pp. 5–6; 'Brussels Benedictine Registers', p. 177.

86 H. Foley, *Records of the English Province of the Society of Jesus* (London, 1877), vol. 1, p. 511; 'Poor Clare Registers', p. 49; 'Brussels Benedictine Registers', p. 184; 'Cambrai Records', pp. 40–1.

87 'Ghent Obituary Notices', pp. 20–1, 28–30, 43–6; 'Brussels Benedictine Registers', pp. 177–8, 181, 184–5; *Chronicle of St Monica's*, vol. 1, pp. 34, 69, 116, 260–1; Knell, 'Southcott Family', pp. 5, 9, 11–12, 21; *The Troubles of Our Catholic Forefathers Related by Themselves*, ed. J. Morris (London, 1872), vol. 1, pp. 364–6.

88 *Chronicle of St Monica's*, vol. 1, pp. 87–92, 111–16, 121, 261–3.

89 C. Walker, ' "Doe not supose me a well mortifyed Nun dead to the world": Letter-Writing in Early Modern English Convents', in *Early Modern Women Letter Writers*, ed. J. Daybell (Basingstoke, 2001), pp. 169–70.

90 Priory, St Monica's MS R16/2, Thomas and Jane Worthington to Mary and Dorothy Worthington, *c.* 1691.

91 'Poor Clare Registers', pp. 71–2, 87, 93–4, 112–13, 116, 121, 187; A. M. C. Forster, 'The Chronicles of the English Poor Clares of Rouen – 2', *RH*, 18 (1986), pp. 168–9; *The Great Diurnal of Nicholas Blundell of Little Crosby, Lancashire*, ed. J. J. Bagley (Chester, 1968, 1970), vol. 1, pp. 105–8, 157–60; vol. 2, xii-xiii; *Chronicle of St Monica's*, vol. 1, pp. 138–42, 153–4; vol. 2, p. 192.

92 *Diurnal of Nicholas Blundell*, vol. 1, pp. 200, 206, 255, 290; 'Poor Clare Registers', p. 128.

93 'Brussels Benedictine Registers'; 'Poor Clare Registers'; Forster, 'Poor Clares of Rouen – 2'; *Chronicle of St Monica's*, vols 1 and 2; Priory, MSS C2, J8, M1; Foley, *Records*; *Franciscana*; 'Cambrai Records'; Priory, Bruges List; Durrant, *Flemish Mystics*; 'Sepulchrine Records'; 'Pontoise Registers'; Birt, *Obit Book*; Versailles, 68 H 3, 68 H 4; Nichols, *Herald and Genealogist*; *Diary of the 'Blue Nuns'*; 'Ghent Obituary Notices'.

94 *Chronicle of St Monica's*, vol. 1, pp. 114–15, 193, 239; Durrant, *Flemish Mystics*, pp. 225–6.

95 P. R. B. Knell, 'Some Catholics of Standon, Herts. 1660–1688', *London Recusant*, 2 (1972), p. 89–90; *Diary of the 'Blue Nuns'*, p. 19; *Chronicle of St Monica's*, vol. 1, pp. 194–6; vol. 2, pp. 17–18, 21, 109, 191, 193.

96   Rapley, 'Religious Vocation', pp. 617–18; Hills, 'Cities and Virgins', pp. 34–7, 44–5; Sperling, *Convents and the Body Politic*, pp. 18–29; Perry, *Gender and Disorder*, pp. 77–8; C. Blaisdell, 'Religion, Gender, and Class: Nuns and Authority in Early Modern France', in *Changing Identities in Early Modern France*, ed. M. Wolfe (Durham, NC, 1997), p. 148.

97   B. J. Harris, 'A New Look at the Reformation: Aristocratic Women and Nunneries, 1450–1540', *Journal of British Studies*, 32 (1993), pp. 91–8; M. Oliva, *The Convent and the Community in Late Medieval England: Female Monasteries in the Diocese of Norwich, 1350–1540* (Woodbridge, 1998), pp. 52–61.

98   G. Zarri, 'Gender, Religious Institutions and Social Discipline: The Reform of the Regulars', in *Gender and Society in Renaissance Italy*, ed. J. C. Brown and R. C. Davis (London, 1998), pp. 208–9.

99   Sperling, *Convents and the Body Politic*, pp. 206–15.

100 S. Hanley, 'Engendering the State: Family Formation and State Building in Early Modern France', *French Historical Studies*, 16 (1989), pp. 6–15, 25.

101 Seguin, 'Addicted Unto Piety', pp. 64–31; L. Stone, *The Family Sex and Marriage in England 1500–1800* (London, 1977), p. 96; Bossy, *Catholic Community*, pp. 133, 137–8; D. J. Steel and E. R. Samuel, *Sources for Roman Catholic and Jewish Genealogy and Family History* (London, 1974), pp. 870–5; H. Aveling, 'The Marriages of Catholic Recusants 1559–1642', *Journal of Ecclesiastical History*, 14 (1963), pp. 70–1; M. D. R. Leys, *Catholics in England 1559–1829: A Social History* (London, 1961), pp. 190–1; D. Matthew, *Catholicism in England 1535–1935: Portrait of a Minority: Its Culture and Tradition* (London, 1936), pp. 53–4, 90–1.

102 M. Sena, 'William Blundell and the Networks of Catholic Dissent in Post-Reformation England', in *Communities in Early Modern England: Networks, Place, Rhetoric*, ed. A. Shepherd and P. Withington (Manchester, 2000), pp. 54–75.

103 R. B. Outhwaite, 'Marriage as Business: Opinions on the Rise in Aristocratic Bridal Portions in Early Modern England', in *Business Life and Public Policy: Essays in Honour of D. C. Coleman*, ed. N. McKendrick and R. B. Outhwaite (Cambridge, 1986), p. 24.

104 A. L. Erickson, *Women and Property in Early Modern England* (London, 1993), p. 88.

105 Ibid.

106 Arundel, Franciscan MS 6b, fol. 9, Book of Statutes, 1641; Franciscan MS Annals, fols. 24, 54.

107 Lille, 20 H 1, fol. 90, Constitutions of English Benedictines at Cambrai, 1631.

108 Lancs. RO, DDCl/1168, Mary Caryll to Thomas Clifton, 25 Jan. 1675.

109 *Brief Relation*, p. 54.

110 AAW, A VIII, fols. 89–90, Concerning the Beginning of the Poor Clares in Graveling; Darlington, MS Gravelines Chronicles, fols. 30–1, 34.

111 Lancs. RO, DDCl/1170, Mary Caryll to Thomas Clifton, 24 April 1676.

112 Darlington, MS Gravelines Chronicles, fol. 28. For dowry figures in the Brussels Benedictine house, see Chapter 3.

113 'Records of the English Canonesses of the Holy Sepulchre at Liège, Now at New Hall, 1652–1793', ed. R. Trappes-Lomax, hereafter 'Sepulchrine Records', in *Miscellanea X* (London, CRS 17, 1915), pp. 9–14.

114 Priory, St Monica's MS M1, fols. 2–24, Council Book, 1669–1874.

115 Lancs. RO, DDCl/1167-7, Mary Caryll to Thomas Clifton 3 Jan. 1674 – 13 March 1676, Ann Clifton to same 25 June 1676; M. J. Galgano, 'Negotiations for a Nun's Dowry: Restoration Letters of Mary Caryll OSB and Ann Clifton OSB', *American Benedictine Review*, 24 (1973), pp. 279–98.

116 Lancs. RO, DDCl/973, Direction...for Payment of Dowry...August 19, 1685.

117 Lancs. RO, DDCl/968, Settlement of Sir Thomas Clifton on Anne Clifton, 1677; DDCl/980, Agreement...for Payments to Anne Clifton at Dunkirk... July 16, 1694.

118 AAM, Fonds Kloosters, Englese Benedictijnen/12, Elizabeth Southcott to Jacob Boonen, 13 July 1622; Frances Gawen to same, 1 Sept. 1622; Agnes Lenthall to same, 8 April 1623; Ursula Hewicke to same, 17 May 1623; Eugenia Poulton, Elizabeth Southcott, Magdalen Digby, Lucy Knatchbull and Alexia Blanchard to same, 18 May 1623; Hewicke to same, [1623]; Hewicke to same, 5 April 1625.

119 *Chronicle of St Monica's*, vol. 2, pp. 37–9; Priory, St Monica's MS C2, fols. 538–9, Chronicle, vol. 1, 1548–1837.

120 *Chronicle of St Monica's*, vol. 1, pp. 160–1.

121 'Cambrai Records', pp. 44, 74–5.

122 'Pontoise Registers', pp. 196, 311.

123 Durrant, *Flemish Mystics*, p. 313.

124 Knell, 'Catholics of Standon', pp. 89–90; B. Zimmerman, *Carmel in England 1615–1849* (London, 1889), pp. 231–2.

125 Rapley, 'Religious Vocation', pp. 621–4.

126 Durrant, *Flemish Mystics*, p. 259; Priory, Bruges MS Professions and Obits 1629–1882, fol. 2.

127 Figures based on women entering aged less than 14 years and 11 months. To be professed at the legal age of 16, they would have entered the novitiate aged 15.

128 *Chronicle of St Monica's*, vol. 2, p. 61; *Diary of the 'Blue Nuns'*, p. 2.

129 *Chronicle of St Monica's*, vol. 2, p. 66.

130 A. Baker, 'Life of Dame Gertrude More', in *The Inner Life and the Writings of Dame Gertrude More*, ed. B. Weld-Blundell (London, 1910), vol. 1, pp. 11, 23.

131 Durrant, *Flemish Mystics*, pp. 304–5.

132 *Chronicle of St Monica's*, vol. 1, p. 105.

133 B. Hill, 'A Refuge from Men: The Idea of a Protestant Nunnery', *P&P*, 117 (1987), pp. 107–30.

134 *The Responsa Scholarum of the English College, Rome, Part II, 1622–1685*, ed. A. Kenny (London, CRS 55, 1963), p. 450.

135 Walker, 'Letter-Writing in English Convents', pp. 168–70.

136 BL, Add. MS 36,452, fol. 70, Winefrid Thimelby to Herbert Aston [c.1657].

137 PRO, SP, Flanders: 77/9, fol. 119, Lady Mary Lovel to Lord Treasurer Salisbury, Aug. 1608.

138 AAM, Fonds Kloosters, Englese Benedictijnen/12, Anne Healey to Jacob Boonen, [1629].

139 *Chronicle of St Monica's*, vol. 1, pp. 187–9; vol. 2, p. 103.

140 Ibid., vol. 1, p. 239.

141 Ibid., vol. 1, pp. 256–7

142 I. Grundy, 'Women's History? Writings by English Nuns', in *Women, Writing, History 1640–1740*, ed. I. Grundy and S. Wiseman (London, 1992), pp. 135–7; W. Scheepsma, ' "For Hereby I Hope to Rouse Some to Piety"': Books of Sisters from Convents and Sister-Houses Associated with the *Devotio Moderna* in the Low Countries', in *Women, the Book and the Godly*, ed. L. Smith and J. H. M. Taylor (Cambridge, 1993), pp. 38–40; C. Woodford, 'Women as Historians: the Case of Early Modern German Convents', *German Life and Letters*, 52 (1999), pp. 271–80.

143 Of the 1,109 women in the sample, 4.1 per cent were of unknown nationality.

144 B. Whelan, *Historic English Convents of Today: The Story of the English Cloisters in France and Flanders in Penal Times* (London, 1936), pp. 89–90; Allison, 'English Augustinian Convent', pp. 480–1.

145 *Diary of the 'Blue Nuns'*, p. 19.

146 Ibid., pp. 58–9.

147 *Franciscana*, pp. 29, 31, 42–5, 140, 141–2, 195–6, 200.

148 'Sepulchrine Records', pp. 3, 7, 9, 12.

149 Ibid., pp. 3, 32–4, 49, 105, 173–7, 179, 181, 183.

150 Ibid., pp. 12, 60–2, 64–8, 99, 201–3, 206–16.

151 See Table 1.4.

152 'Cambrai Records', p. 53; *Franciscana*, pp. 17, 19; *Chronicle of St Monica's*, vol. 1, pp. 106, 188–9, 194–6, 199–200, 244, 257–8, 263–5.

153 'Ghent Obituary Notices', pp. 57–8.

154 Priory, St Monica's MS Q29, fol. 63, E. Shirley, 'The Lyfe of Our Moste Reverent Mother, Margrit Clement', 1626.

155 Guilday, *Catholic Refugees*, p. 365.

2 The Monastic Family: Order and Disorder in the Cloister

1 Darlington, MS Gravelines Chronicles, fols. 146–8.

2 A. Pasture, 'Documents Concernant quelques Monastères Anglais aux Pays-Bas au XVIIe Siècle', *Bulletin de l'Institut Historique Belge de Rome*, 10 (1930), pp. 213–14; Darlington, MS Gravelines Chronicles, fols. 26, 30; P. Guilday, *The English Catholic Refugees on the Continent 1558–1795* (London, 1914), pp. 287, 297–9.

3 See Chapter 5 for scholarly interpretations of the disputes.

4 See the fourth part of this chapter and Chapter 5 for analysis of its governance and spiritual dimensions.

5 J. R. Cain, 'Cloister and the Apostolate of Religious Women', *Review for Religious*, 27 (1968), pp. 270–80; F. Medioli, 'An Unequal Law: The Enforcement of *Clausura* Before and After the Council of Trent', in *Women in Renaissance and Early Modern Europe*, ed. C. Meek (Dublin, 2000), pp. 136–52; M. Brennan, 'Enclosure: Institutionalising the Invisibility of Women in Ecclesiastical Communities', in *Women – Invisible in Theology and Church*, ed. E. Schüssler Fiorenza and M. Collins (Edinburgh, 1985), pp. 42–3; for the medieval origins, see J. Tibbetts Schulenburg, 'Strict Active Enclosure and its Effects on the Female Monastic Experience (ca 500–1100)', in *Distant*

Echoes: Medieval Religious Women, vol. 1, ed. J. A. Nichols and L. T. Shank (Kalamazoo, 1984), pp. 51–86.

6 K. Gill, '*Scandala*: Controversies Concerning *Clausura* and Women's Religious Communities in Late Medieval Italy', in *Christendom and its Discontents: Exclusion, Persecution, and Rebellion, 1000–1500*, ed. S. L. Waugh and P. D. Diehl (Cambridge, 1996), pp. 177–8, 199–200.

7 Linda Lierheimer has argued the same for enclosed French Ursulines, 'Redefining Convent Space: Ideals of Female Community among Seventeenth-Century Ursuline Nuns', *Proceedings of the Annual Meeting of the Western Society for French History*, 24 (1997), pp. 211–20.

8 I will use the term 'abbess' collectively to refer generally to female superiors, but will accord individual prioresses their correct title when referring specifically to them.

9 J. K. McNamara, *Sisters in Arms: Catholic Nuns through Two Millennia* (Cambridge, Mass., 1996), pp. 423–4, 426, 428–9; M. E. Wiesner, 'Ideology Meets the Empire: Reformed Convents and the Reformation', in *Germania Illustrata: Essays on Early Modern Germany Presented to Gerald Strauss*, ed. A. C. Fix and S. C. Karant-Nunn (Kirksville, Miss., 1991), pp. 182–3; M. Oliva, *The Convent and the Community in Late Medieval England: Female Monasteries in the Diocese of Norwich, 1350–1540* (Woodbridge, 1998), pp. 11–36.

10 Wiesner, 'Ideology Meets the Empire', pp. 181–95; C. Blaisdell, 'Religion, Gender, and Class: Nuns and Authority in Early Modern France', in *Changing Identities in Early Modern France*, ed. M. Wolfe (Durham, NC, 1997), pp. 147–68; D. Jonathan Grieser, 'A Tale of Two Convents: Nuns and Anabaptists in Münster, 1533–1535', *SCJ*, 26 (1995), pp. 31–47; L. Roper, *The Holy Household: Women and Morals in Reformation Augsburg* (Oxford, 1989), pp. 206–51; McNamara, *Sisters in Arms*, pp. 419–51.

11 McNamara, *Sisters in Arms*, pp. 385–418.

12 *Canons and Decrees of the Council of Trent*, ed. R. J. Schroeder (St Louis, 1941), pp. 220–1, 223, 229–30.

13 Ibid., pp. 221–2. If no one fitted the criteria, it was possible for a woman aged 30 and professed for five years to be appointed.

14 Ibid., pp. 218–19, 226–9.

15 G. Zarri, 'Gender, Religious Institutions and Social Discipline: The Reform of the Regulars', in *Gender and Society in Renaissance Italy*, ed. J. C. Brown and R. C. Davis (London, 1998), p. 206.

16 M. E. Perry, *Gender and Disorder in Early Modern Seville* (Princeton, NJ, 1990), pp. 97–117; G. Zarri, 'From Prophecy to Discipline, 1450–1650', in *Women and Faith: Catholic Religious Life in Italy from Late Antiquity to the Present*, ed. L. Scaraffia and G. Zarri (Cambridge, Mass., 1999), pp. 88–90; J. Bilinkoff, 'Charisma and Controversy: The Case of María de Santo Domingo', in *Spanish Women in The Golden Age: Images and Realities*, ed. M. S. Sánchez and A. Saint-Saëns (Westport, Conn., 1996), pp. 23–35; P. R. Baernstein, 'In Widow's Habit: Women between Convent and Family in Sixteenth-Century Milan', *SCJ*, 25 (1994), pp. 787–807.

17 L. Châtellier, *The Europe of the Devout: The Catholic Reformation and the Formation of a New Society*, trans. J. Birrell (Cambridge and Paris, 1989), pp. 132–5; S. Cohen, *The Evolution of Women's Asylums Since 1500: From Refuges for Ex-Prostitutes to Shelters for Battered Women* (New York, 1992);

Zarri, 'From Prophecy to Discipline', pp. 92–5; Perry, *Gender and Disorder*, pp. 140–62; McNamara, *Sisters in Arms*, pp. 475–9.

18 Perry, *Gender and Disorder*, p. 68.

19 S. Chojnacki, 'Daughters and Oligarchs: Gender and the Early Renaissance State', in *Gender and Society in Renaissance Italy*, p. 84.

20 Roper, *Holy Household*, p. 3.

21 See Chapter 5 for a discussion of this point.

22 H. Peters, *Mary Ward: A World In Contemplation*, trans. H. Butterfield (Leominster, 1994), pp. 246–59, 403–13, 466–521, 559–67; Cain, 'Cloister', pp. 659–71; E. Rapley, *The Dévotes: Women and Church in Seventeenth-Century France* (Montreal and Kingston, 1990), pp. 28–34; M. Rowlands, 'Recusant Women 1560–1640', in *Women in English Society 1500–1800*, ed. M. Prior (London, 1985), pp. 168–74; R. Warnicke, *Women of the English Renaissance and Reformation* (Westport, Conn., 1983), pp. 174–7; Guilday, *Catholic Refugees*, pp. 163–214.

23 W. M. Wright, 'The Visitation of Holy Mary: The First Years (1610–1618)', in *Religious Orders of the Catholic Reformation*, ed. R. L. DeMolen (New York, 1994), pp. 226–31, 236–40; Rapley, *The Dévotes*, pp. 34–41; McNamara, *Sisters in Arms*, pp. 465–7.

24 C. J. Blaisdell, 'Angela Merici and the Ursulines', in *Religious Orders of the Catholic Reformation*, pp. 99–122; Rapley, *The Dévotes*, pp. 48–60; P. Ranft, *Women and the Religious Life in Premodern Europe* (New York, 1996), pp. 101–6; McNamara, *Sisters in Arms*, pp. 460–1, 469–70.

25 Rapley, *The Dévotes*, pp. 64–70, 81–90; McNamara, *Sisters in Arms*, pp. 482–8.

26 See Chapter 3 for a discussion of this problem.

27 Zarri, 'Reform of the Regulars', p. 210.

28 McNamara, *Sisters in Arms*, p. 461.

29 E. B. Weaver, 'The Convent Wall in Tuscan Convent Drama', in *The Crannied Wall: Women, Religion, and the Arts in Early Modern Europe*, ed. C. A. Monson (Ann Arbor, Mich., 1992), p. 73.

30 Zarri, 'Reform of the Regulars', pp. 210–11.

31 U. Strasser, 'Bones of Contention: Cloistered Nuns, Decorated Relics, and the Contest over Women's Place in the Public Sphere of Counter-Reformation Munich', *Archive for Reformation History*, 90 (1999), pp. 281–2.

32 Darlington, MS Gravelines Chronicles, fol. 159.

33 McNamara, *Sisters in Arms*, pp. 530–1.

34 J. Bilinkoff, *The Avila of Saint Teresa: Religious Reform in a Sixteenth-Century City* (Ithaca, NY, 1989), pp. 131–2.

35 McNamara, *Sisters in Arms*, pp. 501–2; A. Sedgwick, 'The Nuns of Port-Royal: A Study of Female Spirituality in Seventeenth-Century France', in *That Gentle Strength: Historical Perspectives on Women in Christianity*, ed. L. L. Coon, K. J. Haldane and E. W. Sommer (Charlottesville, 1990), pp. 178–9, 187.

36 C. Harline, 'Actives and Contemplatives: The Female Religious of the Low Countries Before and After Trent', *CHR*, 81 (1995), pp. 561–2.

37 Roper, *Holy Household*, pp. 230–1; Zarri, 'From Prophecy to Discipline', pp. 106–7.

38 J. G. Sperling, *Convents and the Body Politic in Late Renaissance Venice* (Chicago, 1999), pp. 12–14, 102–8.

39   *Statutes Compyled for the Better Observation of the Holy Rule of ... S. Benedict ... Delivered to the English Religious Woemen of the Monastery of Our Blessed Lady of the Perpetuall Virgin Mary in Bruxelles and to all their Successours*, hereafter *Benedictine Statutes*, (Ghent, 1632), Part 1, pp. 14–15, 18–22; D. Knox, 'Disciplina: The Monastic and Clerical Origins of European Civility', in *Renaissance Society and Culture: Essays in Honor of Eugene F. Rice, Jr*, ed. J. Monfasani and R. G. Musto (New York, 1991), pp. 113–14.

40   [St Augustine], *Rule ... Together with the Constitutions of the English Canonesse Regular's of Our B. Ladyes of Sion in Paris* (Paris, 1636), pp. 283–91.

41   Arundel, Franciscan MS 6b, fols. 50–2, Book of Statutes, 1641. For other examples, see St Colette, *The Declarations and Ordinances made upon the Rule of ... S. Clare* (1622), pp. 57–66, 81–8, 112–25.

42   *The Chronicle of the English Augustinian Canonesses Regular of the Lateran, at St Monica's in Louvain (now at St Augustine's Priory, Newton Abbot, Devon) 1548–1644*, ed. A. Hamilton, hereafter *Chronicle of St Monica's* (London, 1904), vol. I, pp. 29–30.

43   Priory, St Monica's MS Q29, fol. 30, E. Shirley, 'The Lyfe of Our Moste Reverent Mother, Margrit Clement', 1626.

44   A. M. C. Forster, 'The Chronicles of the English Poor Clares of Rouen – I', *RH*, 18 (1986), pp. 59–62.

45   AAM, Fonds Kloosters, Englese Benedictijnen/12, Anne Ingleby to Jacob Boonen, [1623].

46   *Franciscana: The English Franciscan Nuns, 1619–1821 and the Friars Minor of the Same Province 1618–1761*, ed. R. Trappes-Lomax (London, CRS 24, 1922), p. 185; see also 'Obituary Notices of the Nuns of the English Benedictine Abbey of Ghent in Flanders, 1627–1811', hereafter 'Ghent Obituary Notices', in *Miscellanea XI* (London, CRS 19, 1917), p. 44.

47   *Letters from James Earl of Perth ... to his Sister, the Countess of Errol*, ed. W. Jerdan (London, Camden Society 23, 1845), pp. 42–3.

48   C. D. van Strien, 'Recusant Houses in the Southern Netherlands as Seen by British Tourists, *c.* 1650–1720', *Recusant History*, 20 (1991), p. 495.

49   P. Skippon, 'An Account of a Journey Made thro' Part of the Low Countries, Germany Italy and France', in *A Collection of Voyages and Travels*, 3rd edn, ed. A. and J. Churchill (London, 1744), vol. 6, pp. 376–7, 384, 391.

50   Skippon, 'Account of a Journey', p. 469. He incorrectly identified this house as Benedictine.

51   AAM, Mechliniensia/Reg.8, fol. 236c, Visitatio Monastery S. Mariae Ordinis S. Benedicti Anglarum Bruxellen, 10 May 1620. Thanks to Craig Harline for this material. The pagination of the unfoliated French report is his.

52   AAM, Fonds Kloosters, Englese Benedictijnen/12, Anne Ingleby to Jacob Boonen, [1623].

53   DL, Ealing MS Journal 1695–1738, fols. 30–1.

54   AAW, A XXXVI, fols.167–9, Mr Inese's Second Regulations for the Austin Nuns.

55   *Chronicle of St Monica's*, vol. 2, pp. 139–47.

56   Priory, St Monica's MS Qu2, fol. 3, Instructions for a Religious Superior.

57   *The Diary of the 'Blue Nuns' or Order of the Immaculate Conception of Our Lady, at Paris, 1658–1810*, ed. J. Gillow and R. Trappes-Lomax, hereafter *Diary of the 'Blue Nuns'* (London, CRS 8, 1910), pp. 13–14, 17–18, 19–20, 23–4, 28, 40, 46–7, 71–5.

58 Ibid., pp. 14–15, 41, 44–5.

59 [T. Robinson], *The Anatomy of the English Nunnery at Lisbon in Portugall* (London, 1622), pp. 1–2, 7–28.

60 L. Owen, *The Running Register, Recording a True Relation of the State of the English Colledges, Seminaries and Cloysters in all Forraine Parts* (London, 1626), pp. 100–2.

61 J. Richards, '"To Promote a Woman to Beare Rule"': Talking of Queens in Mid-Tudor England', *SCJ*, 28 (1997), pp. 108–15.

62 W. Gouge, *Of Domesticall Duties* (London, 1622), p. 270.

63 J. Goldberg, 'Fatherly Authority: The Politics of Stuart Family Images', in *Rewriting the Renaissance: The Discourse of Sexual Difference in Early Modern Europe*, ed. M. W. Ferguson, M. Quilligan and N. J. Vickers (Chicago, 1986), pp. 3–32; S. Amussen, *An Ordered Society: Gender and Class in Early Modern England* (Oxford, 1988), pp. 34–66.

64 Gouge, *Domesticall Duties*, pp. 271–2, 433, 546–7, 662.

65 Gouge, *Domesticall Duties*, pp. 18–19, sig. 2v; P. Crawford, 'The Construction and Experience of Maternity in Seventeenth-Century England', in *Women as Mothers in Pre-industrial England: Essays in Memory of Dorothy McLaren*, ed. V. Fildes (London, 1990), pp. 12–13, 27–9; K. Charlton, *Women, Religion and Education in Early Modern England* (London, 1999), pp. 202–15.

66 S. Mendelson and P. Crawford, *Women in Early Modern England* (Oxford, 1998), pp. 131–46; L. Gowing, *Domestic Dangers: Women, Words, and Sex in Early Modern London* (Oxford, 1996), pp. 180–231; P. Crawford, 'Katherine and Philip Henry and their Children: a Case Study in Family Ideology', *Transactions of the Historic Society of Lancashire and Cheshire*, 134 (1984), pp. 39–73; A. Wall, 'Deference and Defiance in Women's Letters of the Thynne Family: the Rhetoric of Relationships', in *Early Modern Women's Letter Writing, 1450–1700*, ed. J. Daybell (Basingstoke, 2001), pp. 77–93.

67 V. Larminie, 'Fighting for Family in a Patronage Society: the Epistolary Armoury of Anne Newdigate (1574–1618)', in *Early Modern Women's Letter Writing*, pp. 77–93; B. J. Harris, 'Women and Politics in Early Tudor England', *HJ*, 33 (1990), pp. 259–81.

68 Cited in Rowlands, 'Recusant Women', p. 153.

69 *Calendar of State Papers, Domestic Series, 1581–1590*, ed. R. Lemon (London, 1865), p. 291.

70 J. Bossy, *The English Catholic Community, 1570–1850* (London, 1975), pp. 150–68; Warnicke, *Women of the English Renaissance*, pp. 170–1; Rowlands, 'Recusant Women', pp. 150–6; A. Walsham, *Church Papists: Catholicism, Conformity and Confessional Polemic in Early Modern England* (Woodbridge, 1993), pp. 78–81; M. Questier, *Conversion, Politics and Religion in England, 1580–1625* (Cambridge, 1996), pp. 146–8; F. E. Dolan, *Whores of Babylon: Catholicism, Gender and Seventeenth-Century Print Culture* (Ithaca, NY, 1999), pp. 61–72.

71 Walsham, *Church Papists*, p. 81.

72 Dolan, *Whores of Babylon*, pp. 69–72; Colleen Seguin discusses the subversive actions of Catholic wives and mothers in her doctoral dissertation, '"Addicted Unto Piety"': Catholic Women in England, 1590–1690' (PhD dissertation, Duke University, 1997), esp. chs 1 and 4.

73 Dolan, *Whores of Babylon*, pp. 136–8; Rowlands, 'Recusant Women' pp. 153–4; Bossy, *Catholic Community*, pp. 158–64.

74   C. S. Durrant, *A Link between Flemish Mystics and English Martyrs* (London, 1925), p. 273.

75   *The Responsa Scholarum of the English College, Rome, Part I, 1598–1621*, ed. A. Kenny (London, CRS 54, 1962), pp. 76–7, 108, 118, 142, 186–7, 244–5, 306, 316, 336; *The Responsa Scholarum of the English College, Rome, Part II, 1622–1685*, ed. A. Kenny (London, CRS 55, 1963), pp. 377, 383, 389, 392, 395, 420, 434, 446, 467, 488, 587, 603, 628.

76   Dolan, *Whores of Babylon*, pp. 135–6.

77   See Chapter 4 for a discussion of the cloister's political symbolism.

78   C. Walker, ' "Of Feminine Sexe, but Masculine Virtue": Catholic Women and the Preservation of the Faith in England, 1558–1640' (Honours dissertation, University of Western Australia, 1986), ch. 4.

79   'Ghent Obituary Notices', p. 36; K. Lowe, 'Secular Brides and Convent Brides: Wedding Ceremonies in Italy during the Renaissance and Counter Reformation', in *Marriage in Italy, 1300–1650*, ed. T. Dean and K. J. P. Lowe (Cambridge, 1998), pp. 41–65.

80   Zarri, 'Reform of the Regulars', p. 208. Colleen Seguin also noted the prevalence of familial imagery, Seguin, ' "Addicted Unto Piety" ', ch. 5.

81   S. O'Brien, '*Terra Incognita*: The Nun in Nineteenth-Century England', *P&P*, 121 (1988), p. 136. See also, N. B. Warren, 'Pregnancy and Productivity: The Imagery of Female Monasticism Within and Beyond the Cloister Walls', *Journal of Medieval and Early Modern Studies*, 28 (1998), pp. 531–52.

82   Priory, St Monica's MS Qu2, fols. 2–3.

83   Ibid., fol. 86.

84   Ibid., fol. 21.

85   Ibid., fol. 87.

86   [Augustine], *Rule ... Constitutions*, pp. 505–12.

87   Arundel, Franciscan MS 6b, fols. 59–62; Priory, St Monica's MS E4, fols. 9–19, 27–40, 54–7, Constitutions, 1609; [Augustine], *Rule ... Constitutions*, pp. 121, 314–17, 510–428 [that is, 510r]; *Benedictine Statutes*, Part 2, pp. 3–17, 27–9; *Diary of the 'Blue Nuns'*, pp. 291–3, 297–303; [St Clare], *The Rule of the Holy Virgin S. Clare* (1621), p. 23.

88   Priory, St Monica's MS Qu2, fol. 85.

89   DL, Hazlemere MS 2020, fol. 36, MS Book of Monastic Ceremonies, 1694.

90   Priory, St Monica's MS E4, fols. 23, 70; *Diary of the 'Blue Nuns'*, p. 288; Arundel, Franciscan MS 15, fols. 1–2, Book of Ceremonial for Novice Mistresses; St Colette, *Declarations*, pp. 77–8.

91   Arundel, Franciscan MS 6b, fol. 52.

92   Arundel, Franciscan MS 22, fol. 6, A Copy of the Privileges Granted the Jubilarians.

93   Arundel, Franciscan MS 'General Cerimonies to be Observed throughout the Yeare Unless it be Otherwise Appoynted for Speciall Feasts', fols. 10, 17, 33, 36, 51. This manuscript was listed as the second copy of the second revision of the 1641 statutes. However, a comparison with the 1738 book of ceremonies identified it as the 1648 ceremonial.

94   *Diary of the 'Blue Nuns'*, p. 305.

95   Darlington, MS Gravelines Chronicles, fols. 147–8; 'Registers of the English Poor Clares at Gravelines, including those who Founded Filiations at Aire,

Dunkirk and Rouen, 1608–1837', hereafter 'Poor Clare Registers', in *Miscellanea 9* (London, CRS 14, 1914), p. 37.

96 Priory, St Monica's MS Q29, fol. 4.

97 AAW, A XXXIII, fol. 451, [Marina] Beaumont to English Chapter, 28 May [c.1670].

98 AAM, Fonds Kloosters, Englese Benedictijnen/5, Barbara Melchiora Campbell to archbishop, 24 Jan. 1683.

99 Arundel, Franciscan MS 16, fol. 5, Miscellanea, vol. I, 'Account of the Duties of the Vicaress by Rev. M. Margaret Paul Radcliffe', *c.*1626.

100 Arundel, Franciscan MS 6b, fols. 54–5; *Benedictine Statutes*, Part 2, pp. 19, 21–2; *Diary of the 'Blue Nuns'*, pp. 290–1; [Augustine], *Rule . . . Constitutions* pp. 126–7, 130–1, 134–5.

101 Priory, St Monica's MS E4, fols. 5–10; *Diary of the 'Blue Nuns'*, pp. 287–91; *Benedictine Statutes*, Part 2, pp. 18–23; Arundel, Franciscan MS 6b, fos. 53–6.

102 [Augustine], *Rule . . . Constitutions*, pp. 115, 117. See also Arundel, Franciscan MS 6b, fol. 54; *Diary of the 'Blue Nuns'*, p. 289; *Benedictine Statutes*, Part 2, p. 18.

103 Priory, St Monica's MS E4, fol. 5; Arundel, Franciscan MS 6b, fols. 36, 54; *Benedictine Statutes*, Part 1, p. 15, Part 2, p. 11; St Colette, *Declarations*, p. 73.

104 *Diary of the 'Blue Nuns'*, p. 291. See also [St Benedict], *The Rule of the Most Blissed Father Saint Benedict Patriarke of all Munkes*, (Ghent, 1632), p. 89.

105 D. R. Reinke, ' "Austin's Labour": Patterns of Governance in Medieval Augustinian Monasticism', *Church History*, 56 (1987), p. 167.

106 Priory, St Monica's MS E4, fol. 5.

107 *Benedictine Statutes*, Part 3, pp. 3–9; *Diary of the 'Blue Nuns'*, pp. 304–5, 311; Arundel, Franciscan MS 6b, fols. 66–7.

108 Priory, St Monica's MS E4, fol. 5.

109 [Augustine], *Rule . . . Constitutions*, p. 139.

110 *Diary of the 'Blue Nuns'*, p. 286; [Augustine], *Rule . . . Constitutions*, p. 135.

111 *Diary of the 'Blue Nuns'*, p. 305.

112 The Benedictines at Brussels, Ghent, Pontoise, Dunkirk and Ypres, the Poor Clares, and the Augustinians at Bruges and Louvain elected their abbesses for life, but the 'Blue Nuns', Franciscans, and Sepulchrines held triennial elections, at which it was usually possible for the same woman to be re-elected superior. The Cambrai and Paris Benedictines had quadrennial elections. The Paris Augustinian community initially elected their abbess for life, but to avoid the French royal practice of imposing superiors *in commendam*, they subsequently changed to quadrennial elections.

113 Arundel, Franciscan MS 6b, fol. 61. See also *Benedictine Statutes*, Part 2, pp. 36–41; *Diary of the 'Blue Nuns'*, pp. 292–3.

114 *Benedictine Statutes*, Part 1, pp. 39–49; Arundel, Franciscan MS 6b, fol. 38; Priory, St Monica's MS E4, fols. 69–75; *Diary of the 'Blue Nuns'*, pp. 283, 294–5; Lille, MS 20 H 1, fols. 54–5, Constitutions of English Benedictines at Cambrai, 1631.

115 *Benedictine Statutes*, Part 2, p. 18.

116 DL, Hazlemere MS 3137, fols. 36–7, 43–7, Exact Copies of Original Letters and Papers . . . 1628 and 1638.

117 *Chronicle of St Monica's*, vol. I, p. 31.

118 Cited in Durrant, *Flemish Mystics*, p. 204.

119 Priory, St Monica's MS Qu2, fol. 59. See also Lille, MS 20 H 1, fol. 70; *Benedictine Statutes*, Part 2, pp. 18, 20; [St Benedict], *Rule*, p. 81; *Diary of the 'Blue Nuns'*, p. 290.

120 'Ghent Obituary Notices', p. 38.

121 Matthew 23:37. See A. Loades, *Searching for Lost Coins: Explorations in Christianity and Feminism* (London, 1987), pp. 89–95.

122 C. Walker Bynum, *Jesus as Mother: Studies in the Spirituality of the High Middle Ages* (Berkeley, Ca., 1982), pp. 154–9.

123 Priory, St Monica's MS Q29, fol. 28.

124 Durrant, *Flemish Mystics*, pp. 336–7.

125 C. Harline and E. Put, 'A Bishop in the Cloisters: The Visitations of Mathias Hovius (Malines, 1596–1620)', *SCJ*, 22 (1991), pp. 626–31; AAM, Mechliniensia/Reg.8, fol. 237.

126 *Benedictine Statutes*, Part 3, p. 29.

127 Priory, St Monica's MS Q29, fols. 32–4.

128 Ibid., fols. 30–2.

129 'Abbess Neville's Annals of Five Communities of English Benedictine Nuns in Flanders, 1598–1687', ed. M. J. Rumsey, hereafter 'Abbess Neville's Annals', in *Miscellanea V* (London, CRS 6, 1909), pp. 27–9.

130 Buckfast, Pontoise MS, Mary Knatchbull, 'An Account of the Foundation of the Convent of Boulogne: First Filiation from Ghent, 1653', fols. 3–29.

131 Buckfast, Pontoise MS, Knatchbull, 'Account', fol. 59. The abbess transcribed her correspondence with the bishop.

132 Ibid., fol. 34.

133 Ibid. fols. 62–3.

134 'Abbess Neville's Annals', p. 49; M. Murray-Sinclair, 'Pontoise: The Vicissitudes of a House "Beyond the Seas"' (unpublished paper), p. 7. I am grateful to Sr Mildred for permission to cite her unpublished work.

135 Buckfast, Pontoise MS, Knatchbull, 'Account', fol. 67.

136 AAM, Mechliniensia/Reg.8, fol. 236b.

137 For a few examples, see AAM, Fonds Kloosters, Englese Benedictijnen/12, Potentiana Deacon to Jacob Boonen, 13 Dec. [1622]; Lucy Knatchbull to same, n.d.; Frances Gawen to same 5 April 1623, 13 April 1623, 29 July [1623]; Elizabeth Southcott to same [1622], 23 April 1623; Mary Vavasour to same [1623]; Teresa Gage to same [1623]; Agnes Lenthall to same, n.d.

138 Ibid., Lucy Knatchbull to Jacob Boonen, 16 May 1623; Barbara Duckett to same, n.d.; Frances Gawen to same, 29 July [1623]; Potentiana Deacon to same, 26 Aug. 1623; Ursula Hewicke to same [1623]; Anne Ingleby to same, [1625]. For a detailed account of the grievances (and Mary Percy's response), see BL, Harleian MS 4275, An English Monastery of Benedictines at Brussels in Flanders.

139 AAM, Fonds Kloosters, Englese Benedictijnen/12, Alexia Blanchard to Jacob Boonen, 22 July 1622.

140 Ibid., Lucy Knatchbull to Jacob Boonen, n.d.; Mary Wintour to same, n.d.

141 Ibid., Potentiana Deacon to Jacob Boonen, 13 Dec. [1622].

142 Ibid., Elizabeth Southcott to Jacob Boonen, 23 April 1623.

143 Ibid., Frances Gawen to Jacob Boonen, 23 April 1623.

144 Ibid., Ursula Hewicke to Jacob Boonen, 5 April 1625.

145 DL, Hazlemere MS 3137, fols. 1–5, 35–48, 56–60, 66, 108–11; BL, Harleian MS 4275; Pasture, 'Documents Concernant quelques Monastères Anglais', pp. 156–211; 'Abbess Neville's Annals', pp. 10, 13–14; Guilday, *Catholic Refugees*, pp. 257–64; Arblaster, 'The Infanta and the English Benedictine Nuns: Mary Percy's Memories in 1634', *RH*, 23 (1997), pp. 513, 516, 521, 523, 525–6.

146 P. Arblaster, 'The Monastery of Our Lady of the Assumption in Brussels (1599–1794)', *English Benedictine History Symposium*, 17 (1999), p. 68.

147 AAW, A XXXIV, fols. 349–60, Narrative of the Transaction between the English Conception Nuns and Fr Warner SJ; *Diary of the 'Blue Nuns'*, pp. 25, 29–31.

148 DL, Hazelmere MS 3137, fol. 44.

149 AAW, A XXXIV, fol. 327, Lord Castlemaine to [Abbess Timperley], 27 July 1675.

150 Ibid., fols. 329–31, 333–5, 343, 345–7, 349–60, Abbess Timperley to Lord Castlemaine, [Aug. 1675]; Abbot Montague to same, [Aug. 1675]; Joseph Shirburne to same, 15 Sept. 1675; Abbess Timperley to same, [Sept. 1675].

151 AAM, Fonds Kloosters, Englese Benedictijnen/12, Potentiana Deacon to Jacob Boonen, 13 Dec. [1622].

3   The Monastic Economy: Prayer and Manual Labour

1 Oulton, MS G.11, Appeal to the citizens of Ghent.

2 A. M. C. Forster, 'The Chronicles of the English Poor Clares of Rouen – I', *RH*, 18 (1986), p. 59.

3 *In a Great Tradition: Tribute to Dame Laurentia McLaughlan Abbess of Stanbrook by the Benedictines of Stanbrook* (London, 1956), pp. 18–19.

4 R. C. Trexler, 'Celibacy in the Renaissance: The Nuns of Florence', in *Dependence in Context in Renaissance Florence* (Binghamton, NY, 1994), pp. 354–61, 370–1; S. Chojnacki, 'Daughters and Oligarchs: Gender and the Early Renaissance State', in *Gender and Society in Renaissance Italy*, ed. J. C. Brown and R. C. Davis (London, 1998), pp. 69–75; J. G. Sperling, *Convents and the Body Politic in Late Renaissance Venice* (Chicago, 1999), ch. 1; H. Hills, 'Cities and Virgins: Female Aristocratic Convents in Early Modern Naples and Palermo', *Oxford Art Journal*, 22 (1999), pp. 33–4, 36–7; E. Rapley, *The Dévotes: Women and Church in Seventeenth-Century France* (Montreal and Kingston, 1990), pp. 185–7.

5 Sperling, *Convents and the Body Politic*, pp. 181, 200, 250–6.

6 K. J. P. Lowe, 'Female Strategies for Success in a Male-ordered World: the Benedictine Convent of Le Murate in Florence in the Fifteenth and Early Sixteenth Centuries', in *Women in the Church*, ed. W. J. Sheils and D. Wood (Oxford, 1990), pp. 218–20.

7 M. E. Perry, *Gender and Disorder in Early Modern Seville* (Princeton, NJ, 1990), p. 78.

8 J. Bilinkoff, *The Avila of Saint Teresa: Religious Reform in a Sixteenth-Century City* (Ithaca, NY, 1989), pp. 123–31; J. Bilinkoff, 'Teresa of Jesus and Carmelite Reform', in *Religious Orders of the Catholic Reformation*, ed. R. L. DeMolen (New York, 1994), pp. 176–7.

9 Sperling, *Convents and the Body Politic*, p. 179.
10 Rapley, *The Dévotes*, p. 182.
11 Perry, *Gender and Disorder*, p. 79.
12 Rapley, *The Dévotes*, pp. 180–1; J. K. McNamara, *Sisters in Arms: Catholic Nuns through Two Millennia* (Cambridge, Mass., 1996), p. 535.
13 McNamara, *Sisters in Arms*, p. 535–6.
14 C. Harline, *The Burdens of Sister Margaret* (New York, 1994), pp. 125, 221–2.
15 DL, Hazlemere MS VI.C 3140, fols. [2–3, 14–15], Account Book; DL, Hazlemere MS 1887, Deeds Concerning Purchase of House.
16 DL, Hazlemere MS VI.C 3140, fols. [137–8].
17 *The Chronicle of the English Augustinian Canonesses Regular of the Lateran, at St Monica's in Louvain, 1548–1625*, ed. A. Hamilton, hereafter *Chronicle of St Monica's* (London, 1904), vol. 1, pp. 58–68; Priory, St Monica's MS P1, fols. 1–15, Benefactors' Book, 1609–1970.
18 *Chronicle of St Monica's*, vol. 1, pp. 75–6.
19 *Annals of the English Benedictines at Ghent, now at St Mary's Abbey, Oulton in Staffordshire*, hereafter *Ghent Annals* (Oulton, 1894), p. 152.
20 'Abbess Neville's Annals of Five Communities of English Benedictine Nuns in Flanders, 1598–1687', ed. M. J. Rumsey, hereafter 'Abbess Neville's Annals', in *Miscellanea V* (London, CRS 6, 1909), p. 19.
21 *Chronicle of St Monica's*, vol. I, pp. 61–8.
22 I have included St Monica's which although the first English Augustinian cloister was a filiation from St Ursula's. The other filiations were the Bruges Augustinians; the Benedictines at Ghent, Boulogne-Pontoise, Dunkirk, Ypres and Paris; the Carmelites at Lierre and Hoogstraeten; the Poor Clares in Aire, Rouen and Dunkirk; and the Conceptionists in Paris. Although Cédoz calls the Paris Augustinian house a filiation from the Flemish abbey of Notre-Dame-de-Beaulieu in Douai, I regard it as an initial foundation. See F. Cédoz, *Un Couvent de Religieuses Anglaises à Paris de 1634 à 1884* (Paris and London, 1891), ch. 1.
23 See Chapter 1 for comparative early recruitment in both cloisters.
24 'Abbess Neville's Annals', pp. 19–22; T. Matthew, *The Life of Lady Lucy Knatchbull*, ed. D. Knowles (London, 1931), pp. 91–105.
25 'Abbess Neville's Annals', pp. 24–31.
26 Ibid., pp. 35–7; *Ghent Annals*, pp. 162–4.
27 *Ghent Annals*, pp. 51, 167–8.
28 Lancs. RO, DDCl/1169, Mary Caryll to Thomas Clifton, 22 Feb. 1675.
29 Lancs. RO, DDCl/1170, Mary Caryll to Thomas Clifton, 24 April 1676; DDCl/1177, Anne Clifton to same, 25 June [1676].
30 DL, Hazlemere MS VI.C 3140, fols. [4–24].
31 Ibid., fols. [44–6].
32 Priory, St Monica's MS M1, fol. 3, Council Book, 1669–1874.
33 Lancs. RO, DDCl/1170, Mary Caryll to Thomas Clifton, 24 April 1676.
34 Yorks. Archives Leeds, GC/F8/1, fols. 23, 35, 44, Personal Account Book of Sir Thomas Gascoigne, 2nd Bart (D11), 1661–1678.
35 DL, Hazlemere MS VI.C 3140, fols. [17, 27].
36 BL, Add. MS 28,227, fol. 428, Lucy Herbert to Mary Caryll, 22 July [1717].
37 For a broader discussion, see my '"Doe not supose me a well mortyfied Nun dead to the world"· Letter-Writing in Early Modern English Convents', in *Early*

Modern Women's Letter Writing, 1450–1700, ed. J. Daybell (Basingstoke, 2001), pp. 163–8.

38 DL, Hazlemere MS VI.C 3140, fols. [22, 40–1, 47]; DL, Hazlemere MS 1887, Bond on *Mont de Piété* for life rents of 1890 florins fixed on heads of Lady Abbess and 18 Religious, 7 Oct. 1639.

39 BL, Add. MS 28,226, fol. 117, Mary Caryll to John Caryll, 1699.

40 Ibid., fols. 114, 117, Mary Caryll to John Caryll, 1697, 1699.

41 DL, Hazlemere MS VI.C 3140, fol. [15].

42 A. F. Allison, 'The English Augustinian Convent of Our Lady of Syon at Paris: Its Foundation and Struggle for Survival during the First Eighty Years, 1634–1713', *RH*, 21 (1993), p. 468.

43 BL, Add. MS 28,226, fols. 114, 118, 122, Mary Caryll to John Caryll, 1697, 1699, 1704.

44 Notably, the Third Order Franciscans in 1658, and the Benedictines of Ypres in the 1680s and 1690s. See B. Whelan, *Historic English Convents of Today: The Story of the English Cloisters in France and Flanders in Penal Times* (London, 1936), pp. 54–60, 101–3, 128.

45 Buckfast, Pontoise MS Mary Knatchbull, 'An Account of the Foundation of the Convent of Boulogne: First Filiation from Ghent', fols. 27–68.

46 Ibid., fols. 47–51. The merchants subsequently reneged on their promises and Abbess Knatchbull lost much of the proposed income.

47 Ibid., fol. 94.

48 Forster had used his influence with Henrietta Maria to persuade the authorities to allow the Poor Clare filiation to Rouen in 1644, and he had contributed 1,000–1,500 pistoles towards the building of the convent's church. See A. M. C. Forster, 'The Chronicles of the English Poor Clares of Rouen – 2', *RH*, 18 (1986), p. 189; 'Abbess Neville's Annals', p. 49.

49 'Abbess Neville's Annals', pp. 48–52; M. Murray-Sinclair, 'Pontoise: the Vicissitudes of a House "Beyond the Seas"' (unpublished paper), p. 7.

50 Murray-Sinclair, 'Pontoise', pp. 8, 10.

51 Versailles, 68 H 5, fols. [36–48], Account Book 1653–1703. Thanks to Professor John Bossy for the generous loan of this material.

52 Apart from in 1697 when the yearly accounts ended 4,618 livres in credit. 1702 is the last date for which I have complete figures. Details are missing for the years 1687–91.

53 Cited in P. Guilday, *The English Catholic Refugees on the Continent 1558–1795* (London, 1914), p. 272.

54 'Registers of the English Benedictine Nuns of Pontoise, now at Teignmouth, Devonshire, 1680–1713', hereafter 'Pontoise Registers', in *Miscellanea X* (London, CRS 17, 1915), p. 254.

55 Bodl., Carte MS 30, fol. 541, Mary Knatchbull to Ormonde, 3 March 1660.

56 'Abbess Neville's Annals', pp. 64–5.

57 For a more detailed discussion of this ideology see my 'Combining Martha and Mary: Gender and Work in Seventeenth-Century English Cloisters', *SCJ*, 30 (1999), pp. 399–404.

58 G. Ovitt, Jr, 'The Cultural Context of Western Technology: Early Christian Attitudes toward Manual Labour', in *The Work of Work: Servitude, Slavery, and Labor in Medieval England*, ed. A. J. Frantzen and D. Moffat (Glasgow, 1994),

pp. 71–94; L. J. R. Milis, *Angelic Monks and Earthly Men: Monasticism and its Meaning to Medieval Society* (Woodbridge, 1992), p. 26.

59 L. Eckenstein, *Woman under Monasticism: Chapters on Saint-lore and Convent Life between AD 500 and AD 1500* (Cambridge, 1896), pp. 356–61; P. D. Johnson, *Equal in Monastic Profession: Religious Women in Medieval France* (Chicago, 1991), pp. 144–7.

60 McNamara, *Sisters in Arms*, p. 316.

61 Ibid., pp. 305–12.

62 R. Gilchrist, *Gender and Material Culture: The Archaeology of Religious Women* (London, 1994), pp. 69–73, 85–91; M. Oliva, *The Convent and the Community in Late Medieval England: Female Monasteries in the Diocese of Norwich, 1350–1540* (Woodbridge, 1998), pp. 11–27; E. Power, *Medieval English Nunneries* (Cambridge, 1922), pp. 2–3, ch. 5.

63 Johnson, *Equal in Monastic Profession*, pp. 219–20.

64 Gilchrist, *Gender and Material Culture*, pp. 36–50.

65 McNamara, *Sisters in Arms*, pp. 280–3.

66 Oliva, *Convent and the Community*, pp. 22, 26–7, 73–4, 209–14.

67 *Statutes Compyled for the Better Observation of the Holy Rule of the Most Glorious Father and Patriarch S. Benedict . . . delivered to the English Religious Woemen of . . . Brussels and to all their Successours*, hereafter *Benedictine Statutes* (Ghent, 1632), part 1, p. 55; [St Augustine], *Rule . . . Together with the Constitutions of the English Canonesse Regular's of Our B. Ladyes of Sion in Paris* (Paris, 1636), pp. 281–2.

68 Both the Brussels Benedictines and the Paris Augustinians were specifically commanded not to make anything within the convent for sale. *Benedictine Statutes*, part 3, p. 17; Allison, 'English Augustinian Convent', p. 464.

69 U. Strasser, 'Bones of Contention: Cloistered Nuns, Decorated Relics, and the Contest over Women's Place in the Public Sphere of Counter-Reformation Munich', *Archive for Reformation History*, 90 (1999), pp. 266–7.

70 Whelan, *English Convents*, pp. 66, 68; St Colette, *The Declarations and Ordinances Made upon the Rule of Our Holy Mother, S. Clare* (1622), pp. 57–66, 89–95; M. Richards, 'Community and Poverty in the Reformed Order of St Clare in the Fifteenth Century', *Journal of Religious History*, 19 (1995), pp. 13–16.

71 T. M. Kealy, *Dowry of Women Religious: A Historical Synopsis and Commentary* (Washington, DC, 1941), pp. 9–26; J. H. Lynch, *Simoniacal Entry into Religious Life from 1000 to 1260: A Social, Economic and Legal Study* (Columbus, Ohio, 1976), ch. 4.

72 S. Thompson, *Women Religious: The Founding of English Nunneries after the Norman Conquest* (Oxford, 1991), pp. 169, 171, 174, 181, 182.

73 Milis, *Angelic Monks*, pp. 20–1, 87–91. See also McNamara, *Sisters in Arms*, pp. 142–3.

74 *The Diary of the 'Blue Nuns' or Order of the Immaculate Conception of Our Lady, at Paris, 1658–1810*, ed. J. Gillow and R. Trappes-Lomax, hereafter *Diary of the 'Blue Nuns'* (London, CRS 8, 1910), pp. 9–10.

75 'Pontoise Registers', pp. 254–5.

76 Ibid., p. 250.

77 Ibid., p. 251.

78 Ibid., p. 266.

79   M. W. Sturman, 'Gravelines and the English Poor Clares', *London Recusant*, 7 (1977), p. 4. See also Darlington, MS Aire Register, [Part 4, fols. 1, 17–18]; 'Records of the Nuns of the Second Order', in *Dominicana* (London, CRS 25, 1925), pp. 192–8.

80   DL, Ealing MS Journal 1695–1738, fols. 14, 26, Diurnall of the English Canonesses Regulars of St Augustin's Order established in Paris; Cédoz, *Religieuses Anglaises*, pp. 195–200.

81   *Diary of the 'Blue Nuns'*, p. 38.

82   *Ghent Annals*, pp. 168–70.

83   Milis, *Angelic Monks*, pp. 87–9.

84   Johnson, *Equal in Monastic Profession*, pp. 21–7.

85   *Diary of the 'Blue Nuns'*, p. 38.

86   AAM, Fonds Kloosters, Englese Benedictijnen/7, Anne Forster to archbishop, 10 March 1681.

87   Schroeder, *Canons and Decrees*, p. 218; Priory, St Monica's MS M1, fols. 11–12.

88   Priory, St Monica's MS P1, fol. 83.

89   Priory, St Monica's MS M1, fols. 9, 12.

90   *Diary of the 'Blue Nuns'*, p. 21; C. S. Durrant, *A Link Between Flemish Mystics and English Martyrs* (London, 1925), pp. 256–7, 433.

91   *A Brief Relation of the Order and Institute of the English Religious Women at Liège* (Liège, 1652), p. 54.

92   Guilday, *Catholic Refugees*, p. 305; Whelan, *English Convents*, pp. 88, 90, 106, 259.

93   Arundel, Franciscan MS Annals, fol. 44, Annals of the Religious of the 3rd Order of St Francis of the Province of England from the year 1621 to (1893).

94   Forster, 'Poor Clares of Rouen – 1', pp. 66, 68–76, 94–5; Forster, 'Poor Clares of Rouen – 2', p. 182.

95   *Brief Relation*, p. 54.

96   M. D. R. Leys, *Catholics in England 1559–1829: A Social History* (London, 1961), p. 168.

97   'Records of the English Benedictine Nuns at Cambrai (now Stanbrook), 1620–1793', ed. J. Gillow, hereafter 'Cambrai Records', in *Miscellanea VIII* (London, CRS 13, 1913), p. 58.

98   Forster, 'Poor Clares of Rouen – 2', pp. 168, 182, 190.

99   Ibid., p. 190.

100   'Cambrai Records', p. 58.

101   Guilday, *Catholic Refugees*, p. 417.

102   'Cambrai Records', pp. 52–5.

103   Cédoz, *Religieuses Anglaises*, p. 169.

104   *Diary of the 'Blue Nuns'*, pp. 20, 34, 39.

105   'Pontoise Registers', p. 324.

106   Forster, 'Poor Clares of Rouen – 1', p. 96.

107   *Chronicle of St Monica's*, vol. 2, pp. 186, 191–2, 194, 198–9.

108   P. Skippon, 'An Account of a Journey Made thro' Part of the Low Countries, Germany Italy and France', in *A Collection of Voyages and Travels*, 3rd edn, ed. A. and J. Churchill (London, 1744), vol. 6, p. 391.

109   BL, Add. MS 28,226, fol. 139, Mary Caryll to John Caryll, 29 May 1711.

110 *Brief Relation*, 52–4.

111 DL, Hazlemere MS VI.C 3140, [fol. 48]. Only two women were professed in the 1670s.

112 Oulton, MS G.39, fol. 4, The English Benedictine Monastery at Ghent; *Ghent Annals*, pp. 51, 180.

113 DL, Ealing MS Journal 1695–1738, fol. 5.

114 Cédoz, *Religieuses Anglaises*, p. 41.

115 'Cambrai Records', p. 59.

116 DL, Ealing MS Journal 1695–1738, fols. 8, 10–15, 17, 19–21, 25–30; Cédoz, *Religieuses Anglaises*, pp. 197–9.

117 *Diary of the 'Blue Nuns'*, pp. 25–6. The nuns were apparently unconcerned about Palmer's dubious reputation, choosing instead to capitalise on her Catholicism and her associations with the English Court.

118 *Diary of the 'Blue Nuns'*, p. 296.

119 [Augustine], *Rule...Constitutions*, pp. 279–82; [St Benedict], *The Rule of the Most Blissed Father Saint Benedict Patriarke of all Munkes* (Ghent, 1632), pp. 72–5.

120 Priory, St Monica's MS M1, fols. 14–15. Clothing gowns were not only recycled into 'Church stuff' by the nuns. Many found their way into the 'Imbrodured sute' made for Prioress Marina Plowden's jubilee in 1704. Ibid., fols. 17–18.

121 T. Carre, *Pietas Parisiensis or a Short Description of the Piety and Charitie Comonly Exercised in Paris* (Paris, 1666), p. 145.

122 DL, Ealing MS Journal 1695–1738, fos. 50–1.

123 C. D. van Strien, 'Recusant Houses in the Southern Netherlands as Seen by British Tourists, *c.* 1650–1720', *RH*, 20 (1991), p. 505.

124 'Abbess Neville's Annals', p. 25.

125 'Obituary Notices of the Nuns of the English Benedictine Abbey of Ghent in Flanders, 1627–1811', in *Miscellanea XI* (London, CRS 19, 1917), p. 52.

126 Skippon, 'Account of a Journey', p. 384.

127 AAM, Fonds Kloosters, Englese Benedictijnen/12, Frances Gawen to Jacob Boonen, 13 April 1623.

128 Versailles, 68 H 5, fols. [5, 12].

129 Lancs. RO, RCBu14/132, James Coghlan to Charles Long, 16 Sept. 1799.

130 'Cambrai Records', pp. 35–6.

131 Carre, *Pietas Parisiensis*, pp. 145–6.

132 Priory, St Monica's MS C2, fols. 499–500, Chronicle, vol. 1, 1548–1837.

133 'Records of the English Canonesses of the Holy Sepulchre at Liège, Now at New Hall, 1652–1793', ed. R. Trappes-Lomax, in *Miscellanea X* (London, CRS 17, 1915), p. 46.

134 *Chronicle of St Monica's*, vol. 1, pp. 263–5.

135 Priory, St Monica's MS M1, fol. 4.

136 Priory, St Monica's MS C2, fols. 499–500.

137 [Benedict], *Rule*, pp. 80–1.

138 Carre, *Pietas Parisiensis*, pp. 147–51; Cédoz, *Religieuses Anglaises*, pp. 43–5; Allison, 'English Augustinian Convent', p. 463.

139 *Diary of the 'Blue Nuns'*, pp. 36, 38.

4. Beyond the Cloister: Patronage, Politics and Society

1 Bodl., Clarendon MS 63, fol. 58, Elizabeth Augustina Cary to Col. Grace, 10 Aug. 1659.

2 C. Walker, 'Prayer, Patronage and Political Conspiracy: English Nuns and the Restoration', *HJ*, 43 (2000), pp. 1–23; C. M. K. Bowden, 'The Abbess and Mrs Brown: Lady Mary Knatchbull and Royalist Politics in Flanders in the Late 1650s', *RH*, 24 (1999), pp. 288–308.

3 *Women and Politics in Early Modern England*, ed. J. Daybell (Ashgate, forthcoming); S. Mendelson and P. Crawford, *Women in Early Modern England* (Oxford, 1998), pp. 365–80; N. K. Maguire, 'The Duchess of Portsmouth: English Royal Consort and French Politician, 1670–85', in *The Stuart Court and Europe: Essays in Politics and Political Culture*, ed. R. M. Smuts (Cambridge, 1996), pp. 247–73; S. Kettering, 'The Patronage Power of Early Modern French Noblewomen', *HJ*, 32 (1989), pp. 817–41; B. A. Hanawalt, 'Lady Honor Lisle's Networks of Influence', in *Women and Power in the Middle Ages*, ed. M. Erler and M. Kowaleski (Athens, Ga., 1988), pp. 204–9.

4 K. J. P. Lowe, 'Female Strategies for Success in a Male-ordered World: the Benedictine Convent of Le Murate in Florence in the Fifteenth and Early Sixteenth Centuries', in *Women in the Church*, ed. W. J. Sheils and D. Wood (Oxford, 1990), pp. 218–21.

5 J. G. Sperling, *Convents and the Body Politic in Late Renaissance Venice* (Chicago, 1999), pp. 144–6, 218–25.

6 C. Blaisdell, 'Religion, Gender and Class: Nuns and Authority in Early Modern France', in *Changing Identities in Early Modern France*, ed. M. Wolfe (Durham, NC, 1997), pp. 150–1.

7 J. Baker, 'Female Monasticism and Family Strategy: The Guises and Saint Pierre de Reims', *SCJ*, 28 (1997), pp. 1096–9.

8 M. E. Wiesner, 'Ideology Meets the Empire: Reformed Convents and the Reformation', in *Germania Illustrata: Essays on Early Modern Germany Presented to Gerald Strauss*, ed. A. C. Fix and S. C. Karant-Nunn (Kirksville, Miss., 1991), pp. 182–3.

9 A. M. Roberts, 'Chiara Gambacorta of Pisa as Patroness of the Arts', in *Creative Women in Medieval and Early Modern Italy: A Religious and Artistic Renaissance*, ed. E. A. Matter and J. Coakley (Philadelphia, 1994), pp. 120–54.

10 H. Hills, 'Cities and Virgins: Female Aristocratic Convents in Early Modern Naples and Palermo', *Oxford Art Journal*, 22 (1999), p. 38; M. Winkelmes, 'Taking Part: Benedictine Nuns as Patrons of Art and Architecture', in *Picturing Women in Renaissance and Baroque Italy*, ed. G. A. Johnson and S. F. Matthews Grieco (Cambridge, 1997), pp. 91–110.

11 U. Wiethaus, ' "If I had an Iron Body": Femininity and Religion in the Letters of Maria de Hout', in *Dear Sister: Medieval Women and the Epistolary Genre*, ed. K. Cherewatuk and U. Wiethaus (Philadelphia, 1993), pp. 171–4.

12 J. Bilinkoff, 'A Saint for a City: Mariana de Jesús and Madrid, 1565–1624', *Archive for Reformation History*, 88 (1997), pp. 328–34.

13 R. Maddox, 'Founding a Convent in Early Modern Spain: Cultural History, Hegemonic Processes, and the Plurality of the Historical Subject', *Rethinking History*, 2 (1998), pp. 182–4.

14   U. Strasser, 'Bones of Contention: Cloistered Nuns, Decorated Relics, and the Contest over Women's Place in the Public Sphere of Counter-Reformation Munich', *Archive for Reformation History*, 90 (1999), p. 269.

15   J. Bilinkoff, 'A Spanish Prophetess and Her Patrons: The Case of María de Santo Domingo', *SCJ*, 23 (1992), pp. 27–30.

16   M. Sánchez, *The Empress, the Queen, and the Nun: Women and Power at the Court of Philip III of Spain* (Baltimore, 1998), p. 148.

17   G. Zarri, 'Living Saints: A Typology of Female Sanctity in the Early Sixteenth Century', in *Women and Religion in Medieval and Renaissance Italy*, ed. D. Bornstein and R. Rusconi (Chicago, 1996), pp. 226–7, 242.

18   P. Macey, 'Infiamma il mio cor: Savonarolan Laude by and for Dominican Nuns in Tuscany', in *The Crannied Wall: Women, Religion, and the Arts in Early Modern Europe*, ed. C. A. Monson (Ann Arbor, Mich., 1992), pp. 164–8, 174–5.

19   L. Roper, *The Holy Household: Women and Morals in Reformation Augsburg* (Oxford, 1989), pp. 211–28.

20   P. S. Datsko Barker, 'Caritas Pirckheimer: A Female Humanist Confronts the Reformation', *SCJ*, 26 (1995), pp. 259–72.

21   *A Brief Relation of the Order and Institute of the English Religious Women at Liège* (Liège, 1652), pp. 6–16.

22   BL, Add. MS 5813, fols. 31–4, An Account of the Nunnery of St Monica in Lovain.

23   Oulton, MS G.39, fol. 5, The English Benedictine Monastery at Ghent.

24   C. S. Durrant, *A Link Between Flemish Mystics and English Martyrs* (London, 1925), p. 309.

25   'Abbess Neville's Annals of Five Communities of English Benedictine Nuns in Flanders, 1598–1687', ed. M. J. Rumsey, hereafter 'Abbess Neville's Annals', in *Miscellanea V* (London, CRS 6, 1909), pp. 42, 58–9; *A History of the Benedictine Nuns of Dunkirk* (London, 1958), p. 24.

26   PRO, SP Flanders 77/6, fol. 73. See also SP Flanders: 77/8, fol. 275; P. Arblaster, 'The Infanta and the English Benedictine Nuns: Mary Percy's Memories in 1634', *RH*, 23 (1997), pp. 522–3.

27   'Abbess Neville's Annals', pp. 2–3.

28   Ibid., pp. 10–11; T. Matthew, *The Life of Lucy Knatchbull*, ed. D. Knowles (London, 1931), pp. 83–91; *Annals of the English Benedictines at Ghent, Now at St Mary's Abbey, Oulton in Staffordshire*, hereafter *Ghent Annals* (Oulton, 1894), p. 179.

29   *The Diary of the 'Blue Nuns' or Order of the Immaculate Conception of Our Lady, at Paris, 1658–1810*, ed. J. Gillow and R. Trappes-Lomax, hereafter *Diary of the 'Blue Nuns'* (London, CRS 8, 1910), pp. 25–6, 30–2, 34–8.

30   DL, Ealing MS Journal 1695–1738, fols. 13, 19, 20, 23, 30; F. Cédoz, *Un Couvent de Religieuses Anglaises à Paris de 1634 à 1884* (Paris and London, 1891), p. 199.

31   Durrant, *Flemish Mystics*, pp. 323–7.

32   *Letters from James Earl of Perth, to his Sister, The Countess of Erroll*, ed. W. Jerdan (London, Camden Society 23, 1845), p. 43.

33   *Letters from James Earl of Perth*, p. 44.

34   'Abbess Neville's Annals', pp. 49–50.

35   T. Carre, *Pietas Parisiensis or a Short Description of the Piety and Charitie Comonly Exorcised in Paris* (Paris, 1666), pp. 147–51, A. F. Allison, 'The English

Augustinian Convent of Our Lady of Syon at Paris: Its Foundation and Struggle for Survival during the First Eighty Years, 1634–1713', *RH*, 21 (1993), p. 464; Cédoz, *Religieuses Anglaises*, pp. 43–5.

36 BL, Add. MS 28,230, fol. 259, Benedicta Caryll to John Caryll, 6 Aug. 1744.

37 For a fuller discussion of letters' importance see my ' "Doe not supose me a well mortifyed Nun dead to the world": Letter-Writing in Early Modern English Convents', in *Early Modern Women Letter Writers*, ed. J. Daybell (Basingstoke, 2001), pp. 170–4.

38 Bodl., Carte MS 214, fol. 253, Mary Vavasour to Ormonde, 2 Nov. 1660.

39 BL, Add. MS 28,227, fol. 163, Benedicta Fleetwood to John Caryll, 24 Aug. 1713.

40 Centre for Kentish Studies, U269 C324 (Bundle 58), Mary Knatchbull to Lord Fitzharding, 29 Nov. 1664.

41 Bodl., Clarendon MS 72, fol. 265, Lady More to Mary Knatchbull, 21 May 1660.

42 BL, Add. MS 28,225, fols. 276–7, Mary Wigmore to Mary of Modena, 23 May 1688.

43 BL, Add. MS 28,226, fols. 104, 118, 121, John Caryll to Mary Caryll, 15 July 1695, Mary Caryll to John Caryll, 25 Feb. 1699, 5 Aug. 1702.

44 BL, Add. MS 36,452, fols. 61–2, 64, 65, 67, Winefrid Thimelby to Catherine Thimelby Aston, undated, Winefrid Thimelby to Herbert Aston, undated.

45 BL, Add. MS 28,226, fols. 114, 117, 139, Mary Caryll to John Caryll, 28 March 1697, 15 Feb. 1699, 29 May 1711.

46 Ibid., fols. 119, 116, Maura Knightly to John Caryll, undated, Mary Caryll to same, 2 Dec. 1699; P. Nolan, *The Irish Dames of Ypres: Being a History of the Royal Irish Abbey at Ypres* (Dublin, 1908), pp. 173–216.

47 BL, Add. MS 28,226, fols. 120, 127, 133, 125, Mary Caryll to John Caryll, 25 Jan. 1700, c. 1706, 13 Dec. 1707, John Caryll to Mary Caryll, 17 Nov. 1706.

48 Ibid., fols. 124, 125–6, Mary Caryll to John Caryll, 5 Nov. 1706, John Caryll to Mary Caryll, 17 Nov. 1706.

49 Ibid., fols. 124, 129, 132, 139, 130–1, Mary Caryll to John Caryll, 5 Nov. 1706, c.1706–7, 5 June 1707, 29 May 1711, John Caryll to Mary Caryll, 22 May 1707.

50 BL, Add. MS 36,452, fols. 106, 109, Winefrid Thimelby to Herbert Aston, 13 July 1684, Mary Aston to Gertrude Aston, 9 Sept. 1690; 'Records of the English Canonesses of the Holy Sepulchre at Liège, Now at New Hall, 1652–1793', ed. R. Trappes-Lomax, in *Miscellanea X* (London, CRS 17, 1915), pp. 12, 95, 191.

51 Bodl., Clarendon MS 39, fols. 75–6, 92–4, 160, 200, 162, Anne Cary to Edward Hyde, 4 March 1650, Patrick Cary to Hyde, 18 March 1650, Hyde to Patrick Cary, 25 April, 1650, 22 May 1650, Hyde to Anne Cary, 25 April 1650; Clarendon MS 40, fols. 13, 169–70, 188, Anne Cary to Hyde, 5 June 1650, Patrick Cary to Hyde, 30 Aug. 1650, Hyde to Anne Cary, 14 Sept. 1650.

52 Bodl., Clarendon MS 52, fol. 341; Clarendon MS 64, fols. 197, 258; Clarendon MS 68, fol. 155; Clarendon MS 70, fol. 70; Clarendon MS 71, fos. 119, 268; Clarendon MS 72, fol. 391; Carte MS 30, fols. 541, 543; Carte MS 31, fol. 157; Carte MS 213, fol. 500.

53 Bodl., Clarendon MS 52, fols. 81, 88, Edward Hyde to Mary Knatchbull, 17 July 1656, Peter Talbot to the king, 19 July 1656.

54 Bodl., Clarendon MS 58, fol. 228, Mary Knatchbull to Edward Hyde, Sept. 1658.

55 Bodl., Clarendon MS 72, fols. 365, 392–3, Mary More to Mary Knatchbull, 21 May 1660, Mary Knatchbull to [Edward Hyde], 25 May 1660.

56 AAW, A XXVI, fols. 433–5, Thomas Carre [*vere* Mile Pinckney] to Richard Smith, 23 Nov. 1632; AAW, A XXVII, fol. 93, Mary Tredway to Smith, 2 April 1633.

57 Allison, 'English Augustinian Convent', p. 458.

58 AAW, A XXXII, fols. 485, 523, 527, Thomas Carre to secretary of English Chapter, *c.*1665–6, Mary Tredway to Dean and Chapter, [26 June 1666], Carre to Chapter, 26 June 1666.

59 Allison, 'English Augustinian Convent', pp. 468–9; A. F. Allison, 'The Origins of St Gregory's, Paris', *RH*, 21 (1992), pp. 14–20.

60 The Poor Clares of Gravelines' annals suggest that Abbess Elizabeth Tyldesley was instrumental in the re-establishment of the English province of friars minor in 1618. Darlington, MS Gravelines Chronicles, fols. 142–3.

61 F. Borgia, *The Practise of Christian Workes, Togeather with a Short Rule, How to Live Well*, trans. J. W. (1620), p. 4.

62 V. Puccini, *The Life of the Holy and Venerable Mother Suor Maria Maddalena de Patsi, A Florentine Lady, & Religious of the Order of the Carmelites*, trans. G. B. (1619), pp. 3–4.

63 Bodl., Clarendon MS 68, fol. 155, Edward Hyde to Henry Bennett, 24 Jan. 1660.

64 Peter of Lucca, *A Dialogue of Dying Wel*, trans. R. V. (Antwerp, 1603), sig. A3.

65 PRO, SP 77/6, fol. 73, Erection of Nunnery at Brussels [Nov. 1599]; SP 77/8, fols. 275, 417–18, Thomas Edmonds to Lord Salisbury, 15 April 1607, A List of the Semminaryes, Monasteries, Cloisters, and Colledges; SP 77/11, fols. 25–6, Names of Certaine Principall men of Englishe and Scottish nations, now residinge in the Archd. Provinces; SP 77/17, fol. 2, William Trumbull to Secretary Conway, 15 Jan. 1624; J. Gee, *New Shreds of the Old Snare* (London, 1624), pp. 119–20; L. Owen, *The Running Register, Recording a True Relation of the State of the English Colledges, Seminaries and Cloysters in all Forraine Parts* (London, 1626), pp. 100–8; [T. Robinson], *The Anatomy of the English Nunnery at Lisbon in Portugall* (London, 1622), pp. 31–2; P. Guilday, *The English Catholic Refugees on the Continent 1558–1795* (London, 1914), pp. 14–18, 28–33, 35–6.

66 *English Nunnery at Lisbon*, p. 18.

67 PRO, SP 77/9, fol. 106, Thomas Edmonds to Lord Salisbury, 10 Aug. 1608.

68 Owen, *Running Register*, p. 101.

69 Gee, *New Shreds*, p. 115. See also *English Nunnery at Lisbon*, p. 9.

70 Gee, *New Shreds*, p. 114.

71 *The Life of the Reverend Fa: Angel of Joyeuse* (Douai, 1623), [sig. 5].

72 Anthony of Aca, *The Historie, Life, and Miracles . . . of the Blessed Virgine, Sister Joane of the Crosse*, trans. F. Bell (St Omer, 1625), sig. 2.

73 Matthew, *Life of Lucy Knatchbull*, p. 15.

74 AAW, A VIII, fol. 89, Concerning the Beginning of the Poor Clares in Graveling and their Rule.

75 *Till God Will: Mary Ward Through her Writings*, ed. M. Emmanuel Orchard (London, 1985), p. 34

76   F. M. Steele, *The Convents of Great Britain* (London, 1902), pp. 50–1.

77   A. M. C. Forster, 'The Chronicles of the English Poor Clares of Rouen – I', *RH*, 18 (1986), p. 67.

78   Darlington, MS Aire Register, [Part 4, fol. 17], Benefactors.

79   *Diary of the 'Blue Nuns'*, pp. 15, 22, 23, 27, 46.

80   Durrant, *Flemish Mystics*, pp. 276–8, 290, 297–8, 302–5.

81   E. Scarisbrick, *The Life of the Lady Warner of Parham in Suffolk: In Religion calle'd Sister Clare of Jesus* (London, 1691), pp. 75, 144–9, 190–8, 233–40; *Benedictine Nuns of Dunkirk*, pp. 31–4.

82   *The Stuart Constitution: Documents and Commentary*, ed. J. P. Kenyon (Cambridge, 1966), pp. 44, 46, 245–6.

83   W. Gouge, *The Extent of God's Providence: Set out in A Sermon, preached in Black-Friers Church, 5 Nov. 1623 on occasion of the Downe-fall of Papists at a Jesuites Sermon* (London, 1631), pp. 397–8.

84   Cited in E. S. Worrall, 'What May Happen to a Second-Class Citizen 1', *London Recusant* 2 (1972), p. 70.

85   Cited in ibid.

86   *The Eighteenth-Century Constitution 1688–1815: Documents and Commentary*, ed. E. N. Williams (Cambridge, 1965), p. 333.

87   Cited in C. D. van Strien, 'Recusant Houses in the Southern Netherlands as Seen by British Tourists, *c.*1650–1720', *RH*, 20 (1991), p. 504.

88   Cited in ibid., p. 500.

89   Ibid., p. 502.

90   'Abbess Neville's Annals', p. 31.

91   *The Chronicle of the English Augustinian Canonesses Regular of the Lateran, at St Monica's in Louvain (now at St Augustine's Priory, Newton Abbot, Devon) 1548–1644*, ed. A. Hamilton, hereafter *Chronicle of St Monica's* (London, 1904), vol. 1, p. 239; 'The English Benedictine Nuns of the Convent of Our Blessed Lady of Good Hope in Paris, now at St Benedict's Priory, Colwich, Staffordshire. Notes and Obituaries', ed. J. S. Hansom, in *Miscellanea VII* (London, CRS 9, 1911), pp. 389–90; *Diary of the 'Blue Nuns'*, pp. 10, 14–15, 19–20, 23–4, 28, 40, 44.

92   *Diary of the 'Blue Nuns'*, pp. 13–14, 17–18, 23–4.

93   'Abbess Neville's Annals', pp. 40–2.

94   M. C. E. Chambers, *The Life of Mary Ward (1585–1645)*, ed. H. J. Coleridge (London, 1885), vol. 2, pp. 27–39.

95   *Dominicana* (London, CRS 25, 1925), pp. 48–9.

96   'Registers of the English Poor Clares at Gravelines, including those who Founded Filiations at Aire, Dunkirk and Rouen, 1608–1837', hereafter 'Poor Clare Registers', in *Miscellanea 9* (London, CRS 14, 1914), pp. 34–5.

97   *Franciscana: The English Franciscan Nuns, 1619–1821 and the Friars Minor of the Same Province 1618–1761*, ed. R. Trappes-Lomax (London, CRS 24, 1922), p. 23.

98   'Abbess Neville's Annals', p. 31.

99   For Mary Ward's Institute, see *St Mary's Convent Micklegate Bar York [1686–1887]*, ed. H. J. Coleridge (London, 1887), pp. 5–8; D. Evinson, 'The Catholic Revival in Hammersmith', *London Recusant* 7 (1977), pp. 21, 25–6.

100 Bodl., Clarendon MS 62, fol. 52, [Peter Talbot to Robert Talbot], 21 July 1659.

101 For a discussion of this foundation, see Walker, 'Prayer, Patronage', pp. 16–18.
102 M. Wright, *Mary Ward's Institute: The Struggle for Identity* (Sydney, 1997), pp. 47–8.
103 Oulton, MS G.39, fols. 3–4.
104 *Ghent Annals*, pp. 46–7; Nolan, *Irish Dames of Ypres*, pp. 166–207; BL, Add. MS 38,146, fol. 13, Pass to Lady Mary Butler, Abbess at Dublin and her nuns from William III, 1690.
105 *Diary of the 'Blue Nuns'*, p. 35.
106 Cited in Allison, 'English Augustinian Convent', p. 466; R. Eaton, *The Benedictines of Colwich 1829–1929* (London, 1929), p. 39.
107 *Memoirs of Thomas, Earl of Ailesbury* (Westminster, 1890), vol. 2, p. 465; Bodl., Clarendon MS 39, fol. 160, Hyde to Patrick Cary, 25 April 1650; Clarendon MS 71, fol. 268, Mary Knatchbull to Hyde, 26 April 1660.
108 'Abbess Neville's Annals', p. 31.
109 Ibid., pp. 31–2; 'Obituary Notices of the Nuns of the English Benedictine Abbey of Ghent in Flanders, 1627–1811', hereafter 'Ghent Obituary Notices', in *Miscellanea XI* (London, CRS 19, 1917), p. 45.
110 Durrant, *Flemish Mystics*, pp. 262–3; B. Whelan, *Historic English Convents of Today: The Story of the English Cloisters in France and Flanders in Penal Times* (London, 1936), pp. 87–8.
111 Bodl., Carte MS 214, fol. 253, Mary Vavasour to marquis of Ormonde, 2 Nov. 1660.
112 Bodl., Clarendon MS 56, fol. 334, Hyde to Ormonde, 22 Dec. 1657; Clarendon MS 59, fol. 442, Knatchbull to Hyde, 30 Jan. 1659; Clarendon MS 60, fol. 65, Knatchbull to Hyde, 12 Feb. 1659; 'Abbess Neville's Annals', pp. 36–7.
113 Bodl., Clarendon MS 70, fol. 51, Hyde to J. Barwick, 8 March 1660.
114 Bodl., Clarendon MS 64, fols. 183–4, Knatchbull to [Hyde], 16 Sept. 1659; Clarendon MS 66, fol. 167, Knatchbull to [Hyde], Nov. 1659.
115 Bodl., Clarendon MS 64, fol. 105, Knatchbull to Hyde, 8 Sept. 1659.
116 'Abbess Neville's Annals', pp. 17–18; *Ghent Annals*, p. 180.
117 BL, Add. MS 28,225, fol. 126, Knatchbull to Mary of Modena, New Year's Day 1687; *HMC, Calendar of the Stuart Papers Belonging to His Majesty the King Preserved at Windsor Castle* (London, 1902), vol. 1, p. 24.
118 Ibid, p. 22.
119 BL Add. MS 28,225, fol. 293, Knatchbull to Mary of Modena, 24 June 1688.
120 Cited in Allison, 'English Augustinian Convent', p. 484.
121 DL, Ealing MS Journal 1695–1738, fols. 8–9, 11–14, 16, 20, 28, 40.
122 *HMC, Calendar of Stuart Papers*, vol. 1, p. 90.
123 Durrant, *Flemish Mystics*, pp. 316–17.
124 Allison, 'English Augustinian Convent', p. 484.
125 BL Add. MS 28,226, fols. 127, 132, Mary Caryll to John Caryll, [*c.* 1706], 5 June 1707.
126 Durrant, *Flemish Mystics*, pp. 317–24.
127 Guilday, *Catholic Refugees*, p. 271.
128 *Dominicana*, pp. 208–9; Guilday, *Catholic Refugees*, pp. 417–18.
129 Repr. in Guilday, *Catholic Refugees*, pp. 30–32.
130 Cited in 'Poor Clare Registers', p. 115.

131   *Diary of the 'Blue Nuns'*, p. 18.
132   Oulton, MS G.16, Knatchbull to Ormonde, 23 Feb. 1686.
133   G. Burnet, *History of His Own Times*, ed. T. Stackhouse (London, 1906), pp. 25–6.

5   Active in Contemplation: Spiritual Choices and Practices

1   DL, Hazlemere MS 1886, fols. 43–4.
2   R. Po-chia Hsia, *The World of Catholic Renewal 1540–1770* (Cambridge, 1998), p. 140.
3   M. Caffiero, 'From the Late Baroque Mystical Explosion to the Social Apostolate, 1650–1850', in *Women and Faith: Catholic Religious Life in Italy from Late Antiquity to the Present*, ed. L. Scaraffia and G. Zarri (Cambridge, Mass., 1999), pp. 176–204.
4   J. Bilinkoff, *The Avila of Saint Teresa: Religious Reform in a Sixteenth-Century City* (Ithaca, NY, 1989), pp. 135–6.
5   U. Strasser, 'Bones of Contention: Cloistered Nuns, Decorated Relics, and the Contest over Women's Place in the Public Sphere of Counter-Reformation Munich', *Archive for Reformation History*, 90 (1999), pp. 261–7, 282–5.
6   J. K. McNamara, *Sisters in Arms: Catholic Nuns through Two Millennia* (Cambridge, Mass., 1996), p. 493.
7   Hsia, *Catholic Renewal*, p. 143.
8   V. Puccini, *The Life of St Mary Magdalene of Pazzi, a Carmelite Nunn* (London, 1687), p. 10.
9   *The Constitutions of the Society of Jesus*, trans. G. Ganss (St Louis, 1970), pp. 262–3.
10   P. Ranft, *A Woman's Way: The Forgotten History of Women Spiritual Directors* (New York, 2000), pp. 107–10.
11   P. Ranft, 'A Key to Counter-Reformation Women's Activism: The Confessor-Spiritual Director', *Journal of Feminist Studies in Religion*, 10 (1994), p. 17.
12   *Till God Will: Mary Ward Through her Writings*, ed. M. Emmanuel Orchard (London, 1985), pp. 10, 22.
13   T. Matthew, *The Life of Lucy Knatchbull*, ed. D. Knowles (London, 1931), pp. 28–49, 83–95.
14   Matthew, *Life of Lucy Knatchbull*, pp. 30–3; PRO, SP Flanders 77/9, fos. 245–7, Thomas Edmondes to Lord Salisbury, 13 April 1609.
15   PRO, SP Flanders 77/12, fol. 432, William Trumbull to Secretary Conway, 14 Dec. 1617; P. Guilday, *The English Catholic Refugees on the Continent 1558–1795* (London, 1914), pp. 361–2; B. Whelan, *Historic English Convents of Today: The Story of the English Cloisters in France and Flanders in Penal Times* (London, 1936), pp. 93–4.
16   Guilday, *Catholic Refugees*, pp. 362–5; Whelan, *English Convents*, pp. 94–5.
17   Darlington, MS Gravelines Chronicles, fols. 144–63; Guilday, *Catholic Refugees*, pp. 298–9n.
18   AAW, A XXXIV, fol. 327, Lord Castlemaine to [Abbess Timperley], 27 July 1675.
19   AAW, A XXXIV, fol. 349, Narrative of the Transaction between the English Conception Nuns and Fr Warner SJ.

20 *The Diary of the 'Blue Nuns' or Order of the Immaculate Conception of Our Lady, at Paris, 1658–1810*, ed. J. Gillow and R. Trappes-Lomax, hereafter *Diary of the 'Blue Nuns'* (London, CRS 8, 1910), pp. 29–31.

21 AAW, A XXXVI, fols. 645–50, Lawrence Breers to John Bentham, 8 Oct. 1697.

22 'Registers of the English Benedictine Nuns of Pontoise, now at Teignmouth, Devonshire, 1680–1713', hereafter 'Pontoise Registers', in *Miscellanea X* (London, CRS 17, 1915), pp. 261–2.

23 Guilday, *Catholic Refugees*, 257–9, 298.

24 P. Spearritt, 'Prayer and Politics among the English Benedictines of Brussels', (unpublished paper). I am grateful to Dom. Placid for permission to cite his unpublished research.

25 D. Lunn, *The English Benedictines, 1540–1688: From Reformation to Revolution* (London, 1980), p. 201.

26 C. M. Seguin, 'Addicted Unto Piety: Catholic Women in England 1590–1690' (PhD dissertation, Duke University, 1997), pp. 303–11.

27 Guilday, *Catholic Refugees*, pp. 298–9.

28 Lunn, *English Benedictines*, p. 201.

29 AAM, Fonds Kloosters, Englese Benedictijnen/12, Potentiana Deacon to Jacob Boonen, 26 Aug. 1623.

30 Ibid., Flavia Langdale to Jacob Boonen, Feb. 1629.

31 Ibid., Benedicta Hawkins to Jacob Boonen, 17 Feb. 1629.

32 BL, Harleian MS 4275, fols. 8–23, An English Monastery of Benedictines at Brussels in Flanders.

33 AAM, Fonds Kloosters, Englese Benedictijnen/12, Anne Healey to Jacob Boonen, [1629].

34 A. Pasture, 'Documents concernant quelques monastères anglais aux Pays-Bas au XVIIe siècle', *Bulletin de l'Institut Historique Belge de Rome*, 10 (1930), p. 159.

35 *In a Great Tradition: Tribute to Dame Laurentia McLaughlan Abbess of Stanbrook by the Benedictines of Stanbrook* (London, 1956), p. 9.

36 [I. Berinzaga and A. Gagliardi], *Breve Compendio Intorno alla Perfezione Cristiana* (1612). See also A. F. Allison, 'New Light on the Early History of the Breve Compendio: The Background to the English Translation of 1612', *RH*, 4 (1957–8), pp. 4–17.

37 V. Puccini, *The Life of the Holy and Venerable Mother Suor Maria Maddalena de Patsi* (1619), sig. 3*v.

38 B. Canfield, *The Rule of Perfection* (Rouen, 1609). It was jointly dedicated to Winefrid and his other cousins, Jane (Mary) Wiseman of the Louvain Augustinians, and Barbara and Anne Wiseman of the Bridgettine cloister in Lisbon.

39 K. Emery, ' "All and Nothing": Benet of Canfield's Règle de Perfection', *Downside Review*, 306 (1974), pp. 46–61.

40 AAM, Fonds Kloosters, Englese Benedictijnen/12, Agnes Lenthall to Jacob Boonen, 18 Jan. 1629.

41 DL, Hazlemere MS 3137, fols. 85–6, Exact Copies of Original Letters and Papers... 1628 and 1638.

42 A. Rodríguez, *Ejercicio de Perfección y Virtudes Cristianas* (Seville, 1609); J. O'Malley, 'Early Jesuit Spirituality: Spain and Italy', in *Christian Spirituality: Post-Reformation and Modern*, ed. L. Dupré and D. E. Saliers (New York, 1989), pp. 12–17.

43 J. de Guibert, *The Jesuits: Their Spiritual Doctrine and Practice*, trans. W. J. Young (St Louis, 1972), pp. 261–2; A. F. Allison and D. M. Rogers, *The Contemporary Printed Literature of the English Counter-Reformation between 1558 and 1640* (Aldershot, 1994), vol. 2, pp. 106, 181.

44 Bibliothèque Mazarine, MS 4058, fol. 228, A Catalogue of the Manuscript Bookes belonging to the Library of the English Benedictine Nuns of Our B. Lady of Good Hope in Paris; A. Rodríguez, *A Treatise of Mentall Prayer* (1627); A. Rodríguez, *A Short and Sure Way to Heaven* (1630).

45 Guibert, *Jesuits*, p. 263.

46 G. More, *The Spiritual Exercises* (Paris, 1658), pp. 61–5.

47 Matthew, *Life of Lucy Knatchbull*, pp. 146–66.

48 Lunn, *English Benedictines*, p. 199.

49 *Chronicle of the First Monastery Founded at Brussels for English Benedictine Nuns AD 1597* (Bergholt, 1898), pp. 140, 143–4.

50 DL, Hazlemere MS 3137, fol. 37.

51 Pasture, 'Documents concernant quelques monastères anglais', pp. 166–8, 174–8.

52 AAW, A XXXII, fol. 485, Thomas Carre to secretary of English Chapter, [1665].

53 AAW, A XXVI, fol. 434, Thomas Carre to Richard Smith, 23 Nov. 1632; A. F. Allison, 'The English Augustinian Convent of Our Lady of Syon at Paris: Its Foundation and Struggle for Survival during the First Eighty Years', *RH*, 21 (1993), p. 457.

54 AAW, A XXXII, fol. 523, Mary Tredway to Dean and Chapter, 26 June 1666.

55 More, *Spiritual Exercises*, p. 91.

56 *In a Great Tradition*, pp. 9–10.

57 D. Knowles, *The English Mystics* (London, 1927), pp. 150–67; D. Knowles, *The English Mystical Tradition* (New York, 1961), pp. 161–82; P. Spearritt, 'The Survival of Medieval Spirituality among the Exiled English Black Monks', *American Benedictine Review*, 25 (1974), pp. 300–3; G. Mursell, *English Spirituality from Earliest Times to 1700* (London, 2001), pp. 348–53.

58 Lunn, *English Benedictines*, 206.

59 *Contemplative Prayer: Ven. Father Augustine Baker's Teaching Thereon from 'Sancta Sophia'*, ed. B. Weld-Blundell (London, 1907), p. 56.

60 More, *Spiritual Exercises*, pp. 53–7, 101.

61 DL, Hazlemere MS 1886, fol. 43.

62 Lille, 20 H 10, fol. 846, Fragments.

63 'Quadrilogus or a Collection of Four Treatises Concerning the Life and Writings of the Venerable…Augustine Baker', in *Memorials of Father Augustine Baker and other Documents Relating to the English Benedictines*, ed. J. McCann and H. Connolly (London, CRS 33, 1933), p. 139.

64 'Quadrilogus', p. 139.

65 Lille, 20 H 10, fol. 905; 'The English Benedictine Nuns of the Convent of Our Blessed Lady of Good Hope in Paris, now at St Benedict's Priory, Colwich, Staffordshire. Notes and Obituaries', hereafter 'Paris Benedictine Obituaries', ed. J. S. Hansom, in *Miscellanea VII* (London, CRS 9, 1911), pp. 340, 367.

66 *In a Great Tradition*, p. 21.

67 For example, Lille, MS 20 H 10; DL, Hazlemere MS 1886; DL, Gillow MS Baker 4, fols. 55–152, [M. Gascoigne] 'Devotions', ed. A. Baker; DL, Gillow MS,

A Collection of some Familiar Answers upon the Conduct of Soules in a Mistick Life, trans. C. Gascoigne (copied 1659).

68 DL, MS 629/82146, *Advises for Confessors and Spiritual Directors for the Most Part taken out of the lives of late holy persons by the most unworthy Religious S. B. C.*

69 Spearritt, 'Survival of Medieval Spirituality', p. 297.

70 Lille, MS 20 H 10, fol. 902.

71 Ibid., fols. 902–4; DL, Baker MS 33, fols. 329–44, Extracts 'Abbess Catherine Gascoigne's Account of her Spiritual Course'; More, *Spiritual Exercises*, pp. 7–112.

72 A. Baker, 'Life of Dame Gertrude More', in *The Inner Life and the Writings of Dame Gertrude More*, ed. B. Weld-Blundell (London, 1910), vol. 1, pp. 271, 265–6, 279.

73 Bodl., Rawlinson MS A.36, fol. 45, Catherine Gascoigne to Augustine Conyers, 3 March 1655.

74 Ibid., fols. 45, 49, Catherine Gascoigne to Augustine Conyers, 3 March, 1655, Gascoigne to Anselm Crowder, 1655.

75 Ibid., fol. 49, Catherine Gascoigne to Anselm Crowder, 3 March 1655.

76 Ibid., fol. 50.

77 Ibid., fol. 49.

78 More, *Spiritual Exercises*, p. 13.

79 Strasser, 'Bones of Contention', p. 286.

80 C. W. Bynum, 'The Mysticism and Asceticism of Medieval Women: Some Comments on the Typologies of Max Weber and Ernst Troeltsch', in *Fragmentation and Redemption: Essays on Gender and the Human Body in Medieval Religion* (New York, 1991), p. 66.

81 Cited in P. Collinson, 'The Role of Women in the English Reformation Illustrated by the Life and Friendships of Anne Locke', *Studies in Church History*, 2 (1965), p. 259.

82 Stanbrook, Baker MS 2, fols. 189–90, The Book D.

83 P. Mack, *Visionary Women: Ecstatic Prophecy in Seventeenth-Century England* (Berkeley, Ca., 1992), p. 33.

84 [G. Garden], *An Apology for M. Antonia Bourignon* (London, 1699), p. 276.

85 P. Crawford, *Women and Religion in England 1500–1720* (London, 1993), pp. 73–5.

86 Stanbrook, Downside MS D42 (copy), fols. 36–7, A. Baker, 'Life of Dame Margaret Gascoigne of Cambrai'.

87 Also called *disciplina corporis*. For a discussion of its practice in medieval monasticism and translation into lay society, see D. Knox, 'Disciplina: The Monastic and Clerical Origins of European Civility', in *Renaissance Society and Culture: Essays in Honor of Eugene F. Rice, Jr*, ed. J. Monfasani and R. G. Musto (New York, 1991), pp. 107–35, esp. pp. 109–14. Elizabeth Rapley has discussed the practice principally in terms of self-punishment in 'Her Body the Enemy: Self-Mortification in Seventeenth-Century Convents', *Proceedings of the Annual Meeting of the Western Society for French History*, 21 (1994), pp. 25–35.

88 Mack, *Visionary Women*, p. 7.

89 DL, Gillow MS Baker 4, fol. 149.

90 Matthew, *Life of Lucy Knatchbull*, p. 66. For similar comments, see E. Bedingfield, *The Life of Margaret Mostyn (Mother Margaret of Jesus). Religious of the*

Reformed Order of Our Blessed Lady of Mount Carmel (1625–1679), ed. H. J. Coleridge (London, 1884), pp. 116–17, 170–3.

91   More, *Spiritual Exercises*, p. 19.

92   Matthew, *Life of Lucy Knatchbull*, p. 54.

93   *Inner Life... of Dame Gertrude More*, vol. 1, pp. 34–46.

94   'Pontoise Registers', p. 279.

95   *Inner Life... of Dame Gertrude More*, vol. 2, p. 170.

96   Bynum, 'Mysticism and Asceticism', pp. 66–72.

97   G. M. Jantzen, *Power, Gender and Christian Mysticism* (Cambridge, 1995), p. 12.

98   S. F. Matthews Grieco, 'Models of Female Sanctity in Renaissance and Counter-Reformation Italy', in *Women and Faith*, pp. 169–75.

99   G. Zarri, 'From Prophecy to Discipline, 1450–1650', in *Women and Faith*, pp. 110–11.

100   The Paris Benedictine nuns' library included manuscript copies of the revelations of St Bridget and Julian of Norwich, and the life of Carmelite, Anne of St Bartholomew; Bibliothèque Mazarine, MS 4058, fols. 143, 206, A Catalogue of Manuscript Bookes belonging to... the English Benedictine Nuns... in Paris.

101   Anthony of Aca, *The Historie, Life... Extasies and Revelations of... Sister Joane of the Crosse* (St Omer, 1625), sig. *.

102   Puccini, *Maria Maddalena de Patsi*, sig. 3*v.

103   *The Lyf of the Mother Teresa of Jesus, Foundresse of the Monasteries of the Descalced or Bare-Footed Carmelite Nunnes and Fryers... Written by Her Self* (Antwerp, 1611), sig. 2–[***4v].

104   DL, MS 629/82146, [fols. xiii–xv].

105   'Paris Benedictine Obituaries', p. 352. Hereafter referred to as Justina Gascoigne to avoid confusion with her aunt, Abbess Catherine Gascoigne of Cambrai.

106   T. Hunter, *An English Carmelite: The Life of Catharine Burton, Mother Mary Xaveria of the Angels, of the English Teresian Convent at Antwerp*, ed. H. J. Coleridge (London, 1876), pp. 26–9.

107   A. Jacobson Schutte, 'Little Women, Great Heroines: Simulated and Genuine Female Holiness in Early Modern Italy', in *Women and Faith*, pp. 144–58; C. Ferrazzi, *Autobiography of An Aspiring Saint*, ed. A. Jacobson Schutte (Chicago, 1996), pp. 39–40; A. Jacobson Schutte, 'Inquisition and Female Autobiography: The Case of Cecila Ferrazzi', in *The Crannied Wall: Women, Religion, and the Arts in Early Modern Europe*, ed. C. A. Monson (Ann Arbor, Mich., 1992), pp. 108–11; J. C. Brown, *Immodest Acts: The Life of a Lesbian Nun in Renaissance Italy* (New York, 1986).

108   Darlington, MS Gravelines Chronicles, fols. 165–226.

109   'Obituary Notices of the Nuns of the English Benedictine Abbey of Ghent in Flanders, 1627–1811', hereafter 'Ghent Obituary Notices', in *Miscellanea XI* (London, CRS 19, 1917), pp. 25–8.

110   Priory, St Monica's MS Q29, fol. ii, E. Shirley, 'The Lyfe of Our Moste Reverent Mother, Margrit Clement', 1626.

111   Matthew, *Life of Lucy Knatchbull*, p. 18.

112   'Ghent Obituary Notices', p. 14.

113   Matthew, *Life of Lucy Knatchbull*, pp. 191–5.

114 Copies found their way into England. See M. Hodgetts, 'The Yates of Harvington, 1631–1696', *RH*, 22 (1994), p. 163.

115 Bibliothèque Mazarine, MS 1755, fol. 182, Quadrilogus or a Collection of Four treatises Concerning... Fa: Augustin Baker.

116 E. Scarisbrick, *The Life of the Lady Warner of Parham in Suffolk* (London, 1691), pp. 78–81.

117 'Paris Benedictine Obituaries', pp. 361–2.

118 Bedingfield, *Life of Margaret Mostyn*, p. 233; A. Hardman, *Mother Margaret Mostyn: Discalced Carmelite 1625–1679* (London, 1937), p. 80.

119 *A History of the Benedictine Nuns of Dunkirk* (London, 1958), pp. 73–4.

120 A. Hardman, *Two English Carmelites* (London, 1939), pp. 157–8.

121 Priory, St Monica's MS Q29, fols. 45–6, 56–7.

122 Ibid., fols. 48–55.

123 Matthew, *Life of Lucy Knatchbull*, p. 193.

124 'Ghent Obituary Notices', p. 20.

125 Hardman, *Two Carmelites*, pp. 65–7.

126 Ibid., pp. 74–5.

127 Bedingfield, *Life of Margaret Mostyn*, pp. 104–8, 157–8.

128 'Pontoise Registers', p. 289.

129 Ibid., p. 273.

130 Bedingfield, *Life of Margaret Mostyn*, pp. 212–19.

131 Hunter, *English Carmelite*, pp. 240–3.

132 'Paris Benedictine Obituaries', pp. 358–60.

133 Darlington, MS Gravelines Chronicles, fols. 213–18; 'Registers of the English Poor Clares at Gravelines, including those who Founded Filiations at Aire, Dunkirk and Rouen, 1608–1837', hereafter 'Poor Clare Registers', in *Miscellanea 9* (London, CRS 14, 1914), pp. 44–5.

134 C. S. Durrant, *A Link Between Flemish Mystics and English Martyrs* (London, 1925), pp. 335–7.

135 Matthew, *Life of Lucy Knatchbull*, p. 48.

136 More, *Spiritual Exercises*, pp. 61–2.

137 See Chapter 2 for a discussion of the significance of conjugal imagery in monastic governance.

138 'Paris Benedictine Obituaries', pp. 343, 344, 348, 353, 357, 360, 363, 367, 386.

139 Priory, St Monica's MS Q29, fol. 78.

140 Matthew, *Life of Lucy Knatchbull*, p. 54.

141 Bedingfield, *Life of Margaret Mostyn*, pp. 120, 124.

142 Hunter, *English Carmelite*, p. 199.

143 Ibid.

144 C. Walker Bynum, ' "... And Woman His Humanity": Female Imagery in the Religious Writing of the Later Middle Ages' in *Fragmentation and Redemption*, pp. 171–5. See also her 'Women's Stories, Women's Symbols: A Critique of Victor Turner's Theory of Liminality', in *Fragmentation and Redemption*, pp. 27–51.

145 Other than some oblique references to the 'mother-god' of medieval literature through the hen imagery (see below), I have found only two images of the maternal Christ in the spiritual material of the English nuns. Lucy Knatchbull's usage is reminiscent of the nursing Christ, while Margaret Gascoigne

called upon Christ's mother-like protection for the children of God. Matthew, *Life of Lucy Knatchbull*, pp. 44–5, 61; 'Ghent Obituary Notices', p. 7; DL, Gillow MS Baker 4, fol. 128. For maternal imagery in the writings of medieval mystics, see C. Walker Bynum, *Jesus as Mother: Studies in the Spirituality of the High Middle Ages* (Berkeley, 1982); Bynum, '"And Woman His Humanity"'.

146 Bedingfield, *Life of Margaret Mostyn*, p. 12.
147 Ibid., pp. 13–14.
148 Ibid., pp. 18–24.
149 Ibid., pp. 33–7, 40–1.
150 See ibid., pp. 72, 88–91, 96–101, 104–22, 130–55, 163, 268–90, for accounts of her numerous visions. She was also visited by saints at various stages during her life; see ch. 15.
151 Ibid., p. 89.
152 Ibid.
153 Ibid., p. 94.
154 See Chapter 2.
155 Bedingfield, *Life of Margaret Mostyn*, pp. 145–55.
156 Ibid., pp. 160, 190–9; 'Ghent Obituary Notices', p. 38.
157 R. E. Surtz, *The Guitar of God: Gender, Power, and Authority in the Visionary World of Mother Juana de la Cruz, 1481–1534* (Philadelphia, 1990), ch. 2.
158 Bedingfield, *Life of Margaret Mostyn*, pp. 109–11.
159 Ibid., p. 98.
160 Lille, 20 H 10, fols. 842–4.
161 Crawford, *Women and Religion*, p. 75.
162 *Diary of the 'Blue Nuns'*, p. 281.
163 [St Augustine], *Rule... Together with the Constitutions of the English Canonesse Regular's of Our B. Ladyes of Sion in Paris* (Paris, 1636), sig. *.
164 [St Benedict], *The Rule of the Most Blissed Father Saint Benedict Patriarke of all Munkes* (Ghent, 1632), pp. 3–37; Bodl. Rawlinson MS A.442, fols. 2–10, Statutes of the English Convent of St Mary, 1613. See also St Colette, *The Declarations and Ordinances made upon the Rule of... S. Clare* (1622), pp. 153–7.
165 [Augustine], *Rule... Constitutions*, pp. 115–35, 226–9, 270–87; Priory, St Monica's MS E4, fols. 5–57, 76–84, Constitutions, 1609; Arundel, Franciscan MS 6b, fols. 2–66, Book of Statutes, 1641; *Diary of the 'Blue Nuns'*, pp. 280–316.
166 Arundel, Franciscan MS 6b, fols. 23, 45.
167 Lille, 20 H 10, fols. 884–5, 887.
168 DL, Hazlemere MS 1886, fol. 213. See also DL, MS 627/82144, [fol. v], 'Considerations or Reflexions upon the Rule of the Most Glorious Father St Benedict. By a Most Unworthy Religious of his Order'.
169 [Benedict], *Rule*, sig (:).
170 'Ghent Obituary Notices', pp. 43, 50, 63.
171 Bodl., Rawlinson MS A.442, fols. 2–3.
172 Arundel, Franciscan MS 6b, fols. 22–3, 27.
173 Bodl., Rawlinson MS A.442, fols. 9–10; [Benedict], *Rule*, pp. 10–11; Lille, 20 H1, fols. 8–9, Constitutions of English Benedictines at Cambrai, 1631.
174 AAM, Mechliniensia/Reg.8, fol. 236c, Visitatio Monastery S. Mariae Ordinis S. Benedicti Anglarum Bruxellen, 10 May 1620.

175   Lille, 20 H 10, fol. 887.
176   'Records of the English Benedictine Nuns at Cambrai (now Stanbrook), 1620–1793', ed. J. Gillow, hereafter 'Cambrai Records', in *Miscellanea VIII* (London, CRS 13, 1913), p. 78.
177   *Franciscana: The English Franciscan Nuns, 1619–1821 and the Friars Minor of the Same Province 1618–1761*, ed. R. Trappes-Lomax (London, CRS 24, 1922), pp. 185–6; see also pp. 181, 184, 199, 200.
178   *Letters from James Earl of Perth...to his Sister, the Countess of Errol*, ed. W. Jerdan (London, Camden Society 23, 1845), p. 43.
179   Allison, 'English Augustinian Convent', p. 464.
180   [Augustine], *Rule...Constitutions*, p. 26.
181   Arundel, Franciscan MS 'General Cerimonies to be Observed throughout the Yeare Unless it be Otherwise Appoynted for Speciall Feasts', fols. 55–6.
182   Priory, St Monica's MS E4, fols. 22–6; Arundel, Franciscan MS 'General Cerimonies', fols. [46–7], Lille, 20 H 1, fols. 34–40; *Diary of the 'Blue Nuns'*, pp. 287, 315; [Benedict], *Rule*, pp. 44–64.
183   *Diary of the 'Blue Nuns'*, p. 296; see also Arundel, Franciscan MS 6b, fols. 39–41; Lille, 20 H 1, fols. 46–7; *A Brief Relation of the Order and Institute of the English Religious Women at Liège* (Liège, 1652), p. 40.
184   [Augustine], *Rule...Constitutions*, p. 281.
185   Arundel, Franciscan MS 'General Cerimonies', fol. 47.
186   Arundel, Franciscan MS 6b, fol. 49; *Statutes Compyled for the Better Observation of the Holy Rule of...S. Benedict... Delivered to the English Religious Woemen of the Monastery of Our Blessed Lady of the Perpetuall Virgin Mary in Bruxelles and to all their Successours* (Ghent, 1632), part 1, p. 27.
187   Priory, St Monica's MS E4, fol. 25.
188   Priory, St Monica's MS C2, fol. 505, Chronicle, vol. 1, 1548–1837.
189   Durrant, *Flemish Mystics*, p. 340.
190   'Ghent Obituary Notices', p. 17.
191   Ibid., pp. 43–6.
192   Ibid., p. 41.
193   Lille, 20 H 10, fol. 845.
194   'Ghent Obituary Notices', p. 15. Tenebrae was the ritual of successively extinguishing the candles during *matins* and *lauds* upon the last three days of holy week.
195   *Diary of the 'Blue Nuns'*, p. 296.
196   'Pontoise Registers', p. 320. See also *Franciscana*, p. 201.
197   'Poor Clare Registers', p. 103.
198   'Ghent Obituary Notices', pp. 36–7.
199   O'Malley, 'Early Jesuit Spirituality', pp. 6–7.
200   *The Chronicle of the English Augustinian Canonesses Regular of the Lateran, at St Monica's in Louvain (now at St Augustine's Priory, Newton Abbot, Devon) 1548–1644*, ed. A. Hamilton, (London, 1906), vol. 2, pp. 164, 168.
201   Ibid., vol. 1, p. 265.
202   Priory, St Monica's MS C2, fol. 540.
203   'Cambrai Records', pp. 78–9.
204   'Pontoise Registers', pp. 277–82.
205   'Ghent Obituary Notices', p. 78
206   Priory, St Monica's MS C2, [addendum, fol. 1].

207 *Franciscana*, p. 37. Although not entirely clear in her clothing details, the wording implies that Smith was admitted with little or no dowry.
208 C. D. van Strien, 'Recusant Houses in the Southern Netherlands as Seen by British Tourists, *c.* 1650–1720', *RH*, 20 (1991), p. 504.
209 *Letters from James Earl of Perth*, p. 44.
210 *Franciscana*, p. 204.
211 AAM, Fonds Kloosters, Englese Benedictijnen/12, Scholastica Smith, Mary Vavasour *et al.* to Jacob Boonen, 31 March 1629.
212 DL, Baker MS 33, fols. 329, 333–5.

Conclusion

1 Darlington, MS Gravelines Chronicles; Buckfast, Pontoise MS 'An Account of the Blowing-up and Destruction of the Town of Gravelines'.
2 BL, Add. MS 28,229, fol. 320, Lucy Herbert to John Caryll, 17 Feb. [1739].
3 P. Nolan, *The Irish Dames of Ypres: Being a History of the Royal Irish Abbey at Ypres* (Dublin, 1908), pp. 173–216; B. Whelan, *Historic English Convents of Today: The Story of the English Cloisters in France and Flanders in Penal Times* (London, 1936), pp. 54–9.

Bibliography

Manuscript sources

Archdiocesan Archives of Mechelen-Brussels, Mechelen

Fonds Kloosters, Englese Benedictijnen/3, Election of Abbesses.
Fonds Kloosters, Englese Benedictijnen/4, Visitation Records.
Fonds Kloosters, Englese Benedictijnen/5, Confessors.
Fonds Kloosters, Englese Benedictijnen/7, Profession Interviews.
Fonds Kloosters, Englese Benedictijnen/12, Dispute.
Mechliniensia/Reg. 8, Matthias Hovius, Visitation Report, 1620.

Archives Départementales; du Nord, Lille

20 H 1, Constitutions, 1631.
20 H 10, Fragments.
20 H 57, Various Documents.
20 H 58, Rent Book.

Archives Départementales; du Seine-et-Oise, Versailles

68 H 3, Register of Entrants, 1652–1781.
68 H 4, Obit Book.
68 H 5, Account Book 1653–1703.

Bibliothèque Mazarine, Paris

MS 1755, 'Quadrilogus or a Collection of Four treatises Concerning ... Fa: Augustin Baker'.
MS 4058, 'A Catalogue of the Manuscript Bookes belonging to the Library of the English Benedictine Nuns of Our B. Lady of Good Hope in Paris'.

Bodleian Library, Oxford

MSS Carte 30–31, 213–14, Papers of the First Duke of Ormonde.
MSS Clarendon 39–40, 52–72, 77, Clarendon State Papers.
MS Rawlinson A. 36, Thurloe Papers.
MS Rawlinson A. 442, Statutes of the English Convent of St Mary, 1613.

British Library

Add. MS 5813, An Account of the Nunnery of St Monica in Lovain.
Add. MS 28,225, Letters to Mary, Queen of James II, 1685–88.
Add. MS 28,226, Letters and Papers of John Caryll, 1648–1711.
Add. MS 28,227, Family of Caryll Correspondence, vol. 1, 1672–1718.
Add. MS 28,228, Family of Caryll Correspondence, vol. 2, 1719–31.
Add. MS 28,229, Family of Caryll Correspondence, vol. 3, 1732–39.

Add. MS 28,230, Family of Caryll Correspondence, vol. 4, 1740–47.
Add. MS 36,452, Aston Papers.
Add. MS 38,146, Letter-Book of Sir Robert Southwell, 1690.
Egerton MS 2536, Nicholas Papers.
Harleian MS 4275, An English Monastery of Benedictines at Brussels in Flanders.

Centre for Kentish Studies, Maidstone

U269 C324 (Bundle 58), Sackville MSS, Berkeley Correspondence.

Convent of Poor Clares, Cross Bush, Arundel

Franciscan MS 6b, Book of Statutes, 1641.
Franciscan MS 15, Book of Ceremonial for Novice Mistresses.
Franciscan MS 16, Miscellanea, vol. 1.
Franciscan MS 22, A Copy of the Privileges Granted the Jubilarians.
Franciscan MS Annals of the Religious of the 3rd Order of St Francis of the Province of England from the Year 1621 to (1893).
Franciscan MS General Cerimonies to be Observed throughout the Yeare Unless it be Otherwise Appoynted for Speciall Feasts.

Downside Abbey

Baker MS A.64, [Dame Clementina Cary], Fragment of Life of Fr Baker, *c*.1663.
Baker MS 33, Extracts.
Ealing MS Journal 1695–1738, Diurnall of the English Canonesses Regulars of St Augustin's Order established in Paris.
Gillow MS Baker 4, Bonilla, Gascoigne B, Summary, etc.
Gillow MS 'A Collection of some Familiar Answers upon the Conduct of Soules in a Mistick Life', trans. Catherine Gascoigne, *c*.1659.
Hazlemere MS 1886, Dame Barbara Constable, 'The Complaints of Sinners', 1649.
Hazlemere MS 1887, Title Deed Concerning Purchase of House in Brussels, 1538–1639.
Hazlemere MS 1888, 17th Century Papers Concerning the House in Brussels.
Hazelmere MS 1893, Various Papers Concerning the English Benedictine Nuns.
Hazlemere MS 2020, Book of Monastic Ceremonies, 1694.
Hazlemere MS 3137, Exact Copies of Original Letters and Papers Concerning our Monastery in Brussels, 1628 and 1638.
Hazlemere MS VI.C 3140, The Receipts, Disbursements and Debts of our Monastery, 1599–1736.
MS 552/82145, [Dame Barbara Constable], 'Considerations for Preests. Composed of Diverse Collections, gathered out of Severall Authors', *c*. 1653.
MS 627/82144, Considerations or Reflexions upon the Rule of the Most Glorious Father St Benedict. By a Most Unworthy Religious of his Order', *c*.1655.
MS 629/82146, [Dame Barbara Constable], 'Advises for Confessors and Spiritual Directors for the Most Part taken out of the Lives of Late Holy Persons', *c*.1650.

Lancashire Record Office, Preston

DDBl24/23, Blundell Papers, 'Account of the Life and Death of Mrs Blundell, 1707.'

DDCl/968–80, Clifton of Lytham Family Papers, Settlements 1677–94 .
DDCl/1152–77, Clifton of Lytham Papers, Correspondence.
RCBu14/1–54, Coghlan Papers.

Oulton Abbey, Stone

MS G.10, Mary Maynell's Book 'Five Meditations on Your Five Vowes'.
MS G.11, Appeal to the Citizens of Ghent.
MS G.15, Agreement for the Transfer of Dame Mary Bedingfield to Brussels, 1661.
MS G.16, Copies of Letters from Abbess Mary Knatchbull to the Duke of Ormonde.
MS G.17, Book of Chemical and Household Receipts, 1671.
MS G. 26, Dispensary Book of Prescriptions.
MS G. 39, The English Benedictine Monastery at Ghent.

Priory of Our Lady of Good Counsel, Sayers Common, Sussex

St Monica's MS B^{B}3, About Our Rents on Mount Piety at Bruxells.
St Monica's MS C2, Chronicle, vol. 1, 1548–1837.
St Monica's MS E4, Constitutions, 1609.
St Monica's MS F2, A Direction How to Govern Postulants, Novices and Young Professed Religious.
St Monica's MS J8, List of All the Religious Professed from Elizabeth Woodford . . . to 1897.
St Monica's MS M1, Council Book, 1669–1874.
St Monica's MS Qu2, Instructions for a Religious Superior.
St Monica's MS Q29, E. Shirley, 'The Lyfe of Our Moste Reverent Mother, Margrit Clement', 1626.
St Monica's MS P1, Benefactors' Book, 1609–1970.
St Monica's MS R16/2, Worthington Letters.
Bruges MS Professions and Obits, 1629–1882.

Public Record Office, London

SP 77/5–32, State Papers, Flanders, 1598–1659.

St Clare's Abbey, Darlington

MS Gravelines Chronicles.
MS Aire Register.

St Mary's Convent, Buckfast

MS An Account of the Blowing-up and Destruction of the Town of Gravelines.
MS Mary Knatchbull, 'An Account of the Foundation of the Convent of Boulogne: First Filiation from Ghent, 1653'.

Stanbrook Abbey, Worcester

Baker MS 2, The Book D.
Downside MS D42 (copy), Augustine Baker, 'Life of Dame Margaret Gascoigne of Cambrai'.

Westminster Cathedral, Archdiocesan Archives

A Series VIII, XX–XXXVI, Correspondence of the Secular Clergy and Miscellanea.

West Yorkshire Archives, Leeds

GC/F8/1, Personal Account Book of Sir Thomas Gascoigne, 2nd Bart, 1661–1678.

Printed primary sources

'Abbess Neville's Annals of Five Communities of English Benedictine Nuns in Flanders, 1598–1687', ed. M. J. Rumsey, in *Miscellanea V* (London: CRS 6, 1909).

Annals of the English Benedictines at Ghent, Now at St Mary's Abbey, Oulton in Staffordshire (Oulton, 1894).

Anthony of Aca, *The Historie, Life, and Miracles . . . of the Blessed Virgine, Sister Joane of the Crosse*, trans. F. Bell (St Omer, 1625).

Arblaster, P., 'The Infanta and the English Benedictine Nuns: Mary Percy's Memories in 1634', *Recusant History*, 23 (1997), 508–27.

Bedingfield, E., *The Life of Margaret Mostyn (Mother Margaret of Jesus): Religious of the Reformed Order of Our Blessed Lady of Mount Carmel (1625–1679)*, ed. H. J. Coleridge (London, 1884).

[Berinzaga, I. and A. Gagliardi], *Breve Compendio Intorno alla Perfezione Cristiana* (1612).

Borgia, F., *The Practise of Christian Workes, Togeather with a Short Rule, How to Live Well*, trans. J. W. (1620).

A Brief Relation of the Order and Institute of the English Religious Women at Liège (Liège, 1652).

Burnet, G., *History of His Own Times*, ed. T. Stackhouse (London, 1906).

Calendar of State Papers, Domestic Series, 1581–1590, ed. R. Lemon (London, 1865).

Canfield, B., *The Rule of Perfection* (Rouen, 1609).

Carre, T., *Pietas Parisiensis or a Short Description of the Piety and Charitie Comonly Exercised in Paris* (Paris, 1666).

Canons and Decrees of the Council of Trent, ed. R. J. Schroeder (St Louis, 1941).

Chambers, M. C. E., *The Life of Mary Ward (1585–1645)*, ed. H. J. Coleridge, 2 vols (London, 1882–85).

The Chronicle of the English Augustinian Canonesses Regular of the Lateran, at St Monica's in Louvain (now at St Augustine's Priory, Newton Abbot, Devon), ed. A. Hamilton, 2 vols (London, 1904–6).

The Constitutions of the Society of Jesus, trans. G. Ganss (St Louis, 1970).

Contemplative Prayer: Ven. Father Augustine Baker's Teaching Thereon from 'Sancta Sophia', ed. B. Weld-Blundell (London, 1907).

The Diary of the 'Blue Nuns' or Order of the Immaculate Conception of Our Lady, at Paris, 1658–1810, ed. J. Gillow and R. Trappes-Lomax (London: CRS 8, 1910).

Dominicana (London: CRS 25, 1925).

The Early Modern Englishwoman: A Facsimile Library of Essential Works, eds B. S. Travitsky and P. Cullen, vol. 13, *Recusant Translators: Elizabeth Cary and Alexia Grey* (Aldershot, 2000).

The Eighteenth Century Constitution 1688–1815: Documents and Commentary, ed. E. N. Williams (Cambridge, 1965).

Elizabeth Cary, Lady Falkland: Life and Letters, ed. H. Wolfe, RTM vol. 4, MRTS vol. 230 (Cambridge and Tempe, AZ, 2001).

'The English Benedictine Nuns of the Convent of Our Blessed Lady of Good Hope in Paris, now at St Benedict's Priory, Colwich, Staffordshire. Notes and Obituaries', ed. J. S. Hansom, in *Miscellanea VII* (London: CRS 9, 1911).

Ferrazzi, C., *Autobiography of An Aspiring Saint*, ed. A. Jacobson Schutte (Chicago, 1996).

Forster, A. M. C., 'The Chronicles of the English Poor Clares of Rouen – I', *Recusant History*, 18 (1986), 59–102.

—— 'The Chronicles of the English Poor Clares of Rouen – II', *Recusant History*, 18 (1986), 149–91.

Franciscana: The English Franciscan Nuns, 1619–1821 and the Friars Minor of the Same Province 1618–1761, ed. R. Trappes-Lomax (London: CRS 24, 1922).

Foley, H., *Records of the English Province of the Society of Jesus*, 7 vols (London, 1877–84).

Galgano, M. J., 'Negotiations for a Nun's Dowry: Restoration Letters of Mary Caryll OSB and Ann Clifton OSB', *American Benedictine Review*, 24 (1973), 278–98.

[Garden, G.], *An Apology for M. Antonia Bourignon* (London, 1699).

Gee, J., *New Shreds of the Old Snare* (London, 1624).

'Glow-Worm Light': Writings of Seventeenth Century Recusant Women from Original Manuscripts, ed. D. L. Latz (Salzburg, 1989).

Gouge, W., *Of Domesticall Duties* (London, 1622).

—— *The Extent of God's Providence: Set out in A Sermon, Preached in Black-Friers Church, 5 Nov. 1623 on Occasion of the Downe-fall of Papists at a Jesuites Sermon* (London, 1631).

The Great Diurnal of Nicholas Blundell of Little Crosby, Lancashire, ed. J. J. Bagley, 3 vols (Chester, 1968–72).

The Herald and Genealogist, vol. 3, ed. J. G. Nichols (London, 1866).

HMC, *Calendar of the Stuart Papers Belonging to His Majesty the King Preserved at Windsor Castle*, 7 vols (London, 1902–23).

Hunter, T., *An English Carmelite: The Life of Catharine Burton, Mother Mary Xaveria of the Angels, of the English Teresian Convent at Antwerp*, ed. H. J. Coleridge (London, 1876).

The Inner Life and the Writings of Dame Gertrude More, ed. B. Weld-Blundell, 2 vols (London, 1910–11).

Letters from James Earl of Perth . . . to his Sister, the Countess of Errol, ed. W. Jerdan (London: Camden Society 23, 1845).

The Life of the Reverend Fa: Angel of Joyeuse (Douai, 1623).

Lucca, P., *A Dialogue of Dying Wel*, trans. R. V. (Antwerp, 1603).

Matthew, T., *The Life of Lucy Knatchbull*, ed. D. Knowles (London, 1931).

Memoirs of Thomas, Earl of Ailesbury (Westminster, 1890).

Memorials of Father Augustine Baker and other Documents Relating to the English Benedictines, ed. J. McCann and H. Connolly (London: CRS 33, 1933).

More, G., *The Spiritual Exercises* (Paris, 1658).

Mush, J., *An Abstracte of the Life and Martirdome of Mistres Margaret Clitherow* (Mechelen, 1619).

Obit Book of the English Benedictines from 1600–1912, ed. H. N. Birt (Edinburgh, 1913).

'Obituary Notices of the Nuns of the English Benedictine Abbey of Ghent in Flanders, 1627–1811', in *Miscellanea XI* (London: CRS 19, 1917).

Owen, L., *The Running Register, Recording a True Relation of the State of the English Colledges, Seminaries and Cloysters in all Forraine Parts* (London, 1626).

Pasture, A., 'Documents concernant quelques monastères anglais aux Pays-Bas au XVIIe siècle', *Bulletin de l'Institut Historique Belge de Rome*, 10 (1930), 155–223.

Peryn, W., *Spirituall Exercises and Goostly Meditations* (Caen, 1598).

Puccini, V., *The Life of St Mary Magdalene of Pazzi, a Carmelite Nunn* (London, 1687).

——*The Life of the Holy and Venerable Mother Suor Maria Maddalena de Patsi, A Florentine Lady, & Religious of the Order of the Carmelites*, trans. G. B. (1619).

'Records of the English Benedictine Nuns at Cambrai (now Stanbrook), 1620–1793', ed. J. Gillow, in *Miscellanea VIII* (London: CRS 13, 1913).

'Records of the English Canonesses of the Holy Sepulchre at Liège, now at New Hall, 1652–1793', ed. R. Trappes-Lomax, in *Miscellanea X* (London: CRS 17, 1915).

'The Register Book of Professions... of the English Benedictine Nuns at Brussels and Winchester, now at East Bergholt, 1598–1856', ed. J. S. Hansom, in *Miscellanea ix* (London: CRS 14, 1914).

'Registers of the English Benedictine Nuns of Pontoise, now at Teignmouth, Devonshire, 1680–1713', in *Miscellanea X* (London: CRS 17, 1915).

'Registers of the English Poor Clares at Gravelines, including those who Founded Filiations at Aire, Dunkirk and Rouen, 1608–1837', in *Miscellanea ix* (London: CRS 14, 1914).

The Responsa Scholarum of the English College, Rome, ed. A. Kenny, 2 vols (London: CRS 54, 55, 1962–63).

[Robinson, T.], *The Anatomy of the English Nunnery at Lisbon in Portugall* (London, 1622).

Rodríguez, A., *A Short and Sure Way to Heaven* (1630).

——*A Treatise of Mentall Prayer* (1627).

——*Ejercicio de Perfección y Virtutes Cristianas* (Seville, 1609).

Scarisbrick, E., *The Life of the Lady Warner of Parham in Suffolk: In Religion call'd Sister Clare of Jesus* (London, 1691).

Skippon, P., 'An Account of a Journey Made thro' Part of the Low Countries, Germany Italy and France', in *A Collection of Voyages and Travels*, 3rd edn, ed. A. and J. Churchill, 6 vols (London, 1744–6).

Statutes Compyled for the Better Observation of the Holy Rule of...S. Benedict... Delivered to the English Religious Woemen of the Monastery of Our Blessed Lady of the Perpetuall Virgin Mary in Bruxelles and to all their Successours (Ghent, 1632).

[St Augustine], *Rule... Together with the Constitutions of the English Canonesse Regular's of Our B. Ladyes of Sion in Paris* (Paris, 1636).

[St Benedict], *The Rule of the Most Blissed Father Saint Benedict Patriarke of all Munkes* (Ghent, 1632).

[St Clare], *The Rule of the Holy Virgin S. Clare* (1621).

St Colette, *The Declarations and Ordinances made upon the Rule of...S. Clare* (1622).

St Mary's Convent, Micklegate Bar, York (1686–1887), ed. H. J. Coleridge (London, 1887).

The Stuart Constitution: Documents and Commentary, ed. J. P. Kenyon (Cambridge, 1966).

[Teresa of Avila], *The Lyf of the Mother Teresa of Jesus, Foundresse of the Monasteries of the Descalced or Bare-Footed Carmelite Nunnes and Fryers . . . Written by Her Self* (Antwerp, 1611).

Till God Will: Mary Ward Through her Writings, ed. M. Emmanuel Orchard (London, 1985).

The Tragedy of Mariam: The Fair Queen of Jewry with The Lady Falkland: Her Life by One of her Daughters, ed. B. Weller and M. W. Ferguson (Berkeley, 1994).

Troubles of Our Catholic Forefathers Related by Themselves, ed. J. Morris, 3 vols (London, 1872–7).

Women's Worlds in Seventeenth-Century England: A Sourcebook, ed. P. Crawford and L. Gowing (London, 2000).

Secondary sources

Allison, A. F., 'The English Augustinian Convent of Our Lady of Syon at Paris: Its Foundation and Struggle for Survival during the First Eighty Years, 1634–1713', *Recusant History*, 21 (1993), 451–96.

—— 'New Light on the Early History of the Breve Compendio: The Background to the English Translation of 1612', *Recusant History*, 4 (1957–8), 4–17.

—— 'The Origins of St Gregory's, Paris', *Recusant History*, 21 (1992), 11–25.

—— and D. M. Rogers, *The Contemporary Printed Literature of the English Counter-Reformation between 1558 and 1640*, 2 vols (Aldershot, 1989–1994).

Amussen, S., *An Ordered Society: Gender and Class in Early Modern England* (Oxford, 1988).

Arblaster, P., 'The Monastery of Our Lady of the Assumption in Brussels (1599–1794)', *English Benedictine History Symposium*, 17 (1999), 54–93.

Aveling, J. C. H., *The Handle and the Axe: The Catholic Recusants in England from Reformation to Emancipation* (London, 1976).

—— 'The Marriages of Catholic Recusants 1559–1642', *Journal of Ecclesiastical History*, 14 (1963), 68–83.

Baernstein, P. R., 'In Widow's Habit: Women between Convent and Family in Sixteenth-Century Milan', *Sixteenth Century Journal*, 25 (1994), 787–807.

Baker, J., 'Female Monasticism and Family Strategy: The Guises and Saint Pierre de Reims', *Sixteenth Century Journal*, 28 (1997), 1091–108.

Barker, P. S. D., 'Caritas Pirckheimer: A Female Humanist Confronts the Reformation', *Sixteenth Century Journal*, 26 (1995), 259–72.

Bilinkoff, J., *The Avila of Saint Teresa: Religious Reform in a Sixteenth-Century City* (Ithaca, NY, 1989).

—— 'Charisma and Controversy: The Case of María de Santo Domingo', in *Spanish Women in the Golden Age: Images and Realities*, ed. M. S. Sánchez and A. Saint-Saëns (Westport, Conn., 1996), 23–35.

—— 'A Saint for a City: Mariana de Jesús and Madrid, 1565–1624', *Archive for Reformation History*, 88 (1997), 322–37.

—— 'A Spanish Prophetess and Her Patrons: The Case of María de Santo Domingo', *Sixteenth Century Journal*, 23 (1992), 21–34.

Blaisdell, C., 'Religion, Gender, and Class: Nuns and Authority in Early Modern France', in *Changing Identities in Early Modern France*, ed. M. Wolfe (Durham, NC, 1997), 147–68.

Bossy, J., 'The Character of Elizabethan Catholicism', in *Crisis in Europe, 1560–1660*, ed. T. Aston (London, 1965), 223–46.

—— *The English Catholic Community, 1570–1850* (London, 1975).

Bowden, C. M. K., 'The Abbess and Mrs Brown: Lady Mary Knatchbull and Royalist Politics in Flanders in the Late 1650s', *Recusant History*, 24 (1999), 288–308.

Bowerbank, S., 'Gertrude More and the Mystical Perspective', *Studia Mystica*, 9 (1986), 34–46.

Brennan, M., 'Enclosure: Institutionalising the Invisibility of Women in Ecclesiastical Communities', in *Women – Invisible in Theology and Church*, ed. E. Schüssler Fiorenza and M. Collins (Edinburgh, 1985), 38–48.

Broomhall, S., '"In My Opinion": Charlotte de Minut and Female Political Discussion in Sixteenth-Century France', *Sixteenth Century Journal*, 31 (2000), 25–45.

Brown, J. C., *Immodest Acts: The Life of a Lesbian Nun in Renaissance Italy* (New York, 1986).

—— 'Monache a Firenze all'inizio dell'età Moderna', *Quaderni Storici*, 85 (1994), 117–52.

Burr Litchfield, R., 'Demographic Characteristics of Florentine Patrician Families, Sixteenth to Nineteenth Centuries, *Journal of Economic History*, 29 (1969), 191–205.

Bynum, C. W., *Fragmentation and Redemption: Essays on Gender and the Human Body in Medieval Religion* (New York, 1991).

—— *Jesus as Mother: Studies in the Spirituality of the High Middle Ages* (Berkeley, Ca., 1982).

Cameron, J., *A Dangerous Innovator: Mary Ward 1585–1645* (Sydney, 2000).

Cain, J. R., 'Cloister and the Apostolate of Religious Women', *Review for Religious*, 27 (1968), 243–80, 652–71.

Carrafiello, M. L., 'English Catholicism and the Jesuit Mission of 1580–1581', *Historical Journal*, 37 (1994), 761–74.

Cédoz, F., *Un Couvent de religieuses anglaises à Paris de 1634 à 1884* (Paris and London, 1891).

Charlton, K., *Women, Religion and Education in Early Modern England* (London, 1999).

Châtellier, L., *The Europe of the Devout: The Catholic Reformation and the Formation of a New Society*, trans. J. Birrell (Cambridge and Paris, 1989).

Chojnacki, S., 'Daughters and Oligarchs: Gender and the Early Renaissance State', in *Gender and Society in Renaissance Italy*, eds J. C. Brown and R. C. Davis (London, 1998), 63–86.

Chronicle of the First Monastery Founded at Brussels for English Benedictine Nuns AD 1597 (Bergholt, 1898).

Cohen, S., *The Evolution of Women's Asylums Since 1500: From Refuges for Ex-Prostitutes to Shelters for Battered Women* (New York, 1992).

Collinson, P., 'The Role of Women in the English Reformation Illustrated by the Life and Friendships of Anne Locke', *Studies in Church History*, 2 (1965), 258–72.

Cooke, K., 'The English Nuns and the Dissolution', in *The Cloister and the World: Essays in Medieval History in Honour of Barbara Harvey*, ed. J. Blair and B. Golding (Oxford, 1996), 287–301.

Cox, V., 'The Single Self: Feminist Thought and the Marriage Market in Early Modern Venice', *Renaissance Quarterly*, 48 (1995), 513–81.

The Crannied Wall: Women, Religion, and the Arts in Early Modern Europe, ed. C. A. Monson (Ann Arbor, Mich., 1992).

Crawford, P., 'The Construction and Experience of Maternity in Seventeenth-Century England', in *Women as Mothers in Pre-industrial England: Essays in Memory of Dorothy McLaren*, ed. V. Fildes (London, 1990), 3–38.

—— 'Katherine and Philip Henry and their Children: A Case Study in Family Ideology', *Transactions of the Historic Society of Lancashire and Cheshire*, 134 (1984), 39–73.

—— *Women and Religion in England 1500–1720* (London, 1993).

Creative Women in Medieval and Early Modern Italy: A Religious and Artistic Renaissance, ed. E. A. Matter and J. Coakley (Philadelphia, 1994).

Diefendorf, B. B., 'Give Us Back Our Children: Patriarchal Authority and Parental Consent to Religious Vocations in Early Counter-Reformation France', *Journal of Modern History*, 68 (1996), 265–307.

Dolan, F. E., *Whores of Babylon: Catholicism, Gender and Seventeenth-Century Print Culture* (Ithaca, NY, 1999).

Dures, A., *English Catholicism 1558–1642* (London, 1983).

Durrant, C. S., *A Link Between Flemish Mystics and English Martyrs* (London, 1925).

Early Modern Women's Letter Writing, 1450–1700, ed. J. Daybell (Basingstoke, 2001).

Eaton, R., *The Benedictines of Colwich 1829–1929* (London, 1929).

Eckenstein, L., *Woman Under Monasticism: Chapters on Saint-lore and Convent Life between AD 500 and AD 1500* (Cambridge, 1896).

Elkins, S. K., *Holy Women of Twelfth Century England* (Chapel Hill, NC, 1988).

Emery, K., ' "All and Nothing": Benet of Canfield's Règle de Perfection', *Downside Review*, 306 (1974), 46–61.

Erickson, A. L., *Women and Property in Early Modern England* (London, 1993).

Evangelisti, S., 'Wives, Widows, and Brides of Christ: Marriage and the Convent in the Historiography of Early Modern Italy', *Historical Journal*, 43 (2000), 233–47.

Evinson, D., 'The Catholic Revival in Hammersmith', *London Recusant*, 7 (1977), 19–45.

Fletcher, J. R., *The Story of the English Bridgettines of Syon Abbey* (South Brent, 1933).

Gilchrist, R., *Gender and Material Culture: The Archaeology of Religious Women* (London, 1994).

Gill, K., '*Scandala*: Controversies Concerning *Clausura* and Women's Religious Communities in Late Medieval Italy', in *Christendom and its Discontents: Exclusion, Persecution, and Rebellion, 1000–1500*, ed. S. L. Waugh and P. D. Diehl (Cambridge, 1996), 177–203.

Goldberg, J., 'Fatherly Authority: The Politics of Stuart Family Images', in *Rewriting the Renaissance: The Discourse of Sexual Difference in Early Modern Europe*, ed. M. W. Ferguson, M. Quilligan and N. J. Vickers (Chicago, 1986), 3–32.

Gowing, L., *Domestic Dangers: Women, Words, and Sex in Early Modern London* (Oxford, 1996).

Grieser, D. J., 'A Tale of Two Convents: Nuns and Anabaptists in Münster, 1533–1535', *Sixteenth Century Journal*, 26 (1995), 31–47.

Grundy, I., 'Women's History? Writings by English Nuns', in *Women, Writing, History 1640–1740*, ed. I. Grundy and S. Wiseman (London, 1992), 126–38.

Guibert, J., *The Jesuits: Their Spiritual Doctrine and Practice*, trans. W. J. Young (St Louis, 1972).

Guilday, P., *The English Catholic Refugees on the Continent 1558–1795* (London, 1914).

Haigh, C., 'The Continuity of Catholicism in the English Reformation', *Past and Present*, 93 (1981), 37–69.

—— 'From Monopoly to Minority: Catholicism in Early Modern England', *Transactions of the Royal Historical Society*, 31 (1982), 129–47.

—— *Reformation and Resistance in Tudor Lancashire* (Cambridge, 1975).

Hanawalt, B. A., 'Lady Honor Lisle's Networks of Influence', in *Women and Power in the Middle Ages*, ed. M. Erler and M. Kowaleski (Athens, Ga., 1988), 188–212.

Hanley, S. 'Engendering the State: Family Formation and State Building in Early Modern France', *French Historical Studies*, 16 (1989), 4–27.

Hanlon, J. D., 'These Be But Women', in *From the Renaissance to the Counter-Reformation* (New York, 1965), 371–400.

Hardman, A., *Mother Margaret Mostyn: Discalced Carmelite 1625–1679* (London, 1937).

—— *Two English Carmelites* (London, 1939).

Harline, C., 'Actives and Contemplatives: The Female Religious of the Low Countries Before and After Trent', *Catholic Historical Review*, 81 (1995), 541–67.

—— *The Burdens of Sister Margaret* (New York, 1994).

—— and E. Put, 'A Bishop in the Cloisters: The Visitations of Mathias Hovius (Malines, 1596–1620)', *Sixteenth Century Journal*, 22 (1991), 611–39.

Harris, B. J., 'A New Look at the Reformation: Aristocratic Women and Nunneries, 1450–1540', *Journal of British Studies*, 32 (1993), 89–113.

—— 'Women and Politics in Early Tudor England', *Historical Journal*, 33 (1990), 259–81.

Havran, M. J., *The Catholics of Caroline England* (Stanford, 1962).

Hibbard, C., *Charles I and the Popish Plot* (Chapel Hill, NC, 1983).

—— 'Early Stuart Catholicism: Revisions and Re-revisions', *Journal of Modern History*, 52 (1980), 1–34.

Hill, B., 'A Refuge from Men: The Idea of a Protestant Nunnery', *Past and Present*, 117 (1987), 107–30.

Hills, H., 'Cities and Virgins: Female Aristocratic Convents in Early Modern Naples and Palermo', *Oxford Art Journal*, 22 (1999), 31–54.

—— 'Iconography and Ideology: Aristocracy, Immaculacy and Virginity in Seventeenth-Century Palermo', *Oxford Art Journal*, 17 (1994), 16–31.

A History of the Benedictine Nuns of Dunkirk (London, 1958).

Hodgetts, M., 'The Yates of Harvington, 1631–1696', *Recusant History*, 22 (1994), 152–81.

Hsia, R. P., *The World of Catholic Renewal 1540–1770* (Cambridge, 1998).

In a Great Tradition: Tribute to Dame Laurentia McLaughlan Abbess of Stanbrook by the Benedictines of Stanbrook (London, 1956).

Jantzen, G. M., *Power, Gender and Christian Mysticism* (Cambridge, 1995).

Johnson, P. D., *Equal in Monastic Profession: Religious Women in Medieval France* (Chicago, 1991).

Kealy, T. M., *Dowry of Women Religious: A Historical Synopsis and Commentary* (Washington, DC, 1941).

Kettering, S., 'The Patronage Power of Early Modern French Noblewomen', *Historical Journal*, 32 (1989), 817–41.

Knell, P. R. B., 'Some Catholics of Standon, Herts, 1660–1688', *London Recusant*, 2 (1972), 87–102.

—— 'The Southcott Family in Essex, 1575–1642', *Essex Recusant*, 14 (1972), 1–38.

Knowles, D., *The English Mystical Tradition* (New York, 1961).

—— *The English Mystics* (London, 1927).

Knox, D., 'Disciplina: The Monastic and Clerical Origins of European Civility', in *Renaissance Society and Culture: Essays in Honor of Eugene F. Rice, Jr*, ed. J. Monfasani and R. G. Musto (New York, 1991), 107–35.

Lehfeldt, E. A., 'Convents as Litigants: Dowry and Inheritance Disputes in Early Modern Spain', *Journal of Social History*, 33 (2000), 645–64.

Leys, M. D. R., *Catholics in England 1559–1829: A Social History* (London, 1961).

Lierheimer, L., 'Redefining Convent Space: Ideals of Female Community among Seventeenth-Century Ursuline Nuns', *Proceedings of the Annual Meeting of the Western Society for French History*, 24 (1997), 211–20.

Loades, A., *Searching for Lost Coins: Explorations in Christianity and Feminism* (London, 1987).

Lowe, K. J. P., 'Female Strategies for Success in a Male-ordered World: The Benedictine Convent of Le Murate in Florence in the Fifteenth and Early Sixteenth Centuries', in *Women in the Church*, ed. W. J. Sheils and D. Wood (Oxford, 1990), 209–21.

—— 'Patronage and Territoriality in Early Sixteenth-Century Florence', *Renaissance Studies*, 7 (1993), 258–71.

—— 'Secular Brides and Convent Brides: Wedding Ceremonies in Italy during the Renaissance and Counter Reformation', in *Marriage in Italy, 1300–1650*, ed. T. Dean and K. J. P. Lowe (Cambridge, 1998), 41–65.

Lunn, D., *The English Benedictines, 1540–1688: From Reformation to Revolution* (London, 1980).

Lynch, J. H., *Simoniacal Entry into Religious Life from 1000 to 1260: A Social, Economic and Legal Study* (Columbus, Ohio, 1976).

McCann, J., 'Some Benedictine Letters in the Bodleian', *Downside Review*, 30 (1931), 465–81.

McGrath, P., *Papists and Puritans under Elizabeth I* (London, 1967).

McNamara, J. K., *Sisters in Arms: Catholic Nuns through Two Millennia* (Cambridge, Mass., 1996).

Mack, P., *Visionary Women: Ecstatic Prophecy in Seventeenth-Century England* (Berkeley, Ca., 1992).

Maddox, R., 'Founding a Convent in Early Modern Spain: Cultural History, Hegemonic Processes, and the Plurality of the Historical Subject', *Rethinking History*, 2 (1998), 173–98.

Maguire, N. K., 'The Duchess of Portsmouth: English Royal Consort and French Politician, 1670–85', in *The Stuart Court and Europe: Essays in Politics and Political Culture*, ed. R. M. Smuts (Cambridge, 1996), 247–73.

Marotti, A. F., 'Alienating Catholics in Early Modern England: Recusant Women, Jesuits and Ideological Fantasies', in *Catholicism and Anti-Catholicism in Early Modern English Texts*, ed. A. Marotti (London, 1999), 1–34.

Mathew, D., *Catholicism in England 1535–1935: Portrait of a Minority: Its Culture and Tradition* (London, 1936).

Medioli, F., 'An Unequal Law: The Enforcement of *Clausura* Before and After the Council of Trent', in *Women in Renaissance and Early Modern Europe*, ed. C. Meek (Dublin, 2000), 136–52.

Mendelson S. and P. Crawford, *Women in Early Modern England* (Oxford, 1998).

Milis, L. J. R., *Angelic Monks and Earthly Men: Monasticism and its Meaning to Medieval Society* (Woodbridge, 1992).

Monson, C., *Disembodied Voices: Music and Culture in an Early Modern Italian Convent* (Berkeley, Ca., 1995).

Muldoon, A. R., 'Recusants, Church-Papists, and "Comfortable" Missionaries: Assessing the Post-Reformation English Catholic Community', *Catholic Historical Review*, 86 (2000), 242–57.

Mullett, M. A., *Catholics in Britain and Ireland, 1558–1829* (Basingstoke, 1998).

Nolan, P., *The Irish Dames of Ypres: Being a History of the Royal Irish Abbey at Ypres* (Dublin, 1908).

Mursell, G., *English Spirituality from Earliest times to 1700* (London, 2001).

Norberg, K., 'The Counter Reformation and Women: Religious and Lay', in *Catholicism in Early Modern History: A Guide to Research*, ed. J. W. O'Malley (St Louis, 1988), 133–46.

Norman, M., 'Dame Gertrude More and the English Mystical Tradition', *Recusant History*, 13 (1976), 196–211.

O'Brien, S., '*Terra Incognita*: The Nun in Nineteenth-Century England', *Past and Present*, 121 (1988), 110–40.

Oliva, M., *The Convent and the Community in Late Medieval England: Female Monasteries in the Diocese of Norwich, 1350–1540* (Woodbridge, 1998).

O'Malley, J., 'Early Jesuit Spirituality: Spain and Italy', in *Christian Spirituality: Post-Reformation and Modern*, ed. L. Dupré and D. E. Saliers (New York, 1989), 3–27.

Outhwaite, R. B., 'Marriage as Business: Opinions on the Rise in Aristocratic Bridal Portions in Early Modern England', in *Business Life and Public Policy: Essays in Honour of D. C. Coleman*, ed. N. McKendrick and R. B. Outhwaite (Cambridge, 1986), 21–37.

Ovitt, G., 'The Cultural Context of Western Technology: Early Christian Attitudes toward Manual Labour', in *The Work of Work. Servitude, Slavery, and Labor in Medieval England*, ed. A. J. Frantzen and D. Moffat (Glasgow, 1994), 71–94.

Peters, H., *Mary Ward: A World In Contemplation*, trans. H. Butterfield (Leominster, 1994).

Perry, M. E., *Gender and Disorder in Early Modern Seville* (Princeton, NJ, 1990).

Power, E., *Medieval English Nunneries, c.1275–1525* (Cambridge, 1922).

Pritchard, A., *Catholic Loyalism in Elizabethan England* (London, 1979).

Questier, M., *Conversion, Politics and Religion in England, 1580–1625* (Cambridge, 1996).

—— 'The Politics of Religious Conformity and the Accession of James I', *Historical Research*, 71 (1998), 14–30.

Ranft, P., 'A Key to Counter-Reformation Women's Activism: The Confessor-Spiritual Director', *Journal of Feminist Studies in Religion*, 10 (1994), 7–26.

—— *A Woman's Way: The Forgotten History of Women Spiritual Directors* (New York, 2000).

—— *Women and the Religious Life in Premodern Europe* (New York, 1996).

Rapley, E., *The Dévotes: Women and Church in Seventeenth-Century France* (Montreal and Kingston, 1990).

—— 'Her Body the Enemy: Self-Mortification in Seventeenth-Century Convents', *Proceedings of the Annual Meeting of the Western Society for French History*, 21 (1994), 25–35.

—— *A Social History of the Cloister: Daily Life in the Teaching Monasteries of the Old Regime* (Montreal and Kingston, 2001).

—— 'Women and Religious Vocation in Seventeenth-Century France', *French Historical Studies*, 18 (1994), 613–31.

Reinke, D. R., ' "Austin's Labour": Patterns of Governance in Medieval Augustinian Monasticism', *Church History*, 56 (1987), 157–71.

Religious Orders of the Catholic Reformation, ed. R. L. DeMolen (New York, 1994).

Richards, J., ' "To Promote a Woman to Beare Rule": Talking of Queens in Mid-Tudor England', *Sixteenth Century Journal*, 28 (1997), 108–15.

Richards, M., 'Community and Poverty in the Reformed Order of St Clare in the Fifteenth Century', *Journal of Religious History*, 19 (1995), 10–25.

Roper, L., *The Holy Household: Women and Morals in Reformation Augsburg* (Oxford, 1989).

Rowlands, M., 'Recusant Women 1560–1640', in *Women in English Society 1500–1800*, ed. M. Prior (London, 1985), 149–80.

Sánchez, M., *The Empress, the Queen, and the Nun: Women and Power at the Court of Philip III of Spain* (Baltimore, 1998).

Scheepsma, W., ' "For Hereby I Hope to Rouse Some to Piety": Books of Sisters from Convents and Sister-Houses Associated with the *Devotio Moderna* in the Low Countries', in *Women, the Book and the Godly*, ed. L. Smith and J. H. M. Taylor (Cambridge, 1993), 27–40.

Sedgwick, A., 'The Nuns of Port-Royal: A Study of Female Spirituality in Seventeenth-Century France', in *That Gentle Strength: Historical Perspectives on Women in Christianity*, ed. L. L. Coon, K. J. Haldane and E. W. Sommer (Charlottesville, 1990), 176–89.

Sena, M., 'William Blundell and the Networks of Catholic Dissent in Post-Reformation England', in *Communities in Early Modern England: Networks, Place, Rhetoric*, ed. A. Shepherd and P. Withington (Manchester, 2000), 54–75.

S. M. F., *Hidden Wheat: The Story of an Enclosed Franciscan Community 1621–1971* (Glasgow, 1971).

Spearritt, P., 'The Survival of Medieval Spirituality among the Exiled English Black Monks', *American Benedictine Review*, 25 (1974), 287–316.

Sperling, J. G., *Convents and the Body Politic in Late Renaissance Venice* (Chicago, 1999).

Steel, D. J. and E. R. Samuel, *Sources for Roman Catholic and Jewish Genealogy and Family History* (London, 1974).

Steele, F. M., *The Convents of Great Britain* (London, 1902).

Stone, L., *The Family Sex and Marriage in England 1500–1800* (London, 1977).

Strasser, U., 'Bones of Contention: Cloistered Nuns, Decorated Relics, and the Contest over Women's Place in the Public Sphere of Counter-Reformation Munich', *Archive for Reformation History*, 90 (1999), 255–88.

Strien, C. D. van, 'Recusant Houses in the Southern Netherlands as Seen by British Tourists, *c.* 1650–1720', *Recusant History*, 20 (1991), 495–511.

Sturman, M. W., 'Gravelines and the English Poor Clares', *London Recusant*, 7 (1977), 1–8.

Surtz, R. E., *The Guitar of God: Gender, Power, and Authority in the Visionary World of Mother Juana de la Cruz, 1481–1534* (Philadelphia, 1990).

Taggard, M. N., 'Picturing Intimacy in a Spanish Golden Age Convent', *Oxford Art Journal*, 23 (2000), 99–111.

Thompson, S., *Women Religious: The Founding of English Nunneries after the Norman Conquest* (Oxford, 1991).

Tibbetts Schulenburg, J., 'Strict Active Enclosure and its Effects on the Female Monastic Experience (ca 500–1100)', in *Distant Echoes: Medieval Religious Women*, vol. 1, ed. J. A. Nichols and L. T. Shank (Kalamazoo, 1984), 51–86.

Trexler, R. C., 'Celibacy in the Renaissance: The Nuns of Florence', in *Dependence in Context in Renaissance Florence* (Binghamton, NY, 1994), 343–72.

—— 'Le Célibat à la Fin du Moyen Age: Les Religieuses de Florence', *Annales ESC*, 27 (1972), 1329–50.

Walker, C., 'Combining Martha and Mary: Gender and Work in Seventeenth-Century English Cloisters', *Sixteenth Century Journal*, 30 (1999), 397–418.

—— '"Doe not supose me a well mortifyed Nun dead to the world": Letter-Writing in Early Modern English Convents', in *Early Modern Women Letter Writers*, ed. J. Daybell (Basingstoke, 2001), 159–76.

—— 'Prayer, Patronage and Political Conspiracy: English Nuns and the Restoration', *Historical Journal*, 43 (2000), 1–23.

Walsham, A., *Church Papists: Catholicism, Conformity and Confessional Polemic in Early Modern England* (Woodbridge, 1993).

Warnicke, R., *Women of the English Renaissance and Reformation* (Westport, Conn., 1983).

Warren, N. B., 'Pregnancy and Productivity: The Imagery of Female Monasticism Within and Beyond the Cloister Walls', *Journal of Medieval and Early Modern Studies*, 28 (1998), 531–52.

Weber, A., 'Spiritual Administration: Gender and Discernment in the Carmelite Reform', *Sixteenth Century Journal*, 31 (2000), 123–46.

Whelan, B., *Historic English Convents of Today: The Story of the English Cloisters in France and Flanders in Penal Times* (London, 1936).

Wiesner, M. E., 'Ideology Meets the Empire: Reformed Convents and the Reformation', in *Germania Illustrata: Essays on Early Modern Germany Presented to Gerald Strauss*, ed. A. C. Fix and S. C. Karant-Nunn (Kirksville, Miss., 1991), 181–95.

Wiethaus, U., '"If I had an Iron Body": Femininity and Religion in the Letters of Maria de Hout', in *Dear Sister: Medieval Women and the Epistolary Genre*, ed. K. Cherewatuk and U. Wiethaus (Philadelphia, 1993), 171–91.

Winkelmes, M., 'Taking Part: Benedictine Nuns as Patrons of Art and Architecture', in *Picturing Women in Renaissance and Baroque Italy*, ed. G. A. Johnson and S. F. Matthews Grieco (Cambridge, 1997), 91–110.

Women and Politics in Early Modern England, ed. J. Daybell (Ashgate, forthcoming).

Wolfe, H., 'Reading Bells and Loose Papers: Reading and Writing Practices of the English Benedictine Nuns of Cambrai and Paris', in *Early Modern Women's Manuscript Writings*, ed. V. Burke and J. Gibson (Aldershot, 2002).

Women and Faith: Catholic Religious Life in Italy from Late Antiquity to the Present, ed. L. Scaraffia and G. Zarri (Cambridge, Mass., 1999).

Wood, J. M., 'Breaking the Silence: The Poor Clares and the Visual Arts in Fifteenth-Century Italy', *Renaissance Quarterly*, 48 (1995), 262–86.

Woodford, C., 'Women as Historians: the Case of Early Modern German Convents', *German Life and Letters*, 52 (1999), 271–80.

Worrall, E. S., 'What May Happen to a Second-Class Citizen 1', *London Recusant*, 2 (1972), 68–71.

Wright, M., *Mary Ward's Institute: The Struggle for Identity* (Sydney, 1997).

Zarri, G., 'Gender, Religious Institutions and Social Discipline: The Reform of the Regulars', in *Gender and Society in Renaissance Italy*, ed. J. C. Brown and R. C. Davis (London, 1998), 193–212.

——'Living Saints: A Typology of Female Sanctity in the Early Sixteenth Century', in *Women and Religion in Medieval and Renaissance Italy*, ed. D. Bornstein and R. Rusconi (Chicago, 1996), 219–303.

——'Ursula and Catherine: The Marriage of Virgins in the Sixteenth Century', in *Creative Women in Medieval and Early Modern Italy: A Religious and Artistic Renaissance*, ed. E. A. Matter and J. Coakley (Philadelphia, 1994), 237–78.

Zimmerman, B., *Carmel in England 1615–1849* (London, 1889).

Theses and unpublished works

Murray-Sinclair, M., 'Pontoise: The Vicissitudes of a House "Beyond the Seas"' (unpublished paper).

Seguin, C., '"Addicted Unto Piety": Catholic Women in England, 1590–1690' (PhD d[Gilchrist, R., *Gender and Material Culture: The Archaeology of Religious Women* (London, 1994)]issertation, Duke University, 1997).

Spearritt, P., 'Prayer and Politics among the English Benedictines of Brussels' (unpublished paper).

Walker, C., '"Of Feminine Sexe, but Masculine Virtue": Catholic Women and the Preservation of the Faith in England, 1558–1640' (Honours dissertation, University of Western Australia, 1986).

Index